Family Favourites Cookbook

Distributed in Australia by:
Cobra Import Export Pty Ltd
Unit 2, 410 Botany Road
Alexandria
Sydney
NSW 2015
Australia

This edition not for resale outside Australia.

First published 1993 by C. J. Publishing (Chanel Publishers Ltd)
This edition published 1993

ISBN 0-908808-26-7

Copyright © Text: Alison Holst
          Photography: Alison Holst
          J. Wattie Foods
          Seasmoke

Publisher: Cliff Josephs
Photographer: Sal Criscillo
Food Styling: Alison Holst and Clare Ferguson
Illustration: Clare Ferguson
Home Economists: Alison Holst and Jane Ritchie
Props: Kathy Heath
Design: Alison Holst and Barbara Nielsen
Produced by Stylus Publishing Services Ltd
Typeset by Typocrafters Ltd
Printed by Everbest, Hong Kong

Family Favourites Cookbook

Alison Holst

Introduction

I feel that cooking for yourself, for a partner, for children, and for friends is an important part of life.

The caring cook has many things to consider as she (or he) plans what to buy, prepare, cook, and serve.

Everyday meals need to provide us with energy and the right balance of nutrients for growth and continuing good health. They should not cost more than we can afford, and should not take too much time nor effort to prepare.

This is far from all, however. Most importantly, the food must taste and look so good that everybody who eats it will enjoy it! Food left on plates does nobody any good.

I hope that this book will give you many ideas. Of course, not every recipe will suit every situation. it is up to you to choose what you feel you need. At the back of the book are listed recipes which are lower in fat than usual. You will also find recipes which have been developed especially for barbecues. (If you want to try these recipes, but you do not barbecue regularly, you can grill (broil) them instead.)

The low-priced recipes included in this book have not been listed separately, since this book will be travelling to many places, and food prices will vary.

These recipes have come from many sources. Some ideas are new, but others are my old favourites, simplified and streamlined, making good use of the efficient equipment in the modern kitchen.

As well as recipes for day-to-day cooking, this book includes helpful ideas for the times when you are cooking for larger family groups and friends. At such times you may wish to spend more time and effort to produce memorable meals, especially if you are still keeping a watchful eye on costs. The success of your special meals is likely to depend more on your cooking skills than on the price of the ingredients!

A book like this requires much more than just recipes! I would like to thank the many people who have worked with me to produce it. I hope you will find that my *Family Favourites* is a pleasure to use, practical and instructive.

Good cooking

About the Author

Alison Holst is New Zealand's best-known and most popular food writer and television cook. For 28 years Alison has been the presenter of numerous television series featuring family cooking. In addition to writing weekly columns for nine newspapers, Alison is broadcast regularly on radio and cooks in front of large audiences throughout the country, raising funds for various charities. Alison has promoted New Zealand internationally through radio, television and newspaper columns.

With 40 cookbooks published and sales of more than 2 million copies, Alison has gained recognition worldwide and has received a CBE and QSM for her work. Her particular interest is family cooking, encouraging home cooks to make good use of limited time and modern appliances.

CONTENTS

Soups 8

Starters 18

Light Meals 28

Fish & Seafood 40

Chicken 50

Lamb 58

Beef, Mince & Venison 70

Pork & Sausages 82

Pasta, Rice, Grains & Beans 94

Potatoes 104

Vegetables & Salads 114

Desserts 132

Breads, Scones & Muffins 146

Cakes & Biscuits 156

Sweets & Drinks 168

Preserves 178

Barbecue Basics 186

Eating for Health 188

Losing Weight 190

Index 191

Important Information

The following measures have been used in this book:

1 Tbsp .... 3 tsp
4 Tbsp .... ¼ cup
8 Tbsp .... ½ cup
16 Tbsp .... 1 cup

All the cup and spoon measures are level, unless otherwise stated. (Rounded or heaped measures will upset the balance of ingredients.)

When measuring flour, spoon it into the measure lightly, and level it off without shaking or banging the cup, since this packs down the flour and means that too much is used. Small ¼ and ½ cup measures are useful for measuring these quantities of flour.

Small amounts of ingredients have been measured by spoons. Larger quantities have been given in metric and imperial measurements.

Metric weights should be used in conjunction with a metric (250 ml) measuring cup. Imperial weights should be used in conjunction with an 8 fluid ounce measuring cup. Within a particular recipe you should use one system or the other.

Weights have been rounded off to convenient amounts and are approximate only.

Conversions through the book may not appear to be consistent, since recipes were considered individually when conversions were made.

Abbreviations Used

cm .... centimeter
C .... Celcius
F .... Fahrenheit
ml .... millilitre
l .... litre
g .... gram
kg .... kilogram
oz .... ounce
fl oz .... fluid ounces
lb .... pound
in .... inch
tsp .... teaspoon
Tbsp .... tablespoon

Oven Temperatures and Approximate Equivalents

Celcius	Fahrenheit	Gas
100°C	225°F	¼
125°C	250°F	½
150°C	300°F	2
160°C	325°F	3
170°C	325°F	3
180°C	350°F	4
190°C	375°F	5
200°C	400°F	6
210°C	425°F	7
220°C	425°F	7
230°C	450°F	8
250°C	500°F	9

Always bring the oven to the required temperature before putting in the food which is to be cooked, unless specified.

Most of the oven-baked recipes in this book were cooked in an oven with a fan. The fan circulates heat so that no parts of the oven are much hotter or colder than other parts.

If you use an oven which does not have a fan, you may find that you need to allow a slightly longer cooking time, or slightly higher temperature.

To help you judge when your food is cooked, I have given you other indications of readiness to look for, wherever possible, as well as indicating the probable time required.

Microwave Cooking

Microwave cooking times vary, and cannot be given precisely. Microwave instructions have been given for a 650 Watt microwave oven with a turntable.

High .... 100% power, about 650 Watts
Medium High .... 70% power, about 450 Watts
Medium .... 50% power, about 350 Watts
Defrost .... 30% power, about 220 Watts

Important
Check the power levels and percentages on your own microwave oven, and alter cooking times accordingly, if your oven is different. The first time you microwave a new recipe, always watch it carefully during the second half of its cooking time, in case it is cooking more quickly. As soon as you can smell the food, you know that it is nearly cooked.

Standing time
Food continues to cook after it is taken out of a microwave oven, e.g. a potato keeps baking for 1–2 minutes.

The appearance and texture of the food change during this time:

- crumble toppings become crisper
- cabbage softens and brightens
- cake surfaces dry out

If you wait until food looks and feels cooked before you take it from the oven, you may well find that it is overcooked after standing. If in doubt, undercook. Take food out after the recommended time. You can always put it back in the oven if it is still undercooked after standing. It is much harder to render first aid to overcooked food!

Can Sizes

You may find that you cannot buy cans of the exact size specified in this book. Do not worry if the cans are a little larger or smaller than those specified. Small differences are unlikely to make a difference to your recipe.

Glossary

baking bran — wheat bran
baking/greasproof paper — bakewell paper
baking soda — bicarbonate of soda
baking tin — baking pan
baking tray — baking sheet
Basmati rice — aromatic long-grain rice
biscuit — cookie
blender — liquidiser
bouillon cubes — stock cubes
bottling — canning
broad beans — fava beans
chickpeas — garbanzo beans
chilli powder — ground dried chillies with no added flavourings

choko — chayote
clam — small round bivalve, replace with cockles
cling wrap — microwave-safe transparent film
crayfish — rock lobster (salt water)
crème fraîche — rich, cultured sour cream
custard powder — use cornflour (cornstarch)
dairy cream — 30% fat, multipurpose cream
double cream — high fat (40%) cream
eggbeater — egg whisk
eggplant — aubergine
essence — extract

evaporated milk — unsweetened condensed milk
flour — unbleached white all-purpose flour
feijoa — subtropical fruit, substitute apples in pies.
glacial acetic acid — white salad cabbage
golden syrup, treacle — molasses
greaseproof paper — baking paper
green prawns — uncooked prawns
green/red pepper — green/red bell pepper
grill — broil
haricot beans — navy beans
hogget — meat from sheep 1–2 years old

icing sugar — confectioner's sugar
icing — frosting
instant coffee — instant coffee powder
instant stock — concentrated powdered stock, replace with stock cubes
jam setting mix — powdered pectin
Japanese soya sauce — Kikkoman soya sauce
kumara — orange-fleshed sweet potato
mandarins — satsumas or clementines
oat flakes — jumbo oats, whole flaked oat grains
minced beef — ground beef
paper towel — kitchen paper
paua — abalone
pipi — bivalve, replace with cockles
reduced cream — 20% milk fat, sterilised and canned
savoury tomatoes — diced tomatoes
scone — biscuit
sieve (verb) — strain
sieve (noun) — strainer
silver beet — Swiss chard, spinach beet

smoked cod's roe — tarama
snow peas — mange tout
soft butter — softened butter
spirits — whisky, gin, brandy, rum
spring onion — scallion
sultanas — seedless raisins
swede — rutabaga
tangelo — cross between tangerine and grapefruit
tasty cheese — sharp cheese
teatowel — dish towel
tomato paste — tomato concentrate
tomato purée — tomato sauce
tomato sauce — tomato ketchup
topmilk — single cream
Trim milk — low-fat milk
Trim pork — New Fashioned Pork in Australia, Pork in the United Kingdom
tuatua — oval bivalve, replace with cockles
vanilla — vanilla extract
vegemite or marmite — yeast extract
wholemeal flour — whole wheat or graham flour
zucchini — courgette

Soup mixes used in some recipes in this book make 3–4 servings of soup.

A 250 g carton of cottage cheese, cream cheese and sour cream is equivalent to 1 cup.

Coconut cream used in these recipes is unsweetened and canned. Replace with liquid made by soaking desiccated coconut in boiling water or dissolve a cake of compressed creamed coconut in warm water.

Food processor: A food processor with a large bowl and a strong motor was used for testing and preparing the recipes in this book. Some food processors would not cope with such large amounts. Follow the instructions given by the maker of your food processor.

One Cup Equivalents

Item	Approximate Weight in Grams	Approximate Weight in Ounces	Item	Approximate Weight in Grams	Approximate Weight in Ounces
allbran	100	3½	frozen strawberries	150	5
almonds slivered	112	4	grated cheese	100	3½
apricots, chopped dried	150	5	green beans	115	4
asparagus pieces	115	4	kibbled wheat	160	5½
banana, mashed	250	8	lentils, brown	190	6½
barley	200	6½	lentils, split red	190	6½
beans, black-eyed	180	6	marrow, chopped	100	3½
beans, cooked red kidney	175	6	mashed potato	250	8
beans, haricot	200	6½	mixed fruit	140	5
beans, red kidney	180	6	moong dahl	185	6
beans, soya	170	6	mushrooms, sliced	85	3
beans, tiger	200	6½	oats, whole grain	90	3
biscuit crumbs	100	3½	onion, diced	140	5
bran, baking	45	1½	Parmesan, grated	125	4
bran, oat	120	4	pasta, dry large	60	2
breadcrumbs, dry	130	4	pasta, dry small	130	4
breadcrumbs, fresh	150	5	peanuts	140	5
bulgar	165	5½	pineapple, crushed*	250	8
butter	225	7	pine nuts	140	5
carrot, grated	170	6	pumpkin purée	250	8
cashew nuts	120	4	rhubarb, chopped	150	5
cauliflower pieces	115	4	rice, brown cooked	190	6½
celery, sliced	125	4	rice, brown raw	195	6½
chickpeas	200	6½	rice, short-grain cooked	150	5
chocolate pieces	160	5½	rice, short-grain raw	185	6
chopped cabbage	115	4	rolled oats	90	3
chopped herbs	25	1	rye, kibbled	160	5½
chopped tomato	175	6	sesame seeds	120	4
cocoa	125	4	spinach, cooked	200	6½
coconut	100	3½	split peas, green	200	6½
cornflour	100	3½	split peas, yellow	200	6½
cornmeal, coarse yellow	170	6	sugar	220	7
cottage cheese	250	8	sugar, brown	200	6½
cream cheese	250	8	sugar, castor	210	7
croutons	50	2	sugar, icing	110	4
cucumber, diced	120	4	sultanas	160	5½
currants	135	4½	sunflower seeds	135	4½
eggplant, diced	100	3½	vegetables, mixed	150	5
flour, pea	140	5	walnuts	75	3½
flour, self-raising	125	4	walnuts chopped	100	3½
flour, soya	90	3	wheatgerm	75	2½
flour, white	125	4	zucchini, grated	150	5
flour, wholemeal	140	5	zucchini, sliced	110	4
frozen peas	110	4			

Note: 1 cup=1 metric 250 ml cup   *from a can of about 400 g (14–16 oz)

Fresh Tomato Soup

SEE PHOTOGRAPH ON PAGE 8

I have eaten homemade tomato soup all my life. My mother made us big steaming bowls of it in autumn, from our garden-fresh tomatoes, and in the winter and spring she used her bottled tomatoes.

Nowadays I use canned tomatoes in tomato juice when I do not have fresh tomatoes in the garden, and I serve my soup cold on hot days, as well as hot on cold days!

Stale bread (or crusts) thickens tomato soup better than anything else. Please try using it. Firm-textured brown bread is best of all, but you can use whatever bread you have!

For 4–6 servings:
1–1.5 kg (2–3 lb) ripe red tomatoes
1–2 slices bread
1 tsp salt
1 Tbsp sugar
½ tsp dried basil
½ tsp dried oreganum
1–2 cloves garlic, chopped
1 onion, chopped
finely chopped parsley (optional)
about 2 tsp wine vinegar
extra ingredients for serving — see method

Put the halved or quartered tomatoes into a saucepan with the bread that has been broken into small pieces. Sprinkle with the salt, sugar, basil and oreganum, replacing the dried herbs with larger quantities of fresh to taste, if available. Add the chopped garlic and onion and the finely chopped parsley. Bring to the boil then reduce the heat, cover and cook until tender and mushy, then break up the mixture with a potato masher. Leave to stand for about 5 minutes, then shake and press through a coarse sieve. Add the vinegar, tasting after 1 teaspoonful has been added, and adjusting seasoning if necessary.

Serve as a cold soup with croutons, diced celery, cubed avocado or chopped cucumber, or as a hot soup with a chopped herb garnish.

'Old-Fashioned' Shank Soup

In this substantial, nutritious meal-in-a-bowl soup, a shank is simmered with the rest of the ingredients for about 2 hours, to make the comforting soup you may remember from your childhood. The stock is not fatty and does not need to be strained. Don't be put off by the long list of ingredients. This is the sort of soup where you put in what you have!

For 8 cups of thick soup:
1 lamb, hogget or mutton shank
2 tsp oil
1 large onion
2 cloves garlic
1 carrot
1 stalk celery
1 scrubbed potato
8 cups (2 litres/64 fl oz) water
1 bay leaf
1 tsp dried oreganum
¼ tsp dried thyme
¼ cup (50 g/1½ oz) pearl barley
¼ cup (50 g/1½ oz) 'soup mix'
¼ cup (50 g/1½ oz) moong dahl or red lentils
½ cup (65 g/2 oz) macaroni
1 cup chopped green beans
1 cup chopped zucchini
1 cup chopped cabbage
about 1 tsp salt
pepper to taste
chopped parsley

Put the shank and the oil into a large pan over a moderate heat. Chop the onion, garlic, carrot, celery and potato in the order given, and add to the pan. Turn the shank, and stir the vegetables, heating them through without letting them brown.

Add the water and the next six ingredients, bring to the boil, then lower the heat, cover, and simmer for 1½ hours. Remove the shank, and add the macaroni, the remaining (quick-cooking) vegetables, and salt and pepper to taste.

When the shank is cool enough to work with, remove the meat, and cut it into small pieces. Put the meat and bone back into the soup. At the end of the cooking time, add the parsley, and adjust seasonings if necessary. Discard the bone.

Note:
'Soup Mix' is a mixture of small grains and pulses that you buy ready-mixed for soup. It does not contain any stock.

Variation:
Use an extra hogget or mutton shank to give a meatier soup.

Spiced Pumpkin and Coconut Soup

Pumpkins are good vegetables which we often take for granted. Inexpensive, and available for all the cold months, they make a wonderful base for soups.

Pumpkin soup does not need to be thickened by any other starchy ingredients — in fact the pumpkin purée usually needs to be thinned. This gives the cook great scope, since there are may suitable 'thinning' liquids available. Coconut cream is one.

For 3–4 servings:
1 Tbsp butter
4 cloves garlic
2 tsp ground cumin
1 tsp ground coriander
750 g (1 lb 10oz) pumpkin
1 cup (250 ml/8 fl oz) water
1 cup (250 ml/8 fl oz) coconut cream
½ tsp salt
1 tsp Trappey's hot pepper sauce

Cook the butter and finely chopped garlic together in a large pan with a lid for 1–2 minutes. Add the spices, and cook for another minute or so before adding the pieces of unpeeled pumpkin and the water.

Cover and cook gently for 10 minutes or until the pumpkin is tender, adding more water if it evaporates during this cooking. Leave until cool enough to handle, then peel or scoop out seeds and peel off skin.

Put the remaining flesh in a blender or food processor, purée, then add the coconut cream, salt and hot pepper sauce. Taste and balance the flavours, adding more water or coconut cream if you think it necessary. Sieve the soup to remove any debris, then reheat when required.

Serve with crisp bread rolls and a salad as the main course of a light meal, or as a starter for a spicy Asian meal.

Spiced Pumpkin and Coconut Soup

Carrot and Tangelo Soup

This soup is especially good in early spring, when you feel that warmer weather is on its way and your soups need a lighter, more interesting taste.

For 6–8 servings:
50 g (2 oz) butter
3–4 cloves garlic
2 large onions, chopped
500 g (1 lb) carrots, grated
5 tsp instant chicken stock
2 tsp sugar
4 cups (1 litre/32 fl oz) hot water
½ tsp dried thyme
½ cup (125 ml/4 fl oz) tangelo juice
thinly peeled tangelo rind (optional)
¼ cup (60 ml/2 fl oz) cream (optional)

Melt the butter in a large saucepan and heat until straw coloured. Add the finely chopped garlic and onion and cook for at least 5 minutes until lightly coloured, but not brown.

Add grated carrot to the onion and garlic, with the instant stock, sugar, hot water and thyme, and simmer for about 10 minutes or until the carrot is tender.

Peel the tangelo thinly with a potato peeler and then squeeze the juice from the fruit. Add the juice to the soup and then purée in batches in a blender or food processor.

Reheat and serve, adding the cream if desired. If you like a more intense flavour, stand the rind in a sieve in the saucepan when reheating.

Note:
Soup which is puréed is a different texture from soup which is thickened with flour or cornflour. Add a little cornflour to this soup if you like.

Variation:
Use oranges instead of tangelos if they are more readily available.

Leek and Potato Soup

This soup can be puréed until quite smooth or left slightly rough. Serve at the start of a dinner party or as the main part of a lunch.

For 4–5 servings:
2 large or 4 small leeks
2 Tbsp (30 g/1 oz) butter
3–4 medium-sized potatoes
2 cups (500 ml/16 fl oz) water
2 tsp instant chicken stock
¼–½ cup (60–125 ml/2–4 fl oz) cream
½ cup (125 ml/4 fl oz) milk
salt and freshly ground black pepper or ½ tsp
*   instant green herb stock*

Slice the white part of the leeks and cook gently in the butter in a covered saucepan for about 5 minutes, without browning.

Peel and slice the potatoes. Add the potatoes, water

and chicken stock to the leeks and simmer until the vegetables are tender. Do not overcook.

Purée to the desired thickness, then add the cream and milk. Taste and adjust the seasonings, adding salt and pepper or instant stock.

Serve hot or reheat or serve cold. For cold soup, replace cream with sour cream and purée until very smooth.

Pumpkin and Bacon Soup

Just what you need to cheer yourself up in the middle of winter! What's more, this pumpkin soup is easy to make and inexpensive.

For 3–4 servings:
1 tsp oil
1 rasher bacon, chopped
1 large onion, chopped
2 cloves garlic, chopped
660 g (1½ lb) pumpkin
2 cups (500 ml/16 fl oz) water
1 small chilli (optional)
about 1 cup (250 ml/8 fl oz) milk
about ½ tsp salt

Heat oil and bacon gently in a fairly large saucepan, then add the chopped onion and garlic and then the pumpkin (with its seeds and skin removed), cut into several chunks.

Add the water and chilli. Cover and simmer until the pumpkin is tender, about 15 minutes.

For a smooth soup, purée, then sieve the mixture, discarding as few solids as possible.

Stir in the milk to thin, then add salt as required.

Fennel Soup

Florence fennel makes wonderful soup.

For 4 servings:
2 medium-sized fennel bulbs
50 g (2 oz) butter
1 small onion, finely chopped
1 clove garlic, crushed
2 tsp instant chicken stock
2 cups (500 ml/16 fl oz) water
1 tsp sugar
½ cup (125 ml/4 fl oz) cream
juice ½ lemon

Slice fennel bulbs in half, then in quarters lengthways, then chop pieces into 1 cm (½ inch) cubes crossways. Melt the butter and add the chopped fennel, onion and garlic and cook till translucent. Add the chicken stock, water and sugar, cover and simmer for 15 minutes or until tender. Purée in a food processor or blender till smooth then sieve, discarding fibres. Add cream and lemon juice. Reheat or serve chilled.

Carrot and Tangelo Soup

vg.

Chunky Chowder

Vegetable chowder makes a substantial meal. By adding canned or frozen vegetables to fresh 'staple' vegetables you get a good mixture of flavours, textures and colours in a short time, for a very reasonable price.

For 4–6 servings:
1 medium-sized carrot
1 medium-sized onion
1 leek or celery stalk
1 potato
1 cup (250 ml/8 fl oz) water
1–2 tsp instant chicken or bacon stock
50 g (2 oz) butter
3 Tbsp flour
½ cup (125 ml/4 fl oz) milk
1 (440 g/1 lb) can cream-style corn
1–2 cups frozen or canned peas

Chunky Chowder

Cut the raw vegetables in small chunky pieces. Cook in the water until tender, then add the instant stock.

In another saucepan melt the butter, stir in the flour and cook briefly. Add the liquid drained from the canned peas and the milk, and stir constantly until the sauce boils.

Stir the sauce into the cooked vegetables, add the corn and peas, and bring mixture back to boiling. Simmer gently for 2–3 minutes, and serve with bread rolls or toasted cheese sandwiches.

Variation:
Add pieces of cooked chicken to the mixture just before serving.

14

Green Pea and Potato Chowder

This beautifully coloured, rich, creamy soup is made from everyday ingredients!

For 4 servings:
1 large onion
2 cloves garlic
1 rasher bacon
1 Tbsp butter
2 medium-sized potatoes (300 g/10½ oz)
2 cups (500 ml/16 fl oz) water
1½ tsp instant chicken stock
1 tsp sugar
3–4 mint sprigs
1 cup peas
½ cup (125 ml/4 fl oz) cream

Chop the onion, garlic and bacon and cook gently in the butter in a medium to large saucepan without allowing it to brown.

Scrub and cube the potatoes. Add to the onion, cover and cook gently for 5 minutes, stirring occasionally.

Add the water, chicken stock, sugar and the mint. Cover and simmer until the potatoes are tender, 5–10 minutes. Add the frozen peas and cook for 5 minutes longer. Reserve ½ cup of the cooked vegetables if desired.

Purée soup in a blender or food processor, adding ½ cup cream. Reheat if necessary, without boiling, adding reserved vegetables for garnish if required.

Green Pea and Potato Chowder

Green Soup

Green Soup

It doesn't take much to make an interesting soup! Take care not to overcook the spinach or you will spoil the colour.

For 6–8 servings:
2 large potatoes
1 large onion, chopped, or the light coloured part of 2 leeks
2 tsp instant green herb stock
3 cups (750 ml/24 fl oz) water
250 g (9 oz) spinach
1 cup (250 ml/8 fl oz) milk or ½ cup cream, ½ cup milk

Scrub the potatoes and cut into 1 cm (¼ inch) cubes. Put in a saucepan with the onion or leeks, the stock and water.

Cover and bring to the boil, simmering for about 15 minutes, or until the potatoes are tender. Add the well-washed, chopped spinach and simmer for 3–4 minutes longer. Purée in a blender or food processor, in several batches, if necessary.

Strain the purée back into the saucepan, add the milk (or cream and milk) and season carefully. Thin further, if desired, with extra milk or cream or with stock made by mixing 1 teaspoon of instant stock with each cup of water.

Swirl a little cream on top before serving.

Gardeners' Chowder

This hearty soup is a meal in itself.

For 4 servings:
2 onions, finely chopped
50 g (2 oz) butter
3 medium-sized potatoes
1 apple, peeled and chopped
1 tsp sugar
3 cups (750 ml/24 fl oz) water
3 tsp instant chicken stock
thyme or marjoram
1–2 cups finely chopped green vegetables

Cook the onion until golden brown in the butter. Do not hurry this step.

Scrub and cube the potatoes and add to the onion with the apple, sugar, water, instant stock and seasonings. Simmer for 15 minutes or until the potatoes are tender. Add the chopped vegetables and cook for about 3 minutes longer, until the greens are tender.

Leave to stand for 5 minutes to blend the flavours.

Serve with toast or crusty bread rolls.

Seafood Chowder

This chowder (or chunky soup) is quickly made from ingredients from your store cupboard, and embellished with fresh oysters and mussels if they are available. Even without these additions, however, the flavour is excellent, especially if the chowder is allowed to stand for a few hours after making, for the flavours to blend.

For 4 servings:
2 medium-sized onions
2 stalks celery
1 carrot
25 g (1 oz) butter
1 cup (250 ml/8 fl oz) water
1 tsp instant herb stock
1 tsp instant chicken stock
2–3 medium-sized potatoes
1 can (about 125 g/4½ oz) shrimps or salmon
2 cups (500 ml/16 fl oz) milk
6–12 raw oysters (optional)
about 12 steamed mussels (optional)
about 2 Tbsp cornflour
cold milk

Chop onions and celery coarsely and slice carrot thinly. Cook gently in butter for 5 minutes then add water, instant stocks and potatoes which have been scrubbed rather than peeled, then cut in small cubes.

Cover and simmer gently for 10–15 minutes, until vegetables are tender.

Add shrimps or salmon and all the liquid from can, the milk, and whole or halved oysters and mussels. Bring back to boiling point, then thicken with cornflour mixed to a paste with milk. Remove from heat straight away or oysters and mussels will toughen. Serve sprinkled with chopped parsley.

Oyster Chowder

This is one of my favourite soups. The bacon, potatoes and oysters seem to be perfect companions. Take care not to overcook the oysters, or the chowder will be spoilt.

For 4 main course servings:
4 rashers bacon
2 Tbsp butter
2 large onions
2 large cloves garlic
2 medium–large potatoes
1 cup (250 ml/8 fl oz) liquid (see below)
1 tsp green herb stock
2 cups (500 ml/16 fl oz) milk
24 oysters
2 Tbsp cornflour
extra milk or water
fresh parsley, chives, dill etc.
black pepper or hot pepper sauce
salt

Cut the rinds off the bacon. Put the rinds in a large (preferably non-stick) pan or saucepan, over a low heat. Chop the bacon into neat 5 mm (¼ inch) pieces, and add to the pan. Cook over a fairly low heat until the bacon is lightly browned.

While the bacon cooks, peel and chop the onions into 1 cm (½ inch) cubes, and chop the garlic finely.

Add the butter, the onion, and garlic to the lightly browned bacon. Stir over a medium heat for about 5 minutes, without browning, while you scrub or peel the potatoes and cut them into 1 cm (½ inch) cubes.

Add the potatoes to the pan, stir for about 30 seconds, then add the liquid. To get a cup of liquid, pour the oysters into a sieve, draining their liquid into a bowl underneath. Rinse the oysters with water, collecting this in the bowl, too. Make the liquid up to 1 cup with more water, or with a little white wine. Pour this liquid over the potatoes, add the instant stock, cover, and simmer for about 10 minutes, until the potatoes are tender.

Check to make sure the oysters contain no pieces of shell, then add the milk, the oysters, and the cornflour, mixed to a paste with more milk, or water. Bring to the boil, stirring constantly, then remove from the heat. The oysters will toughen and shrink if they are overcooked.

Add finely chopped parsley, chives, dill, or whatever fresh herbs you have and like. Taste and adjust the seasonings accordingly, with pepper and/or hot pepper sauce, salt, etc.

Reheat briefly before serving. Do not leave the chowder simmering. Serve in large, deep bowls, with crusty bread or crackers, or toast.

Note:
If Bluff or deep-sea oysters are not available, use other oysters for this chowder.

Oyster Chowder

Bagna Cauda

SEE PHOTOGRAPH ON PAGE 18

This hot dip turns any raw vegetable into something special. Its name, translated, means 'Hot Bath'. I know that it contains an odd combination of ingredients, but everybody, from young children to the 'oldies', loves it. When it is hot it covers the vegetables with the thinnest of coatings of well-seasoned cream. If you like you can reheat it occasionally, by 'zapping' it in the microwave oven.

2 Tbsp butter
3 cloves garlic, finely chopped
6 flat anchovy fillets
1 cup (250 ml/8 fl oz) double cream

Melt the butter, add the garlic and cook over a low heat for 1–2 minutes.

Add the anchovy fillets and cream, bring to the boil and simmer for 5 minutes, mashing the anchovies for extra flavour.

Serve hot or warm, reheating on the stove top or in a microwave oven if necessary. (Mixture is thick and of spreading consistency when cool.)

Surround the dipping bowl with a large selection of colourful chilled raw vegetables cut into dipping-sized pieces.

Suitable vegetables include:

carrots
celery
radishes
cucumber
snow peas
cauliflower
crisp spinach leaves
zucchini
young tender beans
asparagus
red, green and yellow peppers
button mushrooms
witloof (endive)
cherry tomatoes

Smoked Roe Savouries

Smoked roe has a distinctive flavour and texture, and is ready to serve as a gourmet snack after minimal preparation.

Roes vary in size and texture. Small, firm, thin roes may be sliced crossways into oval slices. Larger roes may be scooped or spooned out of their containing skin, or may be easily pressed through a coarse sieve to produce an attractive, light-textured product.

Sliced, sieved or mashed roe may be spooned or scooped on to crackers or small tartlet shells within half an hour of serving, garnished with a few capers, a parsley sprig, or sliced green or black olives.

I think that the flavour and texture of smoked roe is at its best when served mounded on hot, buttered, wholegrain toast.

To serve with drinks, quarter small slices of toast, make sure that a little lemon juice and pepper are added, and add a tiny parsley garnish.

For a lunch snack, spread whole slices of toast, and halve or cut into fingers before serving immediately. This is wonderful in cold weather.

Taramasalata

Especially in warm weather, use fresh or frozen roe to make light-textured, mayonnaise-like, universally popular taramasalata.

100 g (3½ oz) smoked roe
2 slices thick bread, broken into pieces
½ onion, chopped
juice of 2 lemons
1–1½ cups (250–375 ml/8–12 fl oz) olive or other oil
salt

Put all the ingredients in a food processor bowl and process briefly to mix. Pour in the oil in a thin stream, stopping when the mixture is thick and creamy. Add a little salt to taste.

Serve as a spread for fresh crusty bread, or as a dip for fresh vegetables. This is a summer meal in itself.

Potted Cheese

Serve potted cheese at room temperature with crackers, baby radishes, or slices of daikon (large white radish).

This recipe provides a good way to use up scrappy pieces of blue cheese leftover from a cheeseboard.

Make it several hours before serving, or store it in the refrigerator for up to 2 weeks.

50 g (2 oz) blue cheese (or a mixture of blue cheese and mature cheddar cheese)
25 g (1 oz) unsalted butter or cream cheese
2 Tbsp sherry or brandy
freshly ground black pepper
pinch of mace or nutmeg

Either mash room temperature blue cheese and butter together with a fork, then beat until smooth, adding remaining ingredients slowly, or combine blue cheese and butter in a food processor, then add liquid and seasonings. Pack into a container. Cover and refrigerate. Remove from refrigerator at least an hour before serving.

Notes:
Exact quantities are not important for this recipe. Use lightly salted or unsalted butter if preferred.

Smoked Roe Savouries

Mexican Bean Dip

This delicious mixture can be used in many ways. Try it as a starter, with corn chips and raw vegetables, use it as a filling for sandwiches or bread rolls, or thin it down and serve it hot over rice as a vegetarian main course.

1 large onion
2 cloves garlic, chopped
1 Tbsp oil
1 red or green pepper (optional)
1–2 tsp cumin
1 tsp oreganum
¼–½ tsp chilli powder
1 (440 g/1 lb) can baked beans
1 Tbsp tomato paste

Chop the onion and garlic and cook in the oil until lightly browned and transparent. Add the chopped pepper, cumin, oreganum and as much chilli powder as you like, and cook for 1–2 minutes longer. Stand baked beans in a sieve for several minutes and keep sauce which drains off. Add beans and tomato paste to pan, heat through, then mash with a fork or potato masher to desired consistency. Add as much of the strained-off sauce as you need for dip, spread or sauce consistency. Serve hot, warm, cold, or reheated.

Note:
Chilli powder makes the dip hot — the other seasonings give the dip its Mexican flavour, but do not make it hotter.

Mexican Bean Dip

Potted Crayfish or Crab

Like many others, I have very pleasant childhood memories of long summer days on the beach investigating rockpools.

In those days I did not imagine that crabs were edible!

Years later, in San Francisco, I found that crabs were a delicacy which commanded very high prices.

Crayfish (rock lobster) tails are a luxury beyond the reach of most families, but crayfish bodies from which the tails have been removed are sometimes available at reasonable prices.

In both crab and crayfish bodies there is a lot of flesh at the top of the legs in the body cavity, as well as in the legs themselves. It can be used in many ways. One of the most elegant is to pot it, to serve for lunch, or as the starter for a dinner party.

For 6 small individual pots:
250 g (9 oz) cooked crab or crayfish flesh
50 g (2 oz) butter
1 anchovy fillet
¼ tsp salt
½ tsp freshly grated nutmeg or mace
freshly ground black pepper
hot pepper sauce
1 Tbsp lemon juice
food colouring (optional)
2 Tbsp finely chopped chives
about 2 Tbsp melted butter
fresh herbs for garnish

Potted Crayfish or Crab

Catch or buy raw crabs. Boil for 5 minutes, then drain and cool. Lift off and discard the top shell of each crab.

Cut each crab in half, down its mid-line. To squeeze out the flesh, press a rolling pin or something else which is heavy on each half, where the legs join the body, and squeeze out the meat.

Or buy cooked crayfish bodies. Lift off and discard the upper back shell.

Break the legs and feelers and remove the flesh, using pliers if necessary. Separate the flesh from the inedible parts at the top of the legs in the body cavity.

Warm the first measure of butter until it is very soft, but not liquid. Put it in a food processor bowl with the anchovy fillet, salt, nutmeg, pepper to taste, and about 8 drops of hot pepper sauce. Process, then add the crab or crayfish flesh and the lemon juice. Process to mix to the texture you want.

The mixture should taste good at this stage. Taste, adjust the seasoning and add a little food colouring if desired.

Add chopped chives and spoon the mixture into six small individual pots, each about the size of an egg cup. Smooth the surface, and pour enough melted butter over each to cover them. Set a herb leaf in the butter. If you do not own individual pots, press the mixture into one fairly shallow dish instead.

Refrigerate for up to 48 hours.

Serve with toast or melba toast.

Spiced Tomato Juice

This makes a good start to a festive meal.

For 8 (125 ml/4 fl oz) servings:
1 litre (32 fl oz) tomato juice
1 tsp onion pulp
freshly ground black pepper
1 tsp Worcestershire sauce
¼ cup (60 ml/2 fl oz) lemon juice
¼ tsp celery salt

Prepare the onion pulp by scraping the cut surface of half an onion with a teaspoon. Mix all the ingredients together in a jug. Chill and serve over ice.

Quick Hummus

Hummus is a bean dip of Middle Eastern origin which has become very popular throughout the Western world.

This very quick but remarkably good version is made from canned garbanzo beans (chick peas). It is a very low-fat dip, since it is thinned down with the bean cooking liquid instead of the usual amount of oil.

If you cannot find canned beans, cook your own (saving the cooking liquid). The fastest-cooking white beans I know are black-eyed beans. They may be used to replace garbanzo beans in this dip.

1 (310 g/11 oz) can garbanzo beans
¼ cup tahini
1 clove garlic, chopped
1 spring onion, chopped
juice of ½ lemon
2 Tbsp oil
drained liquid from canned beans or cooking
  liquid

Drain the canned beans, reserving the liquid. Mix together the beans, tahini, garlic and the chopped spring onion in a food processor. Add the lemon juice and process until smooth, adding the oil then enough of the bean liquid to thin to the consistency you like.

Use with raw vegetables in sandwiches or in filled rolls, or as a dip with triangles of toasted pita bread, melba toast or crackers, or with a selection of raw vegetable crudités.

Choose from several of the following:

cauliflower florets
snow peas
carrots cut in strips or in diagonal slices
spring onions
cucumber or celery strips

Asparagus Squares

Make this the day before if you like. Serve it warm or hot, in small squares with a drink before a meal, or in large pieces (with a salad and bread roll) for lunch or a light meal. Inexpensive 'overgrown' zucchini add bulk and an interesting texture.

For 8–9 main course servings (or snacks for 20 people):
2 cups (400 g/14 oz) zucchini
1 onion, peeled
4 eggs
1½ cups (150 g/5 oz) grated cheese
1 tsp salt
freshly ground black pepper
1 cup (125 g/4½ oz) self-raising flour
1 (340 g/12–13 oz) can asparagus spears, drained
¼ cup (60 ml/2 fl oz) liquid from asparagus

Grate the unpeeled zucchini and onion into a large mixing bowl with the eggs, cheese and seasonings. Mix well with a fork. Add the flour, the drained, chopped asparagus and ¼ cup of the asparagus liquid and mix to combine. Pour the mixture into a non-stick buttered or baking-paper-lined shallow, square 20 cm cake tin and cook at 200°C (400°F) for 25 minutes or until evenly browned and firm to touch. Leave to stand for at least 5 minutes before cutting and serving.

Beavertown Pâté

This pâté is a treat for kidney lovers. Always make it with very fresh kidneys.

50g (2 oz) butter
6 lambs' kidneys
3 rashers bacon
1 onion, chopped
2 cloves garlic
2 hard-boiled eggs
2 anchovies
2 tsp Worcestershire sauce
1 Tbsp whisky or brandy
1 Tbsp finely chopped fresh herbs
freshly ground black pepper

Melt butter in a medium-sized pan. Add the finely chopped kidneys, the bacon from which the rinds have been cut, the onion and the finely chopped garlic.

Cook over a gentle heat for 10 minutes, stirring often.

While hot, purée or chop very finely in a food processor or blender. Add remaining ingredients and blend in thoroughly, adding pepper to taste.

Press mixture into small, straight-sided dishes, levelling off their tops.

Serve chilled, with melba toast or crackers.

Asparagus Squares and Spiced Tomato Juice

Rollmops

Rollmops

Rollmops are a form of pickled herrings.

Herring fillets are rolled and secured with wooden picks, which should be removed before serving. Serve whole or cut into attractive thin round slices with a sharp knife or unrolled and cut into strips or chopped small.

To soften the flavour of the rollmops quite markedly, whether they are served whole or cut up, coat with a little oil and lemon juice, or French dressing, or olive oil. (In the photograph, a dressing made from equal parts Tomato Salsa and olive oil was spooned over the sliced rollmops.)

Serving suggestions:
Slice rollmops and arrange attractively on a platter with tomato wedges or small tomatoes, sliced cucumber, red onion rings, quartered hard-boiled eggs, gherkins, watercress, salad greens, spring onions, etc. Serve with crusty bread rolls, and a selection of dressings.

Chop rollmops and arrange in a block on a plate with other blocks of chopped pickled beetroot, chopped raw apple, chopped mild (red) onion, and chopped cooked new potatoes. Moisten each ingredient with oil and lemon juice dressing for best flavour. Diners can choose and arrange their own selection on plates, in split rolls, or on wholegrain bread, with a sour cream or mayonnaise dressing.

Arrange cut-up rollmops through a warm potato salad with a Mustard and Dill Sauce, and garnish attractively.

Unroll rollmops, dip in French dressing, arrange on strips of hot toast spread with horseradish and cream cheese, and cut diagonally into short lengths.

Tomato Salsa
1 medium-sized onion
2 large cloves garlic
1 tsp ground cumin
1 tsp hot pepper sauce
1 tsp oreganum
1 (425 g/15 oz) can whole peeled tomatoes in juice

Quarter the onion and put into the food processor with the remaining ingredients. Process until the onion is finely chopped, then simmer in a saucepan for 3 minutes. Cool and add more hot pepper sauce or chilli powder, to taste. Refrigerate and use within 3–4 days.

Mustard and Dill Sauce
1–2 Tbsp wine vinegar
2 Tbsp hot water
3 Tbsp Dijon mustard
¼ cup (60 ml/2 fl oz) olive oil
1 Tbsp sugar
¼ tsp salt
1 Tbsp chopped dill leaves or 1 tsp dried dill

Put all the ingredients in a food processor bowl and process to mix thoroughly, then pour into a screw-topped jar to store. Shake well before use.

Smoked Salmon Slices

Slices of smoked salmon turn any event into a special occasion!

Unless you have a steady hand and a very sharp, long-bladed knife, you will probably prefer to buy smoked salmon already sliced.

The very thin slices are often interleaved with plastic for easy removal from the pack, and for instant use.

Sprinkle a little lemon juice over the slices, grind on a touch of freshly ground white or black pepper, and the smoked salmon is ready to serve.

Or Fold or roll a slice (or part of a cut slice), and arrange it attractively on a small square or triangle of firm wholegrain bread, and add a garnish of a small sprig of parsley, dill or chervil.

To serve simply as a first course:

Make elegant arrangements of two or three overlapping slices of salmon on individual plates, with triangles of lightly buttered wholegrain bread, one or more carefully cut lemon wedges, and a few carefully selected choice salad vegetables, *or*

Spread a spoonful of oil and lemon juice dressing on the plate, place the slices of salmon on it, then 'ruffle' the slices, so their surface is wavy. It is easy to move the slices on the film of dressing.) Arrange accompanying ingredients as above.

For a lunch main course:

Elaborate on the theme above, including other salad ingredients, such as slices of avocado, asparagus, etc. Offer one or more dressings (see below).

Wrap slices of smoked salmon around one, two or three stalks of freshly cooked or canned asparagus, or strips of avocado, or marinated cucumber or zucchini strips. 'Tie' each package with a knotted chive, or an individual sprig of parsley, dill, or chervil. Serve with horseradish sauce or another dressing.

For a champagne breakfast or special brunch:

Sprinkle slivers of chopped smoked salmon and very finely chopped chives or other herbs over the surface of nearly cooked scrambled eggs.

For a dramatic presentation at a dinner party:

Just before serving, place one or more strips (or a carefully cut shape) of smoked salmon on top of a folded or rolled cooked fish fillet, add a small fresh herb to garnish too, for a stunning colour combination. Stand it in a pool of sauce, or serve sauce or dressing separately.

Salmon Caviar

Salmon caviar, used to garnish the smoked salmon in the photograph, is not widely available but can be ordered from a delicatessen or through mail order.

Smoked Salmon Slices with Salmon Caviar

LIGHT MEALS

Quick Mini-Pizzas

SEE PHOTOGRAPH ON PAGE 28

Pizzas are now so common and we eat them so often it is hard to believe that, a generation ago, many of us did not know what a pizza was.

My pizza base recipes have changed over the years. This is my most recent, and fastest, yeast one. I usually make individual pizzas with it, although it may be used for one large pizza, too.

For 6–8 individual pizzas, or a 25–35 cm (10–14 inch) pizza base:
1¼ cups (315 ml/10 fl oz) warm water
2 Tbsp sugar
1 Tbsp dried yeast granules
2 Tbsp corn or soya oil
1 cup (125 g/4½ oz) self-raising flour
2 cups (250 g/9 oz) plain flour
1 tsp salt

Measure the water and sugar into a mixing bowl or food processor bowl. Stir or process to dissolve, double-check that the water is lukewarm, then add the yeast, mix or process briefly again, and leave to stand for at least 5 minutes, until the yeast starts to bubble.

Combine the oil, flours and salt in a large mixing bowl. (Replace 1 cup of plain flour with a cup of wholemeal flour if desired.) Stir in the bubbling yeast mixture and mix well. Add a little extra flour if necessary, to make a dough that is firm enough to turn out and knead on a floured board. Knead until smooth and satiny, then cut dough into six to eight pieces for individual pizzas. Roll each of these out to form a 15–18 cm (6–7 inch) circle, and put them on well-oiled baking trays. Leave them to stand for a few minutes while you prepare the toppings you want (see below) then bake at 220°C (425°F) for 10–15 minutes, until the dough is golden brown around the edges and lightly browned when you look underneath it.

Suggestions for pizza toppings:
- grated or sliced Mozzarella or cheddar cheese on each pizza
- lightly sautéed red or ordinary onions
- lightly oiled mushroom slices
- black olives, chopped anchovies or capers
- sautéed or roasted sliced red or green peppers
- commercially made tomato toppings, spaghetti sauce, etc.
- finely cubed ripe tomatoes, squeezed in a cloth to remove extra liquid, then mixed with chopped oreganum
- tomatoes prepared as above, but cooked in a little oil with chopped garlic until thick, instead of being squeezed
- fresh or dried thyme, oreganum, basil, etc.

Home-Style Baked Beans

These beans baked in a herbed tomato sauce bear little resemblance to the more mildly flavoured commercially canned beans. They make a popular main course.

For 4 main course servings:
1½ cups haricot beans
2 onions, chopped
2–3 cloves garlic
2 Tbsp oil
1 (425 g/15 oz) can whole tomatoes, chopped
2 Tbsp tomato paste
2 Tbsp sugar
1 Tbsp dark soya sauce
1 tsp ground cumin
½ tsp marjoram
¼ tsp thyme
black pepper
3 cups (750 ml/24 fl oz) hot water

Cover the beans with boiling water then leave to stand for 2 hours. Drain, add fresh water and boil for 1–2 hours until tender.

Chop the onions into fairly large chunks and roughly crush and chop the garlic. Combine these in a fairly large casserole dish, and coat with the oil. Bake uncovered at 160°C (325°F) for 30–40 minutes, or until the onion browns, stirring occasionally.

In a blender or food processor, or with a potato masher, combine the whole tomatoes, tomato paste and all the flavourings.

Stir the cooked beans, tomato mixture, seasonings and hot water into the onions and garlic, and bake uncovered at 160°C (325°F) for a further 90 minutes, stirring occasionally. If at any stage the mixture seems too thick, add a little more water.

Serve with crusty bread and a green salad or with cooked vegetables.

Spicy Potted Beef

This recipe is a modification of a recipe from a cookbook published in 1915!

The cooked mixture can be refrigerated for about a week. It is delicious served as a complete light meal, with bread rolls or toast, fresh salad vegetables and pickles. It makes a popular sandwich filling, too.

As a starter, make tiny individual pots (sealed with a layer of melted butter) or serve it already spread on crisp crackers or warm toast, with gherkins or slices of dill pickles.

For 2 cups:
500 g (1 lb 2 oz) lean chuck or skirt steak
100 g (3½ oz) butter
1½ Tbsp anchovy sauce
¼ tsp salt
½ tsp Trappey's hot pepper sauce
½ tsp freshly grated nutmeg
½ tsp mace
freshly ground black pepper

Select a heat-resistant glass or stainless steel bowl which will sit on a bread and butter plate inside a large saucepan with a close-fitting lid.

Using a sharp knife, cut the steak into thin slivers, across the muscle fibres if you can see these clearly. Put the steak into the bowl with the butter which has been cut in small cubes, the anchovy sauce, salt, hot pepper sauce, nutmeg and mace. Add black pepper to taste.

Stir to mix ingredients, then cover the bowl with another bread and butter plate or aluminium foil, stand it on the plate in the saucepan, add hot water to come halfway up the side of the bowl, cover the pan and bring to the boil. Once the water boils, turn the heat down very low and cook for 2 hours, without any further attention apart from checking to see that the water is simmering.

Taste the meat to check that it is tender, then tip the meat and liquid into a blender or food processor and purée until smooth. Spoon or pour into one, two, or individual containers, flattening the surface. If the potted meat will not be used for several days, pour enough melted butter over each one to cover the meat completely.

Spicy Potted Beef

Asparagus (or Corn) Flan

This flan forms its own crust as it cooks. Make it with corn for an economical family meal, or dress it up with asparagus when you're entertaining.

For 4 servings:
1 large onion, chopped
2 cloves garlic, chopped
1 Tbsp butter
2 cooked potatoes, cubed
½ cup (125 ml/4 fl oz) milk

Asparagus Flan

3 eggs
¼ cup (60 ml/2 fl oz) liquid from canned
    vegetables
½ tsp salt
½ cup (60 g/2 oz) self-raising flour
1 cup (100 g/3½ oz) grated tasty cheese
1 (340 g/13 oz) can asparagus spears
    or 1 (440 g/1 lb) can whole-kernel corn

Cook onion and garlic in the butter until tender but not brown. Add cubed cooked potato and heat through. Mix milk, eggs, ¼ cup liquid from the canned vegetables, salt and flour until blended, combine with onion mixture and pour into a buttered 23 cm (9 inch) metal pie plate or solid-bottomed flat tin. Cover with grated cheese and the drained asparagus or corn. Bake at 210°C (425°F) for 20–30 minutes or until set in the centre. Serve warm, in wedges.

Self-Crusting Mushroom Quiche

Use a non-stick dark coloured metal flan plate, pie plate, or cake tin when you make this quiche, and you should get good results.

For 4 servings:
2 onions, chopped
2 cloves garlic, chopped
1–2 Tbsp oil or butter
250 g (9 oz) mushrooms, chopped
2 eggs
½ tsp salt
¾ cup (185 ml/6 fl oz) milk
½ cup (60 g/2 oz) self-raising flour
1 cup (100 g/3½ oz) grated tasty cheese
2 tomatoes, sliced

Cook the onions and garlic in the oil or butter over a moderate heat for about 5 minutes, stirring several times. When barely tender, add the mushrooms, raise the heat, and add 1–2 tablespoons of water to start the mushrooms wilting then cooking.

Beat or food-process the eggs, salt and milk together until they are combined, then add the flour and beat or food-process very briefly, until free of lumps. Overmixing may mean that the crust does not form.

Pour about a quarter of the mixture into a 20 cm (8 inch) non-stick pan which has been buttered or sprayed as an extra precaution. Spread the onion and mushroom evenly over it, pour on the rest of the egg mixture, then sprinkle the grated cheese over the whole surface. Jiggle the pan to make sure that everything is fairly flat, then arrange sliced tomatoes in a circle around the edge.

Bake at 200°C (400°F) for 20–30 minutes, or until the centre is firm and the cheese browned. If removing from the pan to serve it, invert on to a sheet of plastic, place a board or serving plate upside down on the bottom of the quiche, then turn everything upside down again, so the quiche is sitting right side up on its serving dish, without its tin.

Sour Cream Onion Pie

This pie has a substantial crust which contrasts well with the rich, creamy filling. With a salad it makes a complete meal.

Crust
1 cup (125 g/4 oz) self-raising flour
¼ cup (25 g/1 oz) grated tasty cheese
¼ cup (60 ml/2 fl oz) milk

Filling
2 large or 4 small onions
25 g (1 oz) butter
2 eggs
1 cup (250 g/9 oz) sour cream
½ tsp salt
paprika or caraway seeds

Toss together in a bowl the flour and grated cheese. Add the milk and mix to form a fairly firm dough.

Roll out on a board with a little extra flour and line a buttered or sprayed 23 cm (9 inch) pie plate, folding the edge under and fluting it.

To make the filling, slice the onions and cook gently in the butter in a covered pan over a low heat for 10 minutes, until the onions are tender but have not browned.

Beat the eggs with the sour cream and salt. Pour on to the cooked onions, mix well and pour into the uncooked crust. Sprinkle with paprika or caraway seeds.

Bake at 220°C (425°F) for 10 minutes, then at 180°C (350°F) for 15–20 minutes, until firm in the centre.

Leek Flan

This flan, freshly baked or reheated, is a popular main course for lunch or dinner.

For a 20–23 cm (8–9 inch) quiche:
1 uncooked pastry pie crust
3 (500 g/1 lb 2 oz) small leeks
1 clove garlic
1 Tbsp butter
½ cup (125 ml/4 fl oz) water
3 eggs
1 cup (100 g/3½ oz) grated Emmentaler (or tasty) cheese
½ cup (125 g/4½ oz) sour cream
¼ cup (60 ml/2 fl oz) milk
¼ tsp salt

Roll bought or home-made pastry thinly to line a 20–23 cm (8–9 inch) flan tin or pie plate.

Slice the carefully washed leeks into 5 mm (¼ inch) pieces. Cook the leeks and the diced garlic in the butter for 2–3 minutes without browning, then add the water and cook until tender. Raise the heat and let the rest of the liquid evaporate.

Beat the eggs, grated cheese, sour cream, milk and salt together.

Remove the leeks from the heat then stir into the egg mixture. Pour filling carefully into prepared crust.

Bake at 220°C (425°F) for about 30 minutes or until the filling has set in the centre. Sprinkle with chopped herbs and/or paprika before serving if desired.

Ham, Cheese and Asparagus Quiche

A quiche like this makes a good main dish to serve to visitors on a warm day.

Serve it with a mushroom salad, a leafy tossed salad and bread rolls. The quiche takes some time to prepare, but it can be made ahead and reheated.

For about 6 servings:
Pastry
1 cup (125 g/4½ oz) flour
50–75 g (2–2½ oz) cold butter
about ¼ cup (60 ml/2 fl oz) cold water

Filling
100 g (3.5 oz) ham pieces
4 spring onions
1 (340 g/13 oz) can asparagus spears
½ cup (50 g/2 oz) grated tasty cheese
5 eggs
1 cup (250 ml/8 fl oz) cream or evaporated milk
½ cup (125 ml/4 fl oz) drained asparagus liquid
freshly ground black pepper

To make the pastry put the flour and cubed butter into a food processor and while the machine runs add the water in a trickle. Take care not to over-process and not to add too much water. Stop processing as soon as you can press the dough particles together to form a ball — before a ball of dough forms while machine is running. Refrigerate for at least 5 minutes. Roll out thinly. Press into a 23 cm (9 inch) flan or quiche pan.

Cut the ham into 5 mm (¼ inch) cubes and chop the spring onions, and sprinkle over the pastry. Arrange the well-drained asparagus on top in a spoke pattern or chop it into chunks for a quiche with a more casual appearance. Cover with the grated cheese.

Lightly beat the eggs, cream and asparagus liquid with the peppers and carefully pour over the filling. Cook at 220°C (425°F) for 30 minutes, or until the centre is set and the quiche has browned.

Variation:
Replace asparagus with cooked spinach (and its cooking liquid) if preferred.

Ham, Cheese and Asparagus Quiche

Summer Picnic Pie

With a picnic pie like this you need only fruit and drink to complete the meal. If you are planning a more elaborate picnic, you can add a cold chicken, crisp bread and salad vegetables as well.

It doesn't take long to make this pie if you have cooked extra vegetables the day before.

For a 23 cm (9 inch) pie:
about 350 g (13 oz) flaky pastry
3 eggs
3 Tbsp milk
2 ham steaks, chopped
    or 4 slices cooked bacon, chopped
2 sprigs mint, chopped
    or 4 spring onions
3–4 cold cooked new potatoes, sliced
1 cup cold cooked peas
salt (optional)

Summer Picnic Pie

Roll pastry in two rounds and use one to line a 23 cm (9 inch) pie plate.

In a large bowl mix eggs with milk to combine whites and yolks. Put aside a tablespoonful for a glaze. To the remainder add chopped ham steaks or bacon, mint or spring onions, cold potatoes and peas.

Add salt only if small amounts of ham or bacon are used. Tip filling into uncooked pastry.

Dampen edge of second piece of pastry. Use to cover filling, folding edges under. Press edges with a fork. Decorate top with pastry scraps and glaze with reserved egg. Cut steam vents in centre.

Bake at 200°C (400°F) for about 30 minutes. Lower heat if pastry browns before this, but do not remove from oven until filling has set.

Interesting Sandwiches

Sandwiches make a really good, practical light meal. They are the perfect answer for lunch to take to school or work or eat at home or outside, picnic style.

Nutritionally, sandwiches are winners, especially if you use only a film of butter or other spread, and combine thin layers of meat, cheese or eggs with generous amounts of salad vegetables and other interesting low-fat extras.

Sometimes, sandwiches prepared at home seem unexciting compared with the appealing (but expensive) sandwiches that you see on sale at lunch bars. They won't if you use a variety of breads, and use a generous selection of fillings. Plan your sandwiches as you plan for other meals. You will probably want to buy several different ingredients each week, just for sandwiches, especially if you start making them regularly.

It is easy for children to get sidetracked and make unwise choices if they take money to buy their own lunches. On the other hand, unless the nutritious lunch you pack gets eaten, it doesn't do anyone any good! Find out what happens at school, and make sure that your sandwiches meet with approval.

If you prepare sandwiches for other people to take away from home, consider making one for yourself to eat at lunchtime, too. It is a good feeling to know that your lunch is already prepared, and it may encourage you to make all your sandwiches more appealing.

If inspiration fails you when you are trying to dream up sandwich fillings, go and look at the fillings in a good sandwich bar or delicatessen. Two good slices of interesting bread, generously filled, tend to be more the order of the day than four or eight thinly filled, dainty little triangles.

Variety is always important, though. Make sandwiches of different shapes and sizes. Make club sandwiches. Fill bread rolls, and lengths of French bread. Buy and split pita or Lebanese breads, and make long substantial rolls from thin sheets of flat bread, if these are available. Look for breads with different colours, flavours and textures. English muffins, rye bread, sour dough and dense country-style loaves are available. Breads freeze well, so you can buy in bulk and use them as required.

If you fill your sandwiches and rolls generously, you may find it hard to hold them together. Plastic cling wrap is a life-saver, and a tightly confined sandwich invariably stays together better when it is unwrapped.

Watch that you do not put next to the bread ingredients which go soggy. If you put, for example, sliced tomato between two lettuce leaves, the bread will not be dampened.

Remember that it is not compulsory to use a spread on bread, when you are using a variety of fillings. You can often dispense with the spread altogether, especially if you are cutting down on fats.

There are many delicious dairy foods to choose from, and some of these are low in fat. Learn what is available and use a good selection.

When cooked meats, mayonnaise, and foods which spoil easily are included as sandwich fillings, check to see that the sandwiches will be stored in a cool place until they are eaten.

Sandwiches for a group to eat at home may be assembled by the diners on the spot. Put out plates of fillings and spreads, preferably in the order in which they should be used.

If you feel that sandwiches alone are not enough, in hot weather serve sandwiches with salads, and in cool weather team them with soups.

Use these instead of butter or margarine:

Alternative sandwich spreads:
- *low-fat cream cheese*
- *low-fat cream cheese mixed with horseradish*
- *cottage cheese, plain, or flavoured. (Cottage cheese used in larger amounts can also form the main part of a filling.)*
- *cheese spreads*
- *peanut butter, or other nut butters*
- *well-seasoned Bean Spread (see page 37)*
- *Hummus (see page 36)*
- *mayonnaise, plain or flavoured (use sparingly)*
- *meat or liver pâté (sparingly,) fish pâté and spreads*
- *unsweetened yoghurt, after straining in a lined sieve, to thicken it*
- *mustard spreads*
- *marmite etc.*

Fillings to use sparingly, with salad vegetables:
- *thinly sliced cold meat and poultry*
- *chopped hard-boiled egg mixtures*
- *thinly sliced sausage and salami*
- *crumbled cooked bacon*
- *grated cheese or soft sliced cheeses*
- *herbs for flavour*

Fillings for generous use:
- *lettuce and other leafy salad greens*
- *finely shredded cabbage*
- *grated carrot*
- *thinly sliced celery*
- *beetroot*
- *cucumber*
- *radishes*
- *tomatoes*
- *thinly sliced cauliflower*
- *asparagus*
- *sweetcorn, plain or creamed*
- *chopped peanuts or other nuts*
- *dried fruit, chopped or minced, with fruit juice to moisten*
- *dates or date spread*
- *bean sprouts and alfalfa sprouts*
- *cracked wheat salads*
- *green and red peppers*
- *raw or marinated mushrooms*
- *potato salads*
- *bean salads*
- *avocado slices (coated with lemon juice)*

Some sandwich fillings need their texture modified for easy spreading, so they hold together well and so they do not seem dry when they are eaten.

Sometimes it pays to mix the spread and filling ingredients together. This can speed up sandwich making. Unlikely mixtures often taste good!

Filling mixtures to use alone or with salad greens:
- *cream cheese or cottage cheese, chopped gherkin and beansprouts, with a little chilli sauce or chutney*
- *cooked (dried) beans mashed with chopped celery, spring onion, chilli sauce and mayonnaise.*
- *peanut butter, mashed baked beans and cooked bacon*
- *grated cheese, chopped celery or spring onion, and mayonnaise*
- *crunchy peanut butter, toasted chopped sunflower seeds and finely chopped sultanas with a little honey*
- *grated cheese with cottage cheese and chopped celery*
- *baked beans mashed with grated cheese*
- *dates, heated with orange juice to soften them, cooled and mixed with chopped nuts, or peanut butter and/or cottage or cream cheese*
- *chopped or minced cooked meat mixed with pickles or tomato sauce, with shredded cabbage or lettuce*
- *tuna mashed with mayonnaise with chopped cucumber or celery, and lettuce*
- *sweetcorn with relish, cream cheese and lettuce*
- *peanut butter with grated carrot, cream cheese and chopped sultanas*

Barbecued Bread Rolls

These are very popular additions to any barbecue. Served with a salad and/or barbecued vegetables, they can make a complete meal.

1 cup (100 g/3½ oz) grated tasty cheese
2 cloves garlic, finely chopped
1 Tbsp tomato sauce
2 Tbsp melted butter
1 French bread stick

Mix together the cheese, garlic, tomato sauce and melted butter. If too thick to spread add more tomato sauce or butter.

Cut the bread into 2 cm (¾ inch) slices, without cutting through the bottom crust, and spread with as much filling as you like.

Cut filled loaf in two pieces, and wrap each in aluminium foil without sealing it.

Barbecue on the grill rack, turning several times, until crisp and browned. This should take 10–15 minutes. Serve warm.

Toasted Roll-ups

These are economical and very popular with children. They go well with soup for a quick weekend lunch.

fresh sandwich bread
melted butter
grated cheese
canned cream-style corn
canned spaghetti

Cut crusts from bread and lightly brush edges and outside with melted butter. Spread other side with corn, sprinkle with grated cheese then lay canned spaghetti across diagonally. Garnish with pepper strips if desired, then fold the two opposite corners over spaghetti, secure with toothpicks, and bake at 200°C (400°F) for about 10 minutes or until golden brown and crisp.

Pita Bread Filling

Pita bread fillings do not need to hold together since they are contained in a pocket. Try the following combination, in amounts that suit you.

- *lettuce leaves*
- *finely chopped celery*
- *grated carrot*
- *chopped gherkin*
- *bean sprouts*
- *chopped cooked potato, or cooked rice or bulgar*
- *grated cheese*
- *mayonnaise*
- *chopped parsley and spring onion*
- *taco, tomato or chilli sauce.*

Use the lettuce leaves to line the pocket bread. Mix the next six ingredients with just enough mayonnaise to moisten. Add herbs, season to taste, adding a little taco, tomato, or chilli sauce.

Bean Spread

1 small onion, chopped
1 clove garlic, chopped
1 Tbsp oil
1 tsp oreganum
1 tsp ground cumin
¼–½ tsp chilli powder
1 (440 g/1 lb) can baked beans, drained
salt to taste

Cook first six ingredients over low heat for about 5 minutes. Add drained beans, cook for 2–3 minutes longer, then mash or food-process, thinning to spread or dip consistency with reserved liquid from the beans. Season to taste, and add a little lemon juice or tomato paste if desired.

Use in sandwiches or as a dip with corn chips and raw vegetables.

Onion Frittata

Over the years my plain, light omelettes have turned into the more substantial, firm, slowly cooked egg-and-vegetable mixtures that are found in Spain and Italy. My frittatas are made more of vegetables than eggs.

For 2 servings:
1 or 2 cloves garlic
2-4 red onions
1-2 stalks red silver beet (optional)
1 Tbsp oil or butter
3 eggs
2 Tbsp grated Parmesan cheese
½ tsp fresh thyme (optional)
pinch salt
freshly ground black pepper
1 Tbsp butter

Chop the garlic finely and cut the onions in 5 mm (½ inch) slices. If using the silver beet stalks, slice them the same thickness and save the leaves for later use.

Heat the oil or butter in a 18-20 cm (7-8 inch) pan, then cook the garlic, onions and silver beet stalks over a moderate heat for a few minutes. Add about a tablespoon of water, cover the pan, and cook until the water has evaporated and the vegetables are tender. Remove the lid and make sure that any liquid has evaporated.

Beat together with a fork the eggs, cheese, thyme, salt and pepper, until the whites and yolks are blended, then stir in the vegetables.

Add the second measure of butter to the hot pan, and when it foams pour in the egg mixture. Lower the heat and cook until the eggs are set around the sides and on the bottom. Sprinkle top with a little extra Parmesan cheese if desired.

To cook the top, cover with a lid, or put the frittata under a grill.

Serve hot or warm, or wrap leftovers to eat cold in packed lunches.

Savoury Apple Crêpes

Crêpes are thin, delicate, tender pancakes which are made in a small pan. As long as they are kept from drying out, they may be made ahead and refrigerated or frozen until required.

They make wonderful wrappers for many mixtures which might seem uninteresting if served alone.

Don't be discouraged if the first crêpes you make are not perfect. Once you get the hang of it, you will find you can turn out a pile of crêpes remarkably quickly and easily.

For 12-20 small crêpes, each about 15cm (6 inches) in diameter:
2 eggs
¾ cup (185 ml/6 fl oz) milk
½ cup (60 g/2 oz) flour
½ tsp salt

Combine ingredients in order given, in a blender or food processor. If mixing in a bowl, add egg then milk to dry ingredients and beat until smooth. Pour a measured quantity (e.g. 2 tablespoons) into a small, smooth-surfaced, well-sprayed or buttered preheated pan.

Immediately tilt pan so batter covers bottom in a thin film. If batter does not spread thinly, add more milk to thin it before making the next crêpe. Do not worry if pancakes are not evenly shaped circles.

When batter no longer looks wet in the centre, ease edges of crêpe from pan. Lift and turn carefully. Dry second side, without necessarily browning it. Remove from pan. Stack crêpes until required. Place them on a plate in a plastic bag to prevent drying out.

Note:
If freezing or refrigerating crêpes, place a piece of plastic between each for easy removal later.

Savoury Apple Crêpe filling
Sauté sliced onions in butter until tender, then add sliced apple and brown lightly. Add a little white wine and chopped sage if available. Cook until tender. Taste and season. Spread on cooked crêpes. Fold or roll the filled crêpes, sprinkle with Parmesan cheese if desired, and reheat if necessary. Serve with maple syrup.

Spinach and Cheese Crêpes

For really successful spinach crêpes, you need to thicken the spinach and season it very carefully.

For 4-6 servings:
1 recipe crêpe batter
1-2 cups cooked, drained, chopped spinach
3 Tbsp butter
3 Tbsp flour
½ tsp salt
1 tsp grated nutmeg
1½ cups (12 fl oz/360 ml) milk
1½ cups (150 g/7½ oz) grated cheese
paprika or Parmesan cheese

Prepare batter and make crêpes, according to recipe given above, using a small pan.

Cook, drain, squeeze and chop spinach.

Make the sauce. Melt the butter, add the flour, salt and nutmeg. Add the milk, ½ cup at a time, boiling and stirring between additions. After the last boiling, add the cheese.

Mix a third of the cheese sauce with the spinach. Spread spinach mixture over the crêpes and roll up. Place the filled crêpes in a well-sprayed ovenware pan. Pour sauce (thinned a little if necessary) over crêpes. Sprinkle with paprika or Parmesan cheese.

Bake at 200°C (400°F) for 20 minutes or until bubbly. Brown surface under grill before serving.

Onion Frittata

FISH &
SEAFOOD

Barbecued Fish

It's hard to beat a meal of freshly caught fish, lightly cooked to perfection on a gas barbecue!

Because fish is delicate, it must be handled carefully for good results. Double-sided hinged grilling baskets enable fish to be turned without breaking up, and make life easier for the barbecue cook.

Barbecued Fish Steaks

Fish steaks are best cooked in a hinged wire basket over a grill rack, or on a hot plate. Use Lemon Butter Baste or Garlic Herb Butter to brush surfaces before cooking. Steaks about 2 cm (¾ inch) thick may cook in 2 minutes per side in the hinged basket. Place brushed fish on the preheated plate, if using the solid plate. Cook for about the same time as you would in a pan on the stove.

Barbecued Fish Fillets

Cook as above, in a hinged basket or on a solid hot plate. It is likely that the thinner edges of fillets may overcook before the centre is cooked. Steaks are easier to cook evenly, if you have the choice.

Barbecued Whole Round Fish

SEE PHOTOGRAPH ON PAGE 40
If you like fishing, you may want to invest in a curved, fish-shaped hinged basket which will cradle your fish while it barbecues over the grill rack. The fresh fish should be gutted (from as small a slit as possible) and the body cavity cleaned and filled with herbs, lemon slices, crushed garlic, sliced onion, etc., for extra flavour. Wild fennel leaves, dill leaves, wild marjoram or wild mint from riverbanks add interesting flavours. (Use only herbs which you can identify.) These items are not to be eaten, but they delicately flavour the flesh.

It is not essential to scale the fish if you intend to peel back the skin before serving the flesh. Some cooks like to cut diagonal slashes in the thick flesh on each side of the fish, since this ensures more even cooking, while others prefer to serve the fish unmarked. Brush both sides of the fish with melted butter, or with Lemon Butter Baste. A layer of grape leaves between the coated fish flesh and the grill basket produces a more evenly cooked result, and is worth trying if you barbecue fish often and have grape leaves available.

Cooking times vary enormously with the size and thickness of the fish, and with the conditions. A thick fish will cook faster if a domed lid or aluminium foil tent is used to keep the top part warm while the bottom grills.

Barbecued Shellfish

SEE PHOTOGRAPH ON PAGE 40
Our family loves to start a barbecue meal with mussels from the supermarket, steamed open. Overcooking toughens shellfish, so you should take them from the heat soon after they open, before this happens.

Make sure that you start with mussels with shells that are tightly closed, or which close quickly when you tap them. Place them on the grill rack or in a flat hinged basket. As soon as shells open slightly, lift from barbecue, drain off liquid, and turn other way up. At this stage put a little Lemon and Garlic Dipping Sauce or Garlic Parsley Butter in each shell if you like. As soon as mussels are firm, before they shrink, remove from heat. Serve on the half shell, on a flat platter, with whatever condiments you fancy.

Spiced Barbecued Sole or Flounder

A small whole flatfish, quickly cooked on a gas barbecue, served with a warmed crusty bread roll and a cucumber and tomato salad, is hard to beat, on a summer evening. Since a small fish cooks in 2–3 minutes, it is easy to cook one fish after another, until everyone is served.

Mix together in a shaker:
1 tsp chilli powder
1 tsp paprika
1 tsp garlic powder
1 tsp ground cumin
1 tsp salt
1 tsp oreganum

For each fish to be cooked, warm together:
1 tsp butter
1 tsp light soya sauce
1 tsp lemon juice

Allow a 200–300 g (7–10 oz) scaled flatfish for each person. Make three or four parallel diagonal cuts to the bone on each side of the fish, to allow for more even cooking. Brush oil mixture on each side. Place 1 or 2 flatfish in a hinged flat grilling basket for easy turning, sprinkle each side with the seasoning mix, and barbecue over a high heat until the flesh at the thickest part will flake when tested with a fork. This may be as soon as 1 minute for a small fish. Turn and cook the second side. Serve immediately, with a squeeze of lemon or lime juice, and a little extra seasoning.

Lemon Butter Baste

1 large clove garlic, finely chopped
1 Tbsp butter
2 tsp light soya sauce or fish sauce
1 Tbsp lemon juice

Heat garlic with butter until the butter bubbles. Stir in soya or fish sauce and lemon juice.

Brush on chicken or fish before and during cooking.

Mussels in Curried Tomato Sauce

The smaller black-shelled mussels we collected from clean, rocky beaches as children taste very similar to the green-lipped mussels that are now cultivated and sold in fish shops and supermarkets. Use either to make this delicious recipe.

For 2–3 servings:

1 kg (2 lb 2 oz) mussels in the shell (about 12 large mussels)
½ cup (125 ml/4 fl oz) fairly dry white wine
½ cup (125 ml/4 fl oz) water
1 onion, finely chopped
2 cloves garlic, finely chopped
thyme, dill, fennel, or parsley
1 Tbsp butter
½ tsp curry powder
1 Tbsp flour
½ cup (125 ml/4 fl oz) tomato juice
2 Tbsp double cream
about ½ cup peeled tomato flesh

Scrub live mussels and cut off beards with scissors, discarding any mussels which do not close when tapped.

In a large frypan combine the wine, water, onion and garlic. (For speed, chop the onion and garlic with a little of the water in a food processor.) Bring to the boil and simmer gently while chopping any or all of the fresh herbs mentioned. If fresh herbs are not available, used dried herbs. Use amounts to suit your taste. Their flavour will be masked by the curry powder, but the sauce is not as good if they are left out. Add herbs to the frypan.

Mussels in Curried Tomato Sauce

Put the mussels in the simmering liquid, cover, and cook until the shells open wide, then remove them with a slotted spoon or tongs, reserving all liquid. Leave liquid to continue cooking gently while you remove mussels from their shells. Discard shells, and remove any bits you do not like to eat from the mussels. Drain any extra liquid from the mussels into the pan.

Strain the cooking liquid into a bowl, and throw out all the vegetable matter.

Melt the butter in the pan, add the curry powder and cook gently for about a minute, then stir in the flour, the tomato juice and the strained liquid. Stir until smooth and thick, then add the cream. Bring back to the boil, add the cooked mussels and the pieces of tomato, and heat through.

Do not leave the mixture simmering, or the mussels will shrink and toughen. Taste, adjust seasoning if necessary, and sprinkle with more of any fresh herbs used earlier.

Serve in a bowl with crusty bread, on fettucine or other pasta, or with rice. Serve a green salad separately if desired.

Note:

It can be disconcerting eating large mussels in one mouthful. Cut large mussels into smaller pieces before you add them to the sauce.

If you cannot get fresh mussels, use marinated mussels, but do not use the marinating liquid. Use 1 cup (250 ml/8 fl oz) of wine instead of ½ cup when making the sauce.

43

Old-Fashioned Fish Pie

There is something very satisfying about a fish pie. It involves several different steps, but you can get on with one part of the recipe while something else is cooking. Once you have the pie assembled, you can put it aside to bake later, or you can heat it through straight away.

For 4 servings:
about 750 g (1 lb 10 oz) potatoes
2 eggs, hard-boiled
2 leeks (about 600g/1 lb 6 oz)
2 tsp butter
¼ cup (60 ml/2 fl oz) water
1 (310 g/11 oz) can smoked fish fillets
2 Tbsp butter
½ tsp curry powder
2 Tbsp flour
1½ cups (375 ml/12 floz) liquid (see below)
milk for mashed potatoes
2 Tbsp grated Parmesan cheese

Peel the potatoes thinly, cut them into quarters and boil them until tender in a covered saucepan in lightly salted water. Wash the eggs, and put them in to hard-boil while the potatoes cook, remove them after 10–15 minutes.

Cut the carefully washed leeks into 1 cm (¼ inch) slices. Remove the dark outer leaves as you get further up the leek, but slice the tender inside leaves, too. Put the leeks with the 2 teaspoons butter and the water, in a covered pan. Cook for about 5 minutes or until tender-crisp, and still bright green, then drain, reserving liquid.

Open the can of fish, drain off and reserve the liquid, and break the drained fish into chunks in a lightly buttered or sprayed ovenware casserole dish, about 18×23 cm (7×9 inches). Spread the cooked, drained leeks over the fish, and add the hard-boiled egg, chopped into pieces.

Put the fish liquid and leek cooking liquid in a measuring cup, and make up to 1½ cups (375 ml/12 fl oz) with milk.

In the empty leek saucepan, melt the second measure of butter with the curry powder, then add the flour, and heat until it bubbles. Stir in a third of the liquid and heat constantly until it comes to the boil, add the next third, and stir and heat until it boils again, then add the remaining liquid, and repeat. Let the sauce simmer gently for about 5 minutes. Taste. Sauce should have a mild but interesting flavour, and need no extra seasoning. Pour over the fish, leek, and egg. Mix carefully and spread evenly over the dish.

Drain and mash the potatoes, adding as much milk as you need to get a smooth, creamy mixture. Spoon over fish and sauce mixture, sprinkle top with the Parmesan cheese, then roughen surface with a fork.

Reheat at about 180°C (350°F), until potato topping is lightly browned and crisp, and bottom is bubbling.

This should take about 20 minutes if the fish pie has just been prepared, or 30–45 minutes if pie has been made ahead and refrigerated.

Variation:
For a thicker fish layer, use fish from 2 cans if preferred, but discard all the liquid from 1 can, or sauce will be too salty. Do not change the quantities of any other ingredients.

Tomato-Baked Fish Fillets

A low-fat tomato topping on these fish fillets looks attractive and tastes good.

Always take care not to overcook fish, since it dries out, toughens and spoils.

For 2 servings:
2 skinless, boneless fish fillets (about 150g/5 oz) each)
flour for coating
1 small onion, finely chopped
1 tsp oil or butter
1 tsp water
½ cup finely chopped tomato
¼ tsp salt
¼ tsp sugar
1 tsp tomato paste
pinch each dried basil and oreganum
dash hot pepper sauce

Cut each fish fillet lengthways and coat lightly with flour. Arrange the fish in a lightly oiled dish, in one layer.

Cook the onion in the oil and water in a small frypan until tender. Stir in the remaining ingredients and stir briefly over the heat to combine.

Spread the warm topping over the fillets and bake uncovered at 200°C (400°F) for 8 minutes, or until the fillets in the centre of the dish will flake.

Serve on or with rice, with a green leafy salad.

Lemon and Garlic Dipping Sauce

2 Tbsp lemon juice
2 cloves garlic
1 small dried chilli
2 Tbsp sugar
2 Tbsp fish sauce or light soya sauce
2 Tbsp hot water
1 spring onion, finely chopped

Process all ingredients except spring onion together in a blender or food processor until finely chopped. Pour through a sieve, and add spring onion. Use as a dipping sauce or pour a few drops over barbecued fish, shellfish, lamb and vegetables.

Old-Fashioned Fish Pie

Sautéed Groper

This is a quick and easy way to cook a groper steak.

For each serving:
a 250 g (9 oz) groper steak, 1 cm (¼ inch) thick
flour

To microwave:
Lighly flour the groper steak. Preheat a microwave browning dish on Full power for 5 minutes. Add 1 teaspoon of butter or oil, then the fish. Microwave on Full power for 1 minute. Turn, microwave for about 1½ minutes, or until cooked as desired.

To sauté:
Sauté the floured steak in butter or oil in a heavy pan over a moderate heat for 2–3 minutes per side.

Serve with Summer Sauce (see below).

Variation:
Use thick fillet of snapper instead of groper.

Summer Sauce

This sauce is interesting and tangy and leftover sauce is good with cooked vegetables.

1 egg yolk
3 Tbsp lemon juice
2 tsp capers
1 tsp caper liquid
2 anchovy fillets
1 shallot, chopped
1 tsp mixed mustard
1 sprig fresh parsley
1 Tbsp chopped fresh herbs, e.g. dill leaves,
   chives, etc.
¾ cup (185 ml/6 fl oz) olive, corn or soya oil

Place all the ingredients except the oil in a blender or food processor bowl. Process briefly to mix then add the oil in a continuous steady stream until the sauce thickens to a fairly thin pouring consistency.

Serve with Sautéed Groper (see above).

Note:
Use within 24 hours for best flavour.

Fish Fillets with Curry Cream Glaze

These fish fillets are coated with a creamy mixture flavoured with dill leaves and curry powder. This is a delicious Scandinavian combination of flavours. Although it sounds rich, only a small amount of cream is used in the recipe.

For 2 servings:
1 clove garlic, finely chopped
1 tsp butter
½ tsp curry powder
2 skinless, boneless fish fillets, about 150–200 g
   (5–7 oz) each

½ cup (125 ml/4 fl oz) white wine
2 Tbsp low-fat cream
1 tsp chopped fresh dill or ½ tsp dried dill leaf
about 1 tsp cornflour
extra wine

Chop the garlic very finely and cook it gently in the butter, in a pan big enough to hold the fish in one layer, for about a minute. Stir in the curry powder, then the wine. Bring to the boil, then add the fish, cut in pieces, the cream and the dill.

Turn the fish so that it has been coated with the cooking liquid, then cover the pan and simmer gently for about 5 minutes, or until the fish is opaque in its thickest part. Turn after about 2 minutes.

Mix the cornflour to a cream with a little more wine, and pour about half of it into the fish, shaking the pan gently. Add the rest if necessary. The final sauce should coat the pieces of fish. Taste the sauce and adjust the seasonings.

Serve with rice, green beans, and a tomato or other salad.

Barbecued Foiled Fish

It is almost impossible to successfully barbecue fillets of soft-fleshed fish because they will not keep their shape.

Aluminium foil-wrapped fish parcels barbecue well, however. In this recipe the fish is given a delicious Oriental flavour before it is enclosed in individual parcels.

For 4 servings:
750 g (1 lb 10 oz) boneless fish fillets, cut in pieces
3 Tbsp lemon juice
2 Tbsp light soya sauce or fish sauce
1 tsp pepper sauce
1 Tbsp chopped coriander leaf or spring onion
1 Tbsp oil
2 tsp cornflour
1 tsp finely chopped garlic, optional

Combine all ingredients in an unpunctured plastic bag, and knead gently to mix. Refrigerate until required.

Make four squares of doubled foil, put quarter of the fish on each, then fold foil over fish and seal edges, rolling foil over several times and excluding the air. Finished packages should be about 10×15 cm (4×6 inches).

Cook over a grill rack for preference, or on a hot plate. In good conditions, fish should cook in 2–3 minutes per side. Test one package if necessary. Flesh should be milky white, and liquid slightly thickened.

Serve packets on plates so diners can unfold or cut open their own portions. Serve with lemon wedges, salad and heated bread rolls.

Sautéed Groper

Oven-Fried Fish Fillets

Oven-Fried Fish Fillets

This is the 'fried' fish that I have cooked, over the past 30 years, when I did not want my house to smell like a fish and chip shop long after the meal was eaten.

Serve chips with the fish if you like, but at other times try slipping the cooked fish into a heated, but not too crusty, split bun.

For 4 servings:
4 skinless, boneless fish fillets, about 100–150 g
(3½–5 oz)
¼ cup (60 ml/2 fl oz) milk
1 tsp salt or flavoured salt
few drops hot pepper sauce (optional)
½ cup (50 g/2 oz) dry breadcrumbs
25–50 g (1–2 oz) butter

Check that the fillets have no bones, and trim them if necessary.

Mix the milk, salt and pepper sauce in a small bowl.

Measure the crumbs on to a shallow plate or a paper towel. Coat the fillets first with seasoned milk, then with crumbs.

Have the oven preheated to its highest heat, about 230°C (450°F).

Select a shallow baking dish (preferably metal, with a non-stick finish) that will hold the fillets in one layer, without too much space between them, and melt the butter in it until it is bubbling but has not burned.

Turn each fillet in the hot pan so that the side coated first is uppermost. Arrange fillets so they are not touching.

Bake at 230°C (450°F) for 10–15 minutes, until the flesh in the centre of each fillet will flake, and until the coating has browned in parts. Take care not to overcook or the fish will be dry.

Serve promptly.

Variation:
Replace about half the breadcrumbs with Parmesan cheese for extra flavour and colour.

Whitebait Patties

It may seem expensive to use 100 g of whitebait but it is not as dear as many takeaways (for two people). Remember this before you decide that whitebait is a treat that you cannot afford.

For 2 servings:
2 eggs
3 brown bread toast slices
2 spring onions
1 sprig parsley
100 g (3½ oz) whitebait
¼ tsp salt
few drops hot pepper sauce
about 1 Tbsp butter

Beat the eggs in a shallow bowl, using a fork. Beat only enough to combine the whites and yolks.

Crumb the bread, preferably using a food processor, otherwise breaking it up, leaving it to stand in the egg, then working it with your fingers until it disintegrates. Wholegrain bread gives the patties a good texture and flavour.

Add the very finely chopped onion and parsley. These are best added to the crumbed bread in the food processor, and cut in briefly.

Stir the rinsed whitebait into the egg-and-crumb mixture, with the salt and hot pepper sauce.

Heat a large, preferably non-stick pan, add half the butter, and as soon as it melts and bubbles put in spoonfuls of the whitebait mixture, making four fairly large patties.

Cook until lightly browned on both sides, using the rest of the butter when necessary, usually 4–5 minutes altogether.

Serve immediately, with lemon wedges.

Note:
The whitebait used in this recipe are the small, translucent matchstick-sized variety.

Tarakihi with Lemon Cream Sauce

I have always regarded steamed or poached fish as 'comfort food'. I notice with interest that, in the past 10 years, fish cooked like this has become very popular restaurant fare.

Poached fish certainly contains fewer calories than fried fish, but the delicious sauces that coat the poached fish often owe their flavour and texture to butter and cream, so do not take it for granted that you are eating a low calorie dish.

For 2 servings:
2 fillets tarakihi or other firm fine-textured fish,
*   about 100–150 g (3½–5 oz) each*
2 cloves garlic, finely chopped
2 tsp butter
½ cup (125 ml/4 fl oz) water
1 Tbsp lemon juice
thinly peeled rind of ½ lemon
¼ tsp dried thyme
1 tsp flour
2 Tbsp sour cream
1 spring onion, finely chopped

Cut each fillet into two lengthways strips, removing the thin strip of fish containing the bones.

Cook garlic in 1 teaspoon of the butter for about 1 minute, without letting it brown at all. Add the water, lemon juice, rind and thyme, then add the fillets, cover and cook gently for about 2 minutes per side, or until the centre of each piece is opaque. Remove each fillet as soon as it is cooked. Keep cooked fillets on warmed plates in a warm oven.

Strain the cooking liquid into a small container pressing to get all the flavour.

Melt the remaining butter in the same pan, stir in the flour over a low heat, then add the strained liquid, the cream and the spring onion. Cook, stirring constantly until smooth and of coating consistency. Taste and adjust seasoning, adding a little salt, pepper and maybe a pinch of sugar if necessary. Thin sauce with a little extra water if it becomes too thick.

You should finish up with just enough sauce to pour over the four fillets to coat them.

Serve with mashed or new potatoes, zucchini and young carrots.

Herbed Baked Fish

The microwave oven must have made life easier for many cooks who have a fishing enthusiast in the family. It is easy to cook a little fish, exactly as it came from the water an hour or so earlier, then to lift off and discard the skin and scales, and to remove the flesh carefully, leaving the skeleton and even the gut intact.

The cooked fish can be seasoned and eaten as it is, or stirred into batter and fried, if you feel that fried fish *must* be served.

Larger whole fish microwave well, too.

Gut the fish, but scale it only if you want to eat the skin. Cut several slashes down to the bone, on each side, where the flesh is thickest, for most even cooking. Fill the central body cavity with fresh herbs, slices of lemon, chopped onion or shallot, and crushed garlic cloves.

Turn the fish in plain or garlic-flavoured melted butter, then wrap in greaseproof paper or parchment, or cover both the fish and plate with plastic cling wrap. Vent this in several places, and microwave on Full power, allowing 45–50 seconds per 100 g (3½ oz) fish.

If the whole fish is too big to fit, remove its head and tail before weighing and preparing it. (You can always cook these briefly, then arrange them at each end of the cooked fish before serving, with large parsley garnishes to mask your surgery!)

Bake even larger fish in a conventional oven. Prepare as above, wrapping in aluminium foil rather than plastic cling wrap or paper. Bake a 2 kg (4 lb 5 oz) trout at 180°C (350°F) for about 25 minutes.

The times given here are guides only. Before the estimated time has been reached, test the flesh at the thickest part; to see if it has turned milky, and will flake.

Skin and fillet the cooked fish before serving with its buttery cooking juices.

Orange Groper Steaks

These steaks are popular with everyone who eats them!

For a stronger orange flavour add more orange rind, for a milder one, use less.

For 1 serving:
1 small or ½ a large groper steak
flour for coating
2 tsp oil
2 Tbsp orange juice
1 tsp light soya sauce
½ tsp finely grated orange rind
1 spring onion, chopped

Lightly coat the groper steaks with flour, and brown on each side in a hot pan containing the oil.

Add the remaining ingredients to the hot pan. Turn steaks in the liquid as it thickens, then cover the pan and cook very gently until the steaks are cooked in the centre. Pour remaining glaze over the steaks when serving.

CHICKEN

Festive Roast Chicken

SEE PHOTOGRAPH ON PAGE 50

There are times when you want a special occasion meal for a reasonable price.

A chicken goes a long way when you serve it with Stuffing Balls (see below). A frozen chicken, thawed slowly in the refrigerator, costs less than a fresh chicken and, carefully cooked, tastes just as good.

Buy a 1.5 kg (3 lb) chicken for 6 servings. Thaw if necessary. Remove giblets, etc. and pat dry. (Put some of the uncooked stuffing ball mixture in the neck cavity if you like.) Tuck wing tips under bird's neck. For extra flavour put herbs, lemon slices, chopped onion or garlic loosely in main cavity. Do not tie the legs together. Rub the skin with oil, melted butter or a teaspoon each of lemon juice and soya sauce.

Roast uncovered at 170°C (325°F) for 1½–2 hours, until the juice runs clear, not pink, when the flesh is pierced deeply. Leave to stand for about 10 minutes before serving.

Make gravy by stirring 2 tablespoons flour into fat-drained pan drippings over a low heat. Add about 2 cups vegetable liquid and/or water, and simmer until gravy thickens. Strain, adjust seasonings and serve with slices of chicken.

Stuffing Balls

SEE PHOTOGRAPH ON PAGE 50

1 large onion, finely chopped
1 egg
500 g (1 lb 2 oz) sausage meat
1 tsp oreganum
1 tsp garlic salt
1 tsp celery salt
1 cup dry breadcrumbs
1 (440 g/1 lb) can cream-style corn
¼ cup (60 ml/2 fl oz) tomato paste
1 cup (250 ml/8 fl oz) water

Thoroughly mix together all ingredients except the tomato paste and water. Mix the tomato paste and water in a shallow baking dish that will hold 20–30 little meat balls in one layer. Form the meat mixture into small balls and place them in the liquid in the dish. Bake uncovered at 170°C (325°F) for about 40 minutes, turning halfway through the cooking time if you like. Serve with Festive Roast Chicken (see above).

Grandmother's Chicken Casserole

The best container for this type of casserole is one made of heavy metal which can be put directly on the burner to brown the bird, then put into the oven.

If you do not have a heavy, covered metal casserole, brown the chicken in a frying pan, then transfer it to an ovenproof, but not flameproof, casserole. It may take a little longer to cook in this, so adjust cooking times accordingly.

For 4–6 servings:
1 1.5 kg (3 lb) chicken
2 Tbsp oil
2 cloves garlic, optional
½ cup (125 ml/4 fl oz) white wine or stock
½ cup (125 ml/4 fl oz) water or stock
pepper, paprika, etc.
2–3 rashers bacon
1 bunch herbs
6–8 small potatoes
6–8 small carrots
2 stalks celery, chopped
6–8 whole small onions
about 6 small wedges pumpkin
cornflour and water
chopped parsley

Pat the chicken dry, then place it breast up and push down firmly, so the breast is flattened, and will brown more evenly. Heat oil in a large covered heavy metal casserole, then brown the breast side of the chicken in it. Turn and brown the back, too, adding the sliced garlic just before it is ready. Turn off the heat and add the liquid.

Sprinkle with pepper and paprika, put the bacon rashers, whole or cut in short lengths, around the chicken. If you have fresh herbs, tie together some thyme, parsley, lovage and a bayleaf with a string long enough to remove easily before serving. Or add dried herbs to the liquid. Cover the casserole and bake at about 180°C (350°F) for 30 minutes, then add the prepared vegetables, cut in even sizes so they will cook evenly. Cover and cook for another 30–45 minutes, until the chicken is well cooked and the vegetables just cooked.

Skim any visible fat from the liquid around the chicken, and thicken the remaining liquid with cornflour paste, taking care not to break up the vegetables. Stir in a generous amount of parsley, and serve from the casserole, or from a shallow serving plate.

Lemon and Herb Roast Chicken

There is always something especially festive about a roast chicken on a platter, especially if it is garnished nicely and brought to the table for carving and serving while everybody is sitting there waiting.

Make a point of celebrating family festivals with this special emphasis on meal presentation. It is this that will be remembered, rather than fussy recipes or expensive food!

For 4–8 servings:
1 1.5 kg (3 lb) chicken
1 lemon
3 cloves garlic
1 sprig fresh tarragon or ½ tsp dried tarragon
3–4 Tbsp butter, melted
½ cup (125 ml/4 fl oz) white wine
½ tsp salt
fresh ground black pepper

Wash and dry the chicken thoroughly inside and out, using paper towels. Make about eight deep cuts in the lemon.

Almost flatten 2 of the unpeeled garlic cloves and put them with the tarragon (or thyme or several sprigs of other herbs) and the lemon inside the body cavity.

Sit a piece of unpunctured aluminium foil about 30 cm (12 inches) long, in a small roasting pan or other suitable cooking container. Place the chicken on the foil in the empty pan, lifting up the sides of the foil to cradle the chicken. Do not wrap the chicken in the foil.

Warm the butter, wine and seasonings together, chopping the last garlic clove and adding it before brushing the chicken with this mixture. Pour the remaining liquid around the chicken. Bake at 200°C (400°F) for 1 hour, basting several times during cooking with the liquid from around the chicken. The chicken is cooked when the juice from the thickest part of the thigh or drumstick is clear and yellowish rather than pink when pierced with a skewer, and when the skin is golden brown.

Lift the chicken on to a serving plate, garnish with a twist of lemon peel and a bunch of the herbs used in the body cavity, draining all the liquid from the cavity into the pan juices. Skim off and discard the buttery mixture from the cooking liquid, and serve the remaining liquid, unthickened, over the sliced meat if desired.

Note:
The foil cradle stops the wine from evaporating and the butter from spattering as the chicken cooks. It also prevents the pan from getting dirty.

Lemon and Herb Roast Chicken

Paprika-Baked Chicken

Chicken drumsticks and scones, baked together in a large pan, make an excellent casual meal which can be taken outside to eat in the garden, or on the patio.

A salad or corn on the cob will complete an easy dinner!

For 4–6 servings:
2 Tbsp butter
2 Tbsp oil
12 chicken drumsticks
2 Tbsp flour
1 tsp paprika
½–1 tsp curry powder
1 tsp garlic salt
1 tsp castor sugar

Melt the butter with the oil in a large roasting pan, then turn the chicken pieces (which have been dried with a paper towel) in this to coat evenly. Push the chicken pieces to one end of the pan so they are close together in one layer.

Mix the remaining dry ingredients together in a screw-topped jar, then transfer this mixture into a small sieve and shake evenly over the chicken pieces, turning them once, so all sides are coated.

Rearrange the coated chicken pieces in the roasting pan so they are not crowded and bake uncovered at 200°C (400°F) for 40 minutes. Turn them after 20 minutes, then again 10 minutes after this, pushing the chicken to one end of the pan and leaving half the pan empty so Pan-Baked Scones (see below) can be cooked in it, alongside the chicken.

Chicken pieces are cooked when the juices near the bone (at the thick end) run clear, not pink, when pierced. If the chicken is cooked before the scones brown, remove them, and return them to the pan for serving.

Pan-Baked Scones

These scones are turned in the drippings of Paprika-Baked Chicken (see above) so they have extra colour and flavour.

2 cups (250 g/8 oz) flour
4 tsp baking powder
2 Tbsp butter, melted
about ¾ cup (185 ml/6 fl oz) milk

Sift the flour and baking powder into a bowl. Melt the butter, remove from the heat and add the milk. Pour all the liquid into a depression in the middle of the flour, and mix with a knife or firm spatula to make a soft dough, just firm enough to handle. (Add a little more flour or milk if necessary).

Turn the dough out on to a floured board, pat out with the edge of your hand or roll out lightly with a floured rolling pin. For scones to cook with the chicken as above, roll them more thinly than normal. Cut into 12–16 round or square scones and turn each one in the buttery chicken juices before placing fairly close together in the empty end of the roasting pan.

Bake at 200°C (400°F) for about 12 minutes, or until lightly browned top and bottom. Serve scones and chicken hot or warm.

Variation:
Replace drumsticks with other chicken pieces. Alter the times to suit the pieces you use if necessary.

Clare's Apricot Chicken

There are times when the most enthusiastic cook wants an easy recipe.

This put-it-all-in-the-pan-together recipe tastes very good, and is suitable for such occasions. Try it!

For 4–6 servings:
6 chicken drumsticks and 6 wings
2 cups (500 ml/16 fl oz) apple and orange juice
1 onion, chopped
2 tsp grated fresh root ginger
12 dried apricot halves, chopped
½ tsp salt
pinch chilli powder
2 Tbsp toasted sesame seeds

Put everything except the sesame seeds together in a large non-stick pan with a lid. Cover and simmer for 30–45 minutes, until the liquid is thick and syrupy and the chicken is tender and nicely browned. Turn the pieces every 10–15 minutes, checking the heat and the level of the liquid. If it boils down and thickens too quickly, add extra liquid.

Sprinkle with toasted sesame seeds and serve on rice or noodles, with a salad, or with cooked green beans.

Garlic Herb Butter

3–4 cloves garlic, peeled
1 cup parsley sprigs
small sprigs of 1–2 fresh herbs, e.g. thyme, dill, sage or basil
200 g (7 oz) soft (not melted) butter
a little lemon rind
1–2 Tbsp lemon juice
black pepper
hot pepper sauce

Chop together very finely in a food processor the garlic, parsley springs and other fresh herbs. Add butter, lemon rind, and lemon juice. Season with black pepper and hot pepper sauce, process to mix, then refrigerate in a covered dish until needed, up to 2 weeks. Melt small quantities to brush over fish, or skinned chicken breasts or vegetable kebabs before barbecuing.

Paprika-Baked Chicken with Pan-Baked Scones

Barbecued Chicken

Chicken barbecues beautifully! Although you can barbecue it in any form, it makes sense to concentrate on chicken which has been 'broken down' into smallish, flattish pieces, since these will cook more easily, evenl,, and quickly than a whole chicken, chicken halves, or a chicken that has been opened flat. Chicken cuts that have been skinned and boned cook the fastest.

Chickens are young and tender, so you do not have to worry about tenderising the flesh, although you may want to marinate the chicken for extra flavour.

Chicken Cooking Times

Cooking times vary so the suggested times for different chicken pieces that follow should be used as a guide only. You can always tell when chicken is cooked by removing it from the barbecue and piercing the thickest part with a sharp knife. As soon as the juice runs clear, not pink, the chicken is cooked.

Chicken Skin

Chicken skin is much fattier than the flesh underneath it, and can burn readily. Fat from the skin can drip on to hot rocks, the gas burners underneath them, and on to the flat surface under the burners, causing flames and smoke that you do not want.

This is more noticeable on thick pieces of chicken that need long cooking to cook the meat at the thickest part, near the bone.

Possible solutions:
• If you cook skinless chicken pieces, this problem does not arise.
• If you precook the chicken in a microwave oven then brown it, in a shorter time, on your gas barbecue, the fat in the skin will cause less trouble.
• If you cook each piece over a fairly low heat, with the skin side away from the heat, you will need only a short time with the skin facing the heat and dripping.

Barbecued Chicken Breasts

Chicken breasts are light and lean. Skinless, boneless chicken breasts are readily available, and may be barbecued whole or cut in pieces and threaded on a skewer. They cook very quickly, may be marinated for flavour, and should always be brushed with oil or melted butter before they are cooked. They can be glazed towards the end of their cooking time for extra colour and for an attractive appearance. If you overcook them, they will be dry, so you should watch them carefully.

Test them by pressing them in the thickest part. The flesh becomes springier as it cooks. Although you do not want to lose too many juices, you should pierce

the flesh deeply at intervals and remove the breasts from the heat as soon as the juice runs clear rather than pink.

Depending on the heat of the barbecue, this can be as little as 4 minutes per side.

Barbecued Chicken Legs

Thighs and drumsticks are thicker than breast meat and take longer to cook. It is easier to cook them without burning the outside if you skin them first or precook them in a microwave first. Without precooking, they may take up to 30 minutes to barbecue. They are ready when the juices run clear, not pink. (To precook, microwave each thigh for 2 minutes and each drumstick for 1½ minutes at Full power.)

Barbecued Boneless Chicken Thighs

Look for boneless chicken thighs. Opened flat, they cook very quickly, sometimes as quickly as 2 minutes per side. Marinate them in a mixture containing some oil, and brush with extra marinade, or with a glaze as they cook. The flesh is moist and especially delicious.

Barbecued Chicken Wings

Chicken wing pieces cook faster than drumsticks, since they are small. They have a high proportion of skin to flesh, and may drip more than you want if not precooked. They may take 20 minutes or longer from raw.

Sesame Marinade and Glaze

1 large clove garlic, crushed
1 tsp grated root ginger
1 Tbsp light soya sauce
2 tsp sesame oil
a few drops of hot pepper sauce (optional)

Mix together all the ingredients and brush over skinless chicken thighs, breasts, or kebabs.

Grill or cook on the grid of a gas barbecue until juices run clear when pierced, brushing frequently with more marinade. Heat remaining marinade until it boils, and drizzle over cooked chicken.

Note:
Slice thighs and breast meat before serving.

Barbecued Chicken with Apricot and Mustard Glaze

Roast Lamb

SEE PHOTOGRAPH ON PAGE 58

The traditional roast leg of lamb is popular and delicious and is quite at home in the most untraditional situations — for example when it is very carefully trimmed of fat, marinated, cooked on a bed of herbs, served with Roasted Garlic Purée and a selection of just-cooked seasonal vegetables.

leg of lamb
1 Tbsp olive or other oil
2 Tbsp Worcestershire sauce
juice of 1 lemon
2 cloves garlic, crushed
several sprigs rosemary or 1 tsp finely chopped

Trim lamb leg of nearly all visible fat and leave to stand in a marinade made from the next five ingredients, in an unpunctured plastic bag for at least an hour, but overnight if possible. Remove from marinade, lie leg on sprigs of rosemary, and roast uncovered at 160–180°C (325–350°F) for 1½–2 hours, or for the time you like a leg cooked, basting occasionally with marinade.

After cooking, leave to stand in a warm place for 15 minutes before carving.

Roasted Garlic Purée

SEE PHOTOGRAPH ON PAGE 58

1 small head garlic per person
1 Tbsp butter
1 cup (250 ml/8 fl oz) water or stock
1 sprig thyme
6 peppercorns

Cut tops from garlic heads, place in a small covered casserole with the remaining ingredients, and bake beside the lamb for 1 hour. Drain, brush with a little of the lamb marinade (above), and cook in the roasting pan with the lamb for 10–15 minutes.

To serve, squeeze the soft pulp from each clove. The flavour is much milder than you would expect, and goes well with the roast meat.

Minted Lamb Rack

For an elegant, quick and easy dinner for two, I often serve a well-trimmed rack of lamb (cooked in the microwave oven) with noodles and a selection of vegetables cut in julienne strips.

For 2 servings:
1 chined, frenched rack of lamb
concentrated mint sauce
dry mustard
liquid gravy browning or dark soya sauce
freshly chopped herbs

Buy an 8 chop rack which has been 'chined' for easy carving, and 'frenched' to clear the ends of the bones of extra meat. Remove the layer of fat which covers the muscle by running your thumb between the meat and the fat, then by cutting the fatty layer away from the bone.

Make a paste by stirring together about 2 teaspoons mint sauce concentrate, 1 teaspoon dry mustard, and a few drops of gravy browning or soya sauce. Adjust the colour and consistency by adding a little more of any of these, then paint this over the meaty surface.

Sprinkle the surface with any fresh herbs that you like and have, then stand the meat on a microwave roasting pan or on a bread and butter plate inverted on a dinner plate.

Microwave at Full power for 4½ minutes, or until meat in the thickest part of the rack springs back when pressed with a finger, then leave to stand in a warm place for 5–10 minutes.

Carve between the rib bones.

Economical Roast Lamb

A large lamb or hogget* roast is traditional festive fare. When money is limited, shop around for best value. A frozen leg or forequarter costs less than fresh, and is just as good if slowly thawed and carefully cooked. Choose whatever cut gives you the greatest weight of meat for your money. A boned forequarter is delicious when trimmed of all visible fat, brushed on all surfaces with a paste or more or less equal quantities of dark soya sauce and smooth mustard, rolled, and tied with string. A 1.5 kg (3 lb 8 oz) forequarter roasted at 180°C (350°F) takes 1½–1¾ hours.

For ease, trim and roll the meat the day before you want it. Refrigerate until it goes into the oven.

*Hogget is meat from one to two-year-old sheep.

Tomato Salsa

This bright and interesting herby sauce is best made the day before you want it. Serve it with roast lamb instead of gravy and mint sauce to save last minute work.

For 6–10 (each about 2 Tbsp) servings:
1 (425 g/15 oz) can Mexican tomatoes
2 Tbsp cider or wine vinegar
1–2 tsp sugar
½ tsp salt
2 Tbsp grated onion or 3 spring onions, chopped
2 Tbsp very finely chopped celery (optional)
2 Tbsp chopped mint (optional)
pinch chilli powder and cumin to taste (optional)

Mix all ingredients, chopping tomatoes smaller if you like. Refrigerate for up to 3 days and serve warm or at room temperature. Serve with Scalloped Potatoes (see page 112).

Economical Roast Lamb with Tomato Salsa

Barbecued Lamb Forequarter

If you like to carve and eat slices of lean lamb that are nicely browned and full of flavour on the outside and pink, tender and succulent in the centre, try barbecuing an inexpensive boned lamb forequarter from your supermarket. For maximum tenderness, prepare the meat and put it in its marinade in the refrigerator one or even two days before you plan to cook it. Leftovers are good cold.

For 6–8 servings:
1 lamb or hogget* forequarter, boned and rolled
Tex-Mex Marinade or Mediterranean Marinade
(see below)

Remove the net, string or skewers holding the boned shoulder together, and unroll the meat, skin-side down. Using a sharp knife cut away any visible fat and membrane between the muscles, and cut any large chunky muscles so that the whole forequarter lies flat. Turn the meat over so that the skin side is up, and trim away as much fat as you can without the meat falling apart.

Put the trimmed meat in an unpunctured bag with the Tex-Mex or Mediterranean Marinade ingredients, and gently knead to massage the marinade into the meat, working from outside the bag. Squeeze all air from the bag, fasten with a rubber band, and refrigerate until about four hours before the meat is to be barbecued, then bring back to room temperature.

Place the meat, skin side up, on the preheated, oiled grilling rack of the barbecue. Cover with the domed lid that comes with the barbecue, or with a tent made from a doubled piece of aluminium foil. This traps heated air, so the upper surface of the meat is kept warm while the lower surface cooks. When all the lower surfaces are nicely browned, after 10–15 minutes, turn the lamb over and cook the other side. Under good conditions the lamb will cook in 20–30 minutes. The meat should feel springy, not spongy, when cooked. If in doubt, cut a thick part with a sharp knife and see if the centre is done to the stage that you like it. Cook for longer if necessary. Leave to stand, covered, for 10–15 minutes, then carve in slices across the grain of the meat.

Tex-Mex Marinade
1 Tbsp ground cumin
2 tsp oreganum
½–1 tsp chilli powder
juice of 2 or 3 lemons
2 Tbsp Worcestershire sauce
2 Tbsp oil
2–3 cloves garlic, crushed

Mediterranean Marinade
Leave out the chilli and replace the cumin with chopped fresh rosemary leaves or thyme.

*Hogget is meat from one to two-year-old sheep.

Barbecued Lamb Forequarter

Barbecued 'Butterflied' Leg of Lamb

You can open flat and trim a boned leg of lamb so it lies flat, in the same way as the forequarter in the recipe above. The meat is just as delicious, and the slices are bigger, since the leg is made up of several larger muscles than the forequarter. (See photograph opposite.)

The only problem is that you cannot always walk into a supermarket and buy a boned rolled leg, as you can a boned rolled forequarter. You can, however, ask any butcher to 'butterfly' a leg (or the shank end of a leg) of lamb or hogget for you. If you explain that you want to barbecue it in one flattish piece, you may be able to get the outer fatty side trimmed, too. Use Tex-Mex or Mediterranean Marinade (see recipes above), and leave the boned leg to marinate for 24–48 hours, before barbecuing. The cooking time should be about 30–40 minutes (under good conditions), since the meat is thicker.

Barbecued 'Mini' Leg Cuts

A new, exciting butchery ideas is 'seamboning' a leg of lamb or hogget so that you get four neat, compact cuts from each leg. These have no fatty outer layer, and are wonderful for small families. The cuts are:

Lamb Rump or Chump
Lamb Topside
Lamb Silverside
Lamb Thick Flank

All can be barbecued very successfully. I sometimes seambone a leg of hogget myself, 'butterfly' (or cut open and lie flat) the chunky thick flank and topside muscles and marinate then barbecue the four pieces. Depending on appetites and the amount of other food served, they will feed six to eight people. They are easy and neat to carve.

Use Tex-Mex or Mediterranean Marinade or the following marinade.

Sesame Marinade
¼ cup (60 ml/2 fl oz) Kikkoman soya sauce
¼ cup (60 ml/2 fl oz) lemon juice
2 Tbsp sesame oil
1–2 tsp Trappey's hot pepper sauce
2 garlic cloves, crushed

Leave lamb in marinade for at least 24 hours, then barbecue over a high heat on the grilling rack, preferably covered with a domed lid or aluminium foil tent, for 8–12 minutes per side, depending on the conditions and the stage to which you like the meat cooked.

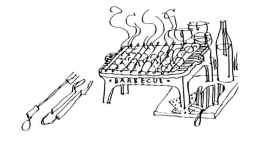

Barbecued Lamb Chops

For thousands and thousands of years, in Mediterranean countries, the delicious smell of pieces of herb-flavoured lamb cooking over open fires has wafted through the countryside.

On a gas barbecue you can cook, quickly and easily, chops cut from the shoulder, ribs, or middle loin. Like all meat which is to be barbecued, the chops should be trimmed of as much visible fat as possible. Well-trimmed meat cooks much faster than meat surrounded by thick layers of fat, and does not drip fat and cause flare-ups.

Rib and middle loin chops are more tender than shoulder chops and may be cooked without marinating. Shoulder chops are best marinated for a few hours before cooking.

East–West Marinade
Good for all chops and cubes of lamb:

1 Tbsp dark or light soya sauce
1 Tbsp lemon juice
½ Tbsp honey
1–2 cloves garlic, crushed
1–2 tsp sesame oil (optional)

Rib and loin chops have an excellent flavour if brushed with any lamb marinade before cooking, and shoulder chops and cubes will be more tender if left to stand in a marinade at room temperature for at least an hour.

Rib Chops and Cutlets
Cut away nearly all outer fat. Cut off knobbly bone with pruners or cutting pliers if you like. (This bone will probably already be removed from cutlets.)

Middle Loin Chops
Trim as much outer fat and other fat as possible, without detaching the tail of the chop. So tail meat does not overcook, roll it up, towards the small eye of very tender meat, and secure with a toothpick.

Noisettes
Trim fat from middle loin chop as above, then cut around T-shaped bone and remove it. Wind tail around both eyes of meat, and push a bamboo skewer through the rolled chop, from one side to the other. Cut off the skewer, and push the halved remaining skewer at right angles to the other. The crossed skewers will keep the roll of lamb flat and in place as it cooks.

Shoulder Chops
Cut off all outer fat, and any bones which are near the edge of the chop. Snip edges to prevent curling during cooking. Bang a few times on both sides with a meat hammer to tenderise if desired. Turn in marinade of your choice and leave to stand at room temperature for an hour, or up to 24 hours in the refrigerator.

Lamb Chops

Lemon-Honey Lamb Cutlets

Lemon–Honey Lamb Cutlets

Cutlets are well-trimmed rib chops from which the upper (angled) bone has been removed.

For 2 servings:
6 lamb cutlets
about 2 tsp soya sauce
¼ cup (60 ml/2 fl oz) lemon juice
½ tsp dried tarragon or ¼ tsp dried mint
1 Tbsp honey
¼ tsp black pepper
1 tsp mustard
1 tsp butter

Trim all the fat from the cutlets, then brush with soya sauce and leave to stand for 5 minutes.

Then pan-cook in a non-stick frypan for 3–4 minutes, depending on the thickness of the chops. Remove from the pan, then add the lemon juice and tarragon (or mint), bring to the boil, stirring the sediment off the bottom of the pan. Add the honey, pepper and mustard and mix thoroughly. Swirl in the butter.

Return the chops to the pan and turn to coat with the sauce.

Glazed Stuffed Noisettes

What better way to celebrate spring than with glazed noisettes made from succulent young lamb chops.

For 4 servings:
8 middle loin lamb chops
8 thin slices side bacon
juice of 2 lemons
¼ cup (60 ml/2 fl oz) red currant, crabapple or
    cranberry jelly
2 tsp mustard

Cut T-bones from the chops and trim if necessary. Cut the bacon rashers so they are as wide as the chops are thick.

Wrap the bacon strips around the noisettes, enclosing the fillings,* if desired, between the two 'eyes' of muscle. Secure the bacon and keep chops flat by pushing two bamboo skewers or two half skewers at right angles through the meat.

Sprinkle with lemon juice and refrigerate until required.

Barbecue or grill for about 5 minutes each side, about 10 cm (4 inches) from the heat.

Heat the remaining lemon juice with the jelly and mustard and brush over the noisettes during the last 2-3 minutes of cooking.

*For fillings use interesting and colourful ingredients and combinations, e.g. prunes and dried apricot or cooked peach pieces, strips of red pepper and wedges of kiwifruit, sautéed mushroom and water chestnut.

Mini-Leg Lamb Steaks

When a leg of lamb is seamboned, the main muscles are cut clear of bone and skin. Some butchers will do this for you. These mini-cuts of chump, silverside, topside and flank may be cooked as small lean roasts, but they may also be cut into small, compact, lean steaks. All these little cuts freeze well, so you can use them as you want them.

Cut any of these mini-leg cuts into 1 cm (¼ inch) slices, and snip any connective tissue around the edge, so the meat does not curl during cooking. Flatten a little more with a meat hammer if you like. Allow about 150 g (5 oz) per serving. For each serving, mix 2 teaspoons of the juice scraped from a halved onion, 1 teaspoon dark soya sauce, and ½ teaspoon oil in a plastic bag. Turn the mini-steaks in this, and leave to stand for at least 10 minutes. Finely grate ¼ teaspoon orange rind and about 1 tablespoon orange juice for each serving.

Heat a heavy pan. When very hot, add the marinated steaks and brown on each side, then lower the heat and cook to the stage you like. Add the orange juice and rind, and turn the steaks in the liquid as it evaporates. Sprinkle with a little chopped mint.

Note:
Trim and bone leg chops, and prepare and cook as above, if preferred.

Lamb Riblets

Flaps, although very cheap, make a tasty meal if carefully cooked.

For 4 servings:
2 hogget flaps* (1-1.2 kg/2 lbs-2½ lbs)
grated rind and juice of ½ orange
2 Tbsp Kikkoman soya sauce
1 Tbsp Worcestershire sauce
2 cloves garlic, crushed
¼ cup (60 ml/2 fl oz) wine or water
1 tsp sesame oil

Using a sharp knife, cut either side of the rib bones and remove them in a sheet, then trim away any large areas of fat. Score the upper and lower surfaces of the meat to form 1 cm (½ inch) diamonds, cutting about 5 mm (¼ inch) deep.

Measure the remaining ingredient into an oven bag without holes punched in it. Put the prepared lamb so it lies flat in the bag, turn the bag so that all surfaces are coated with the liquid, fasten a twist tie round the opening, leaving a finger-sized hole, lie it flat on a sponge-roll tin and bake at 160°C (325°F) for about 1½ hours, or until the meat is very tender, turning several times. Check that there is always some liquid in the bag (as well as the fat that will be poured off later) at all times during the cooking. If it evaporates, add extra water.

When meat is cooked, drain off all liquid, skim and discard fat from it, and keep the small amount of concentrated glaze. Cut the two strips of cooked meat into fingers or 'riblets', drizzle with the glaze, and serve hot on rice.

Variation:
Add smoke-flavoured salt or liquid to the cooking liquid for a barbecued flavour.

*Hogget is meat from one to two-year-old sheep. A 'flap' is the breast section of the carcase. Two flaps should yield about 600 g (1 lb 6 oz) of cooked meat.

Barbecued Lamb Kebabs

To make good kebabs, use 2-3 cm cubes of lean lamb cut from any part of the lamb. Thread on bamboo or metal skewers. Cheapest and most juicy are cubes cut from a boned forequarter or shoulder, or from shoulder chops. Although they may be cooked without marinating, they are tenderised if left to stand in a marinade for at least an hour. Do not choose a marinade with a high sugar content. Buy pre-marinated lamb kebabs if desired. Brush with oil before barbecuing if meat is very lean.

Barbecue over a high heat, for about 5 minutes per side. Cut the centre of one item to check whether it is ready, if necessary. Take particular care not to overcook kebabs — small cubes may require less time.

Glazed Stuffed Noisettes

Chinese Lamb and Vegetables

For 4 servings:
250 g (9 oz) lean lamb, sliced thinly across the
grain
2 cloves garlic, chopped
4 slices root ginger, finely chopped
2 Tbsp water
1 Tbsp cornflour
2 Tbsp oil
¼–½ cup toasted cashew nuts

Vegetables
300 g (10 oz) altogether of the following:
green and red pepper
spring onions
cabbage or spinach
cauliflower
celery
mushrooms

Marinade
1 Tbsp soya sauce
1 Tbsp sherry
1 tsp instant beef stock
1 tsp brown sugar

Mix marinade ingredients.

Slice the lamb thinly and with half the garlic and ginger mix with the marinade. Leave to stand for at least 15 minutes.

In a small bowl mix the water and cornflour and put aside.

Slice all the vegetables so they are suitable for stir-frying.

Heat 1 tablespoon oil in a large pan. Add the remaining garlic and ginger, then the vegetables, adding the longer-cooking ones first. Stir-fry until tender crisp, then remove from the pan.

Reheat the pan again with the remaining oil. Add the lamb and stir-fry over a high heat until the meat changes colour. Add the cashew nuts, the cooked vegetables, then enough of the cornflour paste to glaze both the meat and vegetables.

Serve immediately, on rice or pasta.

Orange Lamb Casserole

This microwaved lamb and vegetable casserole has a good colour and an interesting flavour.

For 4–5 servings:
1 kumara (sweet potato), cubed
25 g (1 oz) butter, melted
1 green pepper, diced
600 g (1 lb 6 oz) cubed lean lamb
1 orange, grated rind and juice
1 Tbsp cornflour
2 tsp instant chicken stock
1 Tbsp soya sauce
2 tsp grated root ginger
1 cup (250 ml/10 fl oz) hot water

Cut the peeled sweet potato into 2 cm (¾ inch) cubes. Place in a lidded microwave dish with the butter, cover and cook on Full power for 5 minutes, stirring after 2 minutes.

Add the pepper and the cubed lamb to the cooked sweet potato.

In a jug mix the grated orange rind and juice, cornflour, chicken stock, soya sauce, root ginger and hot water to a smooth paste. Stir into the meat mixture.

Cover and cook on Full power for 3 minutes, stir well, then cook at Medium (50% power) for 20 minutes, or until the meat is tender.

Leave to stand for 15 minutes before adjusting the seasonings and serving.

Spicy Barbecued Lamb

This sauce turns barbecued lamb into something special!

For 4 servings:
600–700 g (1 lb 6 oz–1 lb 9 oz) cubed shoulder
lamb
2 cloves garlic, chopped
2 tsp grated root ginger
1 tsp freshly ground coriander seed (optional)
2 Tbsp dark soya sauce
2 Tbsp lemon juice
2 Tbsp oil
6–8 drops hot pepper sauce
¼ cup (50 g/2 oz) brown sugar
3 Tbsp peanut butter
¼ cup (60 ml/2 fl oz) water

Cut the lamb into 15 mm (¾ inch) cubes, trimming away all excess fat. Place lamb cubes in an unpunctured plastic bag.

Combine the remaining ingredients, preferably in a food processor bowl, and mix to blend.

Pour 2 tablespoons of the mixture over the cubed lamb and knead the bag to mix. Close the bag, leaving the lamb to marinate for at least 15 minutes before threading on eight soaked bamboo skewers or metal skewers.

Heat the remaining marinade until smooth and thick, adding a little more water or lemon juice if the sauce is thicker than thin cream.

Barbecue lamb close to the heat (or cook under a grill). Brush with the thickened marinade when lamb is nearly cooked.

Cooked lamb should be pink inside and slightly crusty outside.

Orange Lamb Casserole

BEEF, MINCE
& VENISON

Barbecued Steak

Steaks which have been cut 1–2 cm (½–¾ inch) thick are best cooked on a preheated thick metal plate rather than on a grill rack, since it is hard to get the heat on a rack high enough to brown the outside of a thinnish steak without overcooking the centre.

A steak which is 3–5 cm (1½–2 inches) thick should be carved diagonally into thin slices after it is cooked. You will get good results cooking it on the grilling rack or a solid plate.

All steaks will be more tender if they are marinated before they are cooked. The longer they stand in the marinade, the more tender they will be. Marinades tenderise fastest at room temperature. If you have only a few hours in which to marinate steak, leave it at room temperature. You can leave steak in a marinade in the refrigerator for several days if you like. The tougher the steak cut, the longer it should be marinated. Put steak, trimmed of nearly all visible fat, in an unpunctured plastic bag with your chosen marinade, squeeze out all the air, and secure bag with a rubber band.

- Fillet steak is the most tender steak.
- Rib eye and sirloin steaks are not quite as tender as fillet, but have more flavour.
- Rump steaks and cross-cut blade steaks have excellent flavour but are tougher and require marinating and brief cooking for best results. A thick piece of marinated rump is excellent carved after cooking.
- Thin flank or flank skirt steak may be marinated and cooked fairly rare, in one piece, on a hot plate, then thinly sliced across the grain.

Wine Marinade
¼ cup (60 ml/2 fl oz) red or white table wine
1 Tbsp wine vinegar
1–2 cloves garlic, crushed
1 tsp dried oreganum
1–2 Tbsp corn or olive oil

If you are using a not-so-tender steak and have little marinating time, tenderise the steak with a meat hammer as well.

Pat steak dry, oil its surface lightly, then brown on both sides on a thoroughly preheated plate (or on a heavy pan on the barbecue). Lower heat to cook until the centre is cooked as you like it if necessary.

Cooking time can be as little as 3 minutes under good conditions. Brush with any desired glaze at end of cooking time if you like.

Note:
Soya-based marinades are also good for beef.

Steak Diane

This is a delicious way to serve thinly cut fillet steak. Steak Diane is an easy but elegant steak dish, which is especially good for a small number of guests.

For 4 servings:
400–500 g (14 oz–1 lb 2 oz) fillet steak cut 5 mm (¼ inch) thick
2 shallots or 1 medium-sized onion
50 g (2 oz) butter
2 Tbsp Worcestershire sauce
¼ cup finely chopped parsley
2 tsp brandy

Gently bang the thin steaks even thinner, between two sheets of plastic, using a rolling pin.

Chop the shallots or onions very finely. Heat the butter in a frypan and cook the shallots or onion until tender. Push the shallots aside, and raise the heat in the pan, until the butter browns slightly. Add the steaks and brown quickly. Add the sauce to taste and turn the steaks in it. Sprinkle with the finely chopped parsley, add the brandy, turn the steaks again and flame carefully. Serve immediately with the pan juices spooned over the steaks.

White Veal Schnitzels

Pan-Grilled Venison Steaks

For 2 servings:
4 venison back or leg steaks
2 Tbsp oil
2 tsp lemon juice
2 tsp soya or Worcestershire sauce
1 garlic clove, crushed
¼ cup (60 ml/2 fl oz) port wine
¼ cup (60 ml/2 fl oz) any well-flavoured stock
2 tsp green peppercorns
1 tsp liquid from peppercorns
2 Tbsp cream

Marinate steak for at least 1 hour in a marinade made by mixing together the oil, lemon juice, soya sauce and garlic.

Remove the steaks from the marinade and pan-grill briefly over a high heat, taking care not to overcook, until cooked to the desired stage. Remove from the pan.

Add to the pan the remaining ingredients and boil until reduced to at least half the original volume, adjust the seasonings and pour over the steaks.

Note:
Use farm-reared venison.

If necessary butterfly small steaks. Cut double thickness steaks almost in half, leaving a 'hinge', then open them flat so the steaks appear to be double their size.

Variation:
Cook and serve fillet steak following this recipe, if desired.

White Veal Schnitzels

White veal is the meat from young calves. It is lean, with a delicate flavour, and should not be overcooked or served with foods that have very strong flavours.

1 or 2 white veal schnitzels per serving
flour for coating meat
1 Tbsp oil
1 Tbsp butter
¼ cup sliced mushrooms
2 tsp flour
¼ cup (60 ml/2 fl oz) white wine
¼ cup (60 ml/2 fl oz) chicken stock
1 Tbsp capers (optional)
2 Tbsp cream

Lightly flour the schnitzels and cook in the oil and butter in a pan over a moderate heat until very lightly browned on both sides. Remove the meat from the pan.

Add the mushrooms and 2 teaspoons flour to the drippings in the pan, and cook until straw coloured.

Stir in the wine, chicken stock, capers and cream and stir until smooth, diluting with extra wine or water if desired.

Pour over the veal and serve.

Beef Satay

Make these kebabs with sirloin or rump steak. (They are good made with lamb, pork and chicken, too.)

For 4 servings:
750 g (1½ lbs) steak, in 2 cm (¾ inch) cubes
1 tsp ground cumin
1 tsp ground coriander
2 Tbsp dark or light soya sauce
2 Tbsp lemon juice
2 Tbsp oil
2 cloves garlic, crushed
about ¼ tsp chilli powder

Peanut Sauce
¼ cup peanut butter
½ cup (125 ml/4 fl oz) water
2 Tbsp soft brown sugar
1 Tbsp lemon juice
1 Tbsp dark soya sauce

Cube steak and mix with other ingredients in a plastic bag. Refrigerate for 12–24 hours.

Thread steak on 12 bamboo skewers that have been soaked in water, then barbecue on an oiled grilling rack over a high heat for about 4 minutes per side.

Stir remaining marinade into peanut sauce ingredients and bring to boil, thinning with more water if necessary. Brush kebabs with peanut sauce during second half of cooking. Serve extra sauce with skewered beef.

Warm Venison Salad

SEE PHOTOGRAPH ON PAGE 70
Salads made using meat which has been cooked a short time before serving are interesting — and fashionable!

A warm venison salad makes a good first course for a special occasion meal. Allow 50 g (2 oz) venison for each serving. If used for a main course, allow 100g (4 oz) per person.

200 g (8 oz) tender venison, from back or leg cut
into strips 1 cm × 2 cm (½ inch × 1 inch)

Marinade
2 Tbsp white wine
1 Tbsp Worcestershire sauce
1 Tbsp corn or soya oil
2 tsp dark honey
½ tsp finely chopped thyme
1–2 cloves garlic, crushed

Dressing
2 Tbsp wine vinegar
2 Tbsp dry sherry
2 tsp Dijon mustard
2 tsp dark honey
¼ cup corn or soya soil
½ tsp finely chopped thyme
salt to taste

Trim and slice venison, removing the silvery membrane around each muscle if this has not already been done.

Combine marinade ingredients in a plate or unpunctured plastic bag. Add venison and leave for 15–60 minutes.

Remove meat from marinade and pan-cook, preferably in a non-stick pan, over a high heat for 2–3 minutes, until nicely browned on all outer surfaces, but still pink in the centre of the meat. Add a little marinade to glaze meat in last 30 seconds, if desired.

Combine dressing ingredients in a food processor until thick and creamy. Pour a little dressing over cooked venison and leave to stand for 15–30 minutes.

Slice meat thinly just before serving. Toss with mixed, prepared salad greens and enough dressing to moisten the leaves and coat the meat. Serve with warm crusty bread.

Note:
Use farm-reared venison.

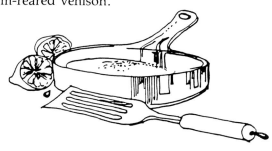

Oriental Steak Salad

SEE PHOTOGRAPH ON PAGE 70
Pan-grilled skirt steak has a very good flavour and is a good price compared with more commonly used steaks. It needs to be treated with care, however, or it may be tough.

The rules to remember if you want tender pan-grilled skirt steak are:

• marinate before cooking
• cook to rare or medium only
• slice thinly, across the grain

A whole skirt steak will make two hot servings, and two delicious cold salad servings.

To pan-grill skirt steak:
Trim the thin edges from a whole skirt (or thin flank or flank-skirt steak). Score lightly in diamond shapes on both surfaces.

Place in a heavy, unpunctured plastic bag with the marinade (see below). Squeeze the air from the bag and marinate for 2–8 hours at room temperature or for longer in the refrigerator.

Remove from marinade, then pan-grill in a heavy, preheated, very hot pan, allowing about 4 minutes per side. Cut centre of meat to check for doneness. Cook a little more if necessary, leave to stand for 5 minutes or longer, then cut across the grain of the meat, with the knife at 45° to the board, making very thin slices.

Marinade
2 Tbsp dark soya sauce
2 Tbsp lemon juice
2 Tbsp corn or soya oil
2 cloves garlic, crushed

74

Salad

To make the salad, pour as much of the dressing (see below) as you like over the thinly sliced warm or cold beef. Turn slices gently to coat, then arrange slices over lightly coated salad greens, in individual plates. Garnish as desired, with herbs or with edible flowers such as nasturtiums or borage.

Dressing

4 shallot bulbs, unpeeled
1–2 garlic cloves (optional)
¼ cup (60 ml/2 fl oz) corn or soya oil
¼ cup (60 ml/2 fl oz) lime or lemon juice
¼ cup (60 ml/2 fl oz) light soya sauce
1 Tbsp sugar
pinch chilli powder

Combine all ingredients in a food processor. Mix, then strain, and bottle until required.

Beef Satay

Beef Mini Roasts

Three of the 'new' small beef roasts that are produced when larger cuts are seamed out, and which make very good quick roasts for small groups are: rump cap, rump eye, and thick flank bullet. You may not see these cuts in meat displays, but good butchers should prepare them if asked.

To roast any of these, rub with oil, then brown on all sides in a well-heated heavy frypan. This should take 5–10 minutes. Transfer meat to a roasting pan and roast, uncovered at 180°C (250°F) for 20–45 minutes, depending on size of meat and the degree of pinkness you like. Stand meat in a warm place, covered with foil, for 10 minutes, while you make gravy, etc. Slice thinly, using a very sharp knife, at 45° to the board.

Cooking guide
rump eye 800 g (1 lb 12 oz), 25–30 minutes
thick flank bullet 1–1.3 kg (2lb 4 oz–3 lb),
    35–40 minutes.

Mustard Gravy
The lean cuts above, cooked as described, should produce very little fat. Drain off any fat, leaving pan drippings only, add a tablespoon of Dijon mustard to the pan, then stir in ¼ –½ cup (60–135 ml/2–4 fl oz) red wine and ½ –¾ cup (125–185 ml/4–6 fl oz) vegetable cooking liquid or stock. Stir over a moderate heat until reduced to ½–¾ cup then serve with the thinly sliced beef.

Corned Beef

When I am away travelling and working for several weeks, even if I am staying in wonderful hotels, and eating in exciting restaurants, I miss some of my old 'comfort foods'. I invariably get a longing for corned beef. It is surprising how seldom one sees it on restaurant or hotel menus.

These days, I often omit the sauces that I used to think were an important part of the corned beef dinner.

1.5–2 kg (3 lb 6 oz–4 lb 4 oz) corned silverside of
    beef
1 onion, stuck with cloves
2 cloves garlic
1 or 2 bay leaves
1 sprig parsley
1 stalk celery
1 sprig thyme
1 sprig dill, if available
6 peppercorns

Put the meat in a deep saucepan. Cover with cold water. Add the seasonings listed, bring to the boil, cover, and simmer gently, so that the surface of the water barely moves, for about 2½ hours.

Select the vegetables that you want to serve with

Corned Beef

the corned beef, e.g. carrots, cabbage, Brussels sprouts, white turnips, potatoes and onions, and cook them separately, using some of the corned beef cooking liquid instead of lightly salted water.

Drain vegetables and butter them lightly.

If desired, make parsley or mustard sauce to serve with the corned beef, using some of the cooking stock, or simply serve the meat with your favourite mild mustard, or horseradish cream.

Drip Stew

A 'drip stew' needs no attention as it cooks. I started to make these stews when my children were young and the house was likely to become chaotic just before dinner. I knew that the meat would cook gently on, regardless of what was happening.

I hope that you will try this method. The resulting mixture has a flavour which is intensely beefy. If you do not want to wait for an hour and a half while your stew cooks, prepare and cook it the night before you want it, while you are getting another meal. Like all stews, it tastes even better when reheated.

For 4 servings:
600 g (1 lb 6 oz) chuck steak
1 onion, chopped
1 Tbsp Worcestershire sauce
bunch of herbs (optional)
freshly ground black pepper
¼ tsp salt
2 tsp cornflour
2 Tbsp sherry or water

Select a bowl of heat-resistant glass or stainless steel, or a small casserole dish which you can sit on a plate inside a large covered saucepan. During the cooking the bowl or casserole should be covered by a plate, an inverted lid, or a piece of aluminium foil which is depressed in the middle. The idea behind this is that the steam from the meat will condense on whatever cover you use, and will drip back down on to the meat from its lowest point, the centre.

Slice the chuck steak into thin strips, discarding fat and thick pieces of gristle. (Small pieces will disappear during the cooking.) Quarter and peel the onions, then slice them thinly, too. Put the meat, onions and Worcestershire sauce in the container and mix together.

Make a herb bundle by picking then wrapping together with a piece of heavy thread or string any herbs which you would like to flavour this, for example, thyme, oreganum, lovage, a bay leaf and parsley, or add a pinch of some of these, dried. Bury the bundle of herbs in the meat. Add the pepper, cover, pour warm water around the bowl so that it comes halfway up the side, and simmer for 1½ hours, until the meat is tender. Look at the meat after an hour, stirring it and removing the bundle of herbs.

When the meat is tender add salt to taste, and stir in the cornflour mixed with the sherry or water. Cook a little longer until the stew has thickened, then serve with a selection of vegetables. Try spooning the meat and gravy over noodles, sometimes, too.

77

Steak and Kidney Pie

Although you can make a pie any shape you like, you should choose a container with a flat rim. If you do not have a pie dish deep enough to hold much meat, spoon extra stew on to the individual plates, alongside the pie.

For 4–6 servings:
750 g (1 lb 8 oz) blade steak
3 Tbsp flour
oil
1 large onion, chopped
about 250 g (4 oz) ox kidney
1 cup (250 ml/8 fl oz) vegetable or meat stock,
    water, wine or a mixture of both
fresh or dried herbs
about ½ tsp salt
pepper
400 g (14 oz) packet flaky pastry
beaten egg (optional)

Remove any fat from the meat, turn it in the flour, and brown well, over a high heat, in a heavy pan, in a small amount of oil. Cut in cubes after browning, and put in a large pan with the chopped onion and kidney, any remaining flour, and the stock or other liquid. Cover and simmer for about an hour, or until tender. Add herbs, salt, and pepper just before the meat is cooked, or when assembling the pie.

Place a pie funnel or a supporting egg cup in the centre of a pie dish or pie plate with a rim, then fill the dish with the cold, thickened cooked meat. Preheat the oven to 230°C (450°F), then roll out the pastry evenly, until it is considerably bigger than the plate, leave it to stand in a cool place for at least 15 minutes, then cut a strip of pastry about 1.5 cm (¾ inch) wide, and press this on to the dampened rim. Lift the pastry carefully on to the pie plate or dish, press it down on to the pastry rim, then trim the edge with a sharp knife. Decorate edge with a knife or fork if you like, but take care not to press down the cut edge. Cut a steam vent above the pastry funnel. Brush with a little beaten egg, decorate with pastry trimmings, then bake at 230°C (450°F) for about 45 minutes, turning the oven down if the pastry browns too much. Use the fan-forced option if you have it.

South Pacific Meat Loaf

Sweet potatoes and spices give this meat loaf an interesting flavour.

For 4 servings:
500 g (1 lb 2 oz) minced lamb or beef
1 egg
1 large onion
1 tsp ground coriander seed or ½ tsp curry powder
1½ tsp salt
500 g (1 lb 2 oz) kumara (sweet potato)

Put the minced meat in a bowl with the egg. Grate the onion, or chop it finely in a food processor, then add the seasonings, using the coriander seed if you like a curry-orange flavour, or the curry powder, and salt.

Scrub and grate the kumara, without peeling them. Mix the grated flesh through the mince as soon as it is prepared, so it does not discolour on standing.

Line a loaf tin about 23×10 cm (9×4 inches) with a sheet of baking paper so the paper goes across the long sides and the bottom, then oil the ends of the tin and press the loaf mixture evenly into it. Cover with foil, and bake at 180°C (350°F) for an hour, then remove the foil and bake uncovered for 30 minutes longer. Cut into thick slices.

Variation:
Use cooked mashed or shredded kumara, and bake for 45–60 minutes.

Beef Port Casserole

This full-flavoured casserole requires little attention as it cooks. If tamarillos are not available, use pineapple or other fruit, and consider adding about a tablespoon of tomato paste to intensify the flavour of the liquid around the meat.

For 4 servings:
4 cross-cut blade steaks (about 600 g/1 lb 4 oz)
2 medium-sized onions, sliced
2 Tbsp oil
2 Tbsp flour
1 Tbsp honey
½ cup (125 ml/4 fl oz) water
½ cup (125 ml/4 fl oz) port wine
2 tsp instant beef stock or 1 tsp salt
2 tamarillos or 4 pineapple rings (optional)

Lay the steaks in one layer in a casserole dish. Slice the onions in rings and brown in a frypan in the oil. Do not hurry this step. Add the flour, stir until it is evenly brown, then add the honey and let it turn golden brown.

Remove from the heat, add water, wine and instant stock (or salt) and pour over the meat.

Cover tightly and bake at 150°C (300°F) for 1 hour.

Add the sliced, peeled tamarillos (or other fruit) and cook for 30 minutes longer.

Serve with baked potatoes and Brussels sprouts or beans.

Variation:
Replace port with sherry.

The flavour of nearly all stews and casseroles improves on standing. Make twice as much as you need and refrigerate half of it to serve several nights later, or make it the day before you need it, if you are planning a special meal with a stew or casserole as the central part of your main course.

Steak and Kidney Pie

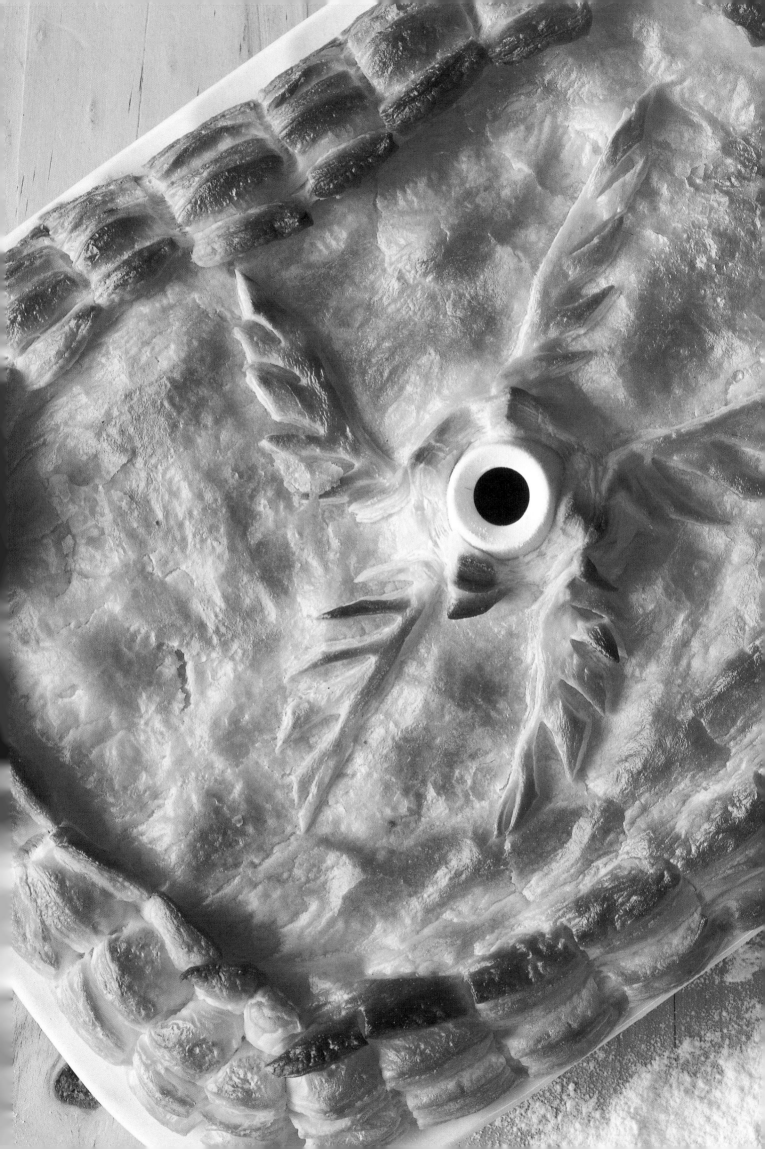

Chilli Beef and Beans

When you add baked beans, tomatoes and interesting seasonings to minced beef, you make a popular chilli mixture that will go a long way and will be ready to eat in less than 30 minutes.

For 6–8 servings:
2 large onions, chopped
2 Tbsp oil
2 large cloves garlic, chopped
500 g (1 lb 2 oz) minced beef
1 tsp paprika
1 tsp ground cumin
1 tsp oreganum

Chilli Beef and Beans

½–1 tsp chilli powder
1 (400 g/14 oz) can whole tomatoes in juice
1 (820 g/1 lb 13 oz) can baked beans
2 Tbsp lemon juice or wine vinegar

Brown the onions in the oil in a large pan, then add the garlic and mince and cook until the meat has browned. Add the seasonings, then the remaining ingredients, cover and simmer for 15–20 minutes.

Serve on rice, with corn chips on the side, or thicken and serve with shredded lettuce, grated cheese, etc., in taco shells.

Little Meat Balls

Little meat balls in tomato sauce on noodles have always been a favourite in our house. This recipe makes a little bit of meat go a long way and still provides a high-protein nutritious meal.

For 4 servings:
1 onion, chopped very finely
about 400 g (14 oz) minced beef
1 egg
¼ cup (60 ml/2 fl oz) milk
¼ cup (20 g/½ oz) rolled oats
¼ cup (20 g/½ oz) wheatgerm
½ tsp salt
1 tsp dried basil
½ –1 tsp dried oreganum

oil for frying
1 tsp dark soya sauce
¼ cup (60 ml/2 fl oz) hot water

Combine first group of ingredients in a large bowl and mix well, adding more rolled oats or wheatgerm if the mixture is too soft to handle, or a little extra milk if it is too dry. (If you have a food processor, use it to chop the onion finely, then add the other ingredients and process until well blended.)

Divide the mixture into halves, then quarters, then eighths, then divide each piece into five or six small balls, working with wet hands to prevent it sticking.

When all the balls are formed, heat a large, preferably non-stick pan, add about a tablespoon of oil, and, while you shake the pan backwards and forwards with one hand, drop in the little balls with the other. Keep the pan moving, over a fairly high heat, until the balls are evenly browned and firm.

Mix teaspoon of dark soya sauce with ¼ cup hot water, and add to the pan, still keeping it moving. This should dislodge any bits from the bottom of the pan, and glaze the meat balls nicely.

If serving with noodles, cook plenty of egg noodles in a large saucepan, in a generous amount of boiling salted water. Drain, rinse, and toss in a little butter or oil, with chopped herbs or a little Parmesan cheese if you like.

For an easy sauce, put in another pan 2 teaspoons cornflour, and chopped fresh parsley, spring onions and other herbs if you have them. Mix with a little of the liquid from a 425 g (15 oz) can of savoury tomatoes, then add the remaining can contents. Bring to the boil, chopping or mashing the tomatoes, then adjust the seasonings.

Add the sauce to the meatballs and reheat them. Serve on egg noodles.

Barbecued Hamburgers

Cook hamburgers on a grill rack or heated metal plate. A hinged basket over a grill rack gives excellent results.

Season beef mince with chopped spring onions or other herbs or spices you particularly like. If you like hamburgers cooked so that they are no longer pink in the middle, mix in fresh breadcrumbs.

Crumble 1 slice of bread per 500 g (1 lb) minced beef, and moisten the mixture with 1–2 tablespoons of milk, wine, or tomato sauce. This makes the texture of the cooked hamburger softer. Mixing 1–2 teaspoons of instant stock or salt into the uncooked mince gives it a good flavour. Shape into four to six patties with wet hands.

Brush with any marinade just before barbecuing, if desired, or glaze just before end of cooking time. Cooking time is about 8 minutes.

Sesame Onion Marinade

Stir together 2 tablespoons Kikkoman soya sauce, 1 tablespoon onion juice (scraped from the cut surface of an onion cut through its equator), and 1 or 2 teaspoons sesame oil. Leave chicken, all meats and fish to stand in this before barbecuing, and brush on during cooking if desired.

Minted Yoghurt Sauce

Stir together ½ cup (250 ml/8 fl oz) plain yoghurt, 1 tablespoon lemon juice, ½ teaspoon each of salt, ground cumin and sugar, a mashed and chopped garlic clove, and 2–3 tablespoons finely chopped mint. Leave to stand for at least 30 minutes, then use some to marinate beef or lamb, and the rest as a sauce over the barbecued meat.

Soya and Sherry Dip

Simmer together until reduced to half original volume ¼ cup (60 ml/2 fl oz) Kikkoman soya sauce, ¼ cup (60 ml/2 fl oz) sherry, 2 tablespoons sugar, and 1 crushed garlic clove. Brush over any quick-cooking meat while it cooks, and drizzle some over the cooked meat.

Apricot Mustard Glaze

Warm together 2 tablespoons apricot jam, 2 teaspoons Dijon-style mustard, and 1 tablespoon dark or light soya sauce. Thin with a little sherry or orange juice if necessary, until it is a good consistency to brush over nearly cooked beef, lamb, chicken, or pork.

PORK & SAUSAGES

Stuffed Roast Loin of Pork

A stuffed loin of pork makes a delicious festive dinner for a large family group. Serve it with thin mustard-flavoured gravy and a good selection of vegetables.

Extras that you might serve alongside the meat are crackling (cooked separately), apple sauce, and tart jelly.

For 6–8 servings:
1.5–2 kg (4–5 lbs) loin of lean pork
mixed mustard
dark soya sauce
about 8 moist prunes
2–3 tamarillos, sliced
6 blanched spinach leaves
about 2 Tbsp fine dry breadcrumbs

2 Tbsp mixed mustard
about 1 cup vegetable liquid and wine
1 tsp apricot jam (optional)

Rub all surfaces of the pork with a paste made from the mustard and soya sauce. Work out where stuffing will lie, then arrange rows of prunes and tamarillo slices on the spinach leaves. Sprinkle with bread-crumbs. Roll up and tie securely in several places, then place on a rack over a roasting pan just big enough to hold the meat. Roast, uncovered at 180°C (350°F), for 1½ to 2 hours.

Remove meat to carving plate, then make thin gravy in the pan. Pour off any fat, stir in about 2 tablespoons mixed mustard, heat until bubbling, then add about a cup of a mixture of vegetable liquid and wine. Add apricot or other jam for sweetness if you like, and boil down until thin cream consistency.

Variations:
Soak prunes and tamarillos in sherry or liqueur before using them in the stuffing.

Replace tamarillos with about 6 cooked peach halves.

Pork and Apple Casserole

It is not always necessary to brown stews and cas-seroles in added butter or oil if the liquid in which the meat simmers is well-flavoured. Fruit and/or vege-tables that simmer with the meat make servings look larger, and add to the flavour.

For 4 servings:
500 g (1 lb 2 oz) cubed lean pork
1 large apple, cubed
1 large onion, chopped
2 stalks celery, sliced
2 Tbsp Worcestershire sauce
2 Tbsp tomato sauce
1 Tbsp brown sugar
¾ tsp salt
½ tsp dried thyme
1 tsp dried sage
1½ cups (375 ml/12 fl oz) water

cornflour to thicken
chopped parsley

Put all the ingredients except the cornflour and parsley into a casserole dish with a well-fitting lid. Cook below the middle of an oven heated to 150°C (300°F) for 1½ hours, stirring once if possible.

When meat is tender, thicken with cornflour paste and sprinkle with chopped parsley. Serve on noodles or with mashed potatoes, with pan-cooked cabbage and carrots.

Pickled Pork

Pickled pork was part of Christmas in our house when I was a child. It is delicious.

If you don't see it at your butchers shop or super-market, ask about it. It may be called pickled pork, cured pork, or salted pork. It is salted by soaking it in brine, but is not smoked like a ham.

For 4–6 servings:
1 (1–1.5 kg/2–3 lb) piece pickled shoulder pork
water to cover for soaking
1–1½ litres (32–48 fl oz) water
1 onion
1–2 cloves garlic
1 carrot
1 stalk celery
about 10 peppercorns
about 6 juniper berries
about 6 allspice seeds
1 bay leaf
1 sprig thyme
1 sprig parsley
1–2 small chillies

If you want a piece of fairly lean meat, buy pork from the shoulder rather than the belly.

Place in a large container, cover with cold water, and leave to stand for 1–3 hours, changing the water after 30 minutes for faster results.

Place in a large pan or cast-iron casserole with fresh water to cover. Try to select a container into which the meat fits snugly.

Add whatever flavourings on the above list that you have, or use other flavourings if you know that you like them. Do not add salt or anything which is salty. Vegetables need not be peeled, but should be scrubbed and chopped roughly. Spices may be crushed if you like for greater flavour.

Bring to the boil and simmer very gently with the lid on, turning the meat occasionally. The meat is cooked when a skewer goes through it easily. This may be as soon as an hour for young shoulder meat.

Lift cooked pork out of the cooking liquid. I put it in a roasting bag with a few spoonfuls of liquid, so it cools without drying out. It can be reheated in a microwave oven or conventional oven in this bag, too.

Use some of the cooking liquid to make a parsley sauce. Throw out the rest.

Serve with new or mashed potatoes, small whole carrots, and cabbage or leeks.

Parsley Sauce

1 Tbsp butter
2 Tbsp flour
½ cup (125 ml/4 fl oz) milk
¼–½ cup (60–125 ml/2–4 fl oz) cooking liquid
about 1 Tbsp dry sherry or white wine (optional)
2–3 Tbsp chopped parsley

Melt the butter in a small pan. Stir in the flour, then add the milk and quarter of a cup of the stock, and

Pickled Pork

bring to the boil, stirring constantly. When the mixture boils, taste it to check on its saltiness. If it is not too salty, add more cooking liquid, but if it is salty, add extra milk instead. Add sherry or white wine for extra flavour if desired, then stir in chopped parsley.

Let the sauce simmer gently for a few minutes, then add extra milk or cooking liquor to bring it to a fairly thin coating consistency. Adjust seasonings to suit your taste.

Barbecued Pork Ribs

It's no use planning a slow-cooking pork rib recipe for a barbecue, because people who are addicted to them just can't wait that long. Although this recipe calls for preliminary work in the kitchen, it is worth it.

For 4 servings:
1–1.5 (2 lb 2oz–2 lb 9 oz) meaty pork ribs
1 cup (250 ml/8 fl oz) water
sprinkling of ground cumin

Sauce
1 onion
2 cloves garlic
1 Tbsp oil
1 tsp ground cumin
½ tsp ground coriander seed
½ cup (125 ml/4 fl oz) tomato sauce
2 Tbsp Worcestershire sauce
2 Tbsp soft brown sugar
1 Tbsp wine or cider vinegar
1 Tbsp tomato concentrate
½ tsp cornflour
½ cup (125 ml/4 fl oz) water
⅛–¼ tsp chilli powder

Cut the pork ribs into sections, each with three or four rib bones, and place in a large saucepan with the water and ground cumin. Cover tightly and simmer for 1½ hours, or until the meat is very tender.

While the pork cooks, make the sauce. Put the first five ingredients into a food processor, chop very finely, transfer to a pan and cook over a moderate heat for about 5 minutes. Measure the remaining ingredients into the pan, using the smaller amount of chilli powder unless a hot sauce is required, and simmer for about 15 minutes.

When required, place the rib sections on the barbecue, heat on each side until they sizzle, then brush with the warm sauce and heat again on both sides. Serve with crusty bread, warmed on the barbecue, or with corn cobs. Coleslaw goes well with either combination.

Peachy Pork Schnitzels

Beans or broccoli and kumara (sweet potato) or pumpkin go well with this.

For 2 servings:
200 g (7 oz) lean pork schnitzels
2 Tbsp sherry
2 tsp dark soya sauce
1 clove garlic, crushed
pinch freshly grated nutmeg
¼ cup canned peach segments, sliced into thinner pieces
2 tsp butter

Barbecued Pork Ribs

Trim any small pieces of connecting tissue and fat from the schnitzels then flatten them evenly with a meat hammer.

Combine the next four ingredients in a large shallow dish and turn schnitzels in this mixture. Leave to stand for at least 5 minutes.

Heat a frypan until very hot, add butter, then before it burns put the schnitzels into the pan. Cook for 15–20 seconds per side until lightly browned, then remove from the pan and add the peaches and any remaining marinade to the pan drippings. Put the schnitzels back in the pan and turn to coat with the peach mixture. Heat through and serve.

- Take care not to overcook lean pork, or it toughens and dries out.
- Always trim connective tissue from the edge of schnitzels, or snip it at intervals, otherwise the schnitzels curl up during cooking.

Barbecued Pork Kebabs

For these kebabs you can buy lean cubed pork, or choose foreloin, butterfly, or medallion pork steaks. Cut the steaks into even 2 cm (¾ inch) cubes, and leave them to stand in their marinade for at least an hour, before grilling them over a high flame, on a preheated gas barbecue.

For 4 servings:
Kebabs
750 g (1½ lb) lean cubed pork
3–4 pineapple rings (optional)
1 red pepper (optional)
1 green pepper (optional)

Marinade
1 Tbsp dark soya sauce
1 rounded Tbsp honey
1 Tbsp sherry
1 Tbsp sesame oil
1 tsp grated fresh ginger
1 tsp Trappey's hot pepper sauce
2 cloves garlic, crushed

Cut the pork into cubes and place them in an unpunctured plastic bag. Measure the marinade ingredients into the bag with the pork, knead gently to mix, squeeze all the air out of the bag, fasten with a rubber band and leave to stand at room temperature for at least an hour, or in the refrigerator overnight.

Divide the cubes into 12 even groups and thread on 12 soaked bamboo skewers, alone or with cubes of pineapple and squares of blanched red and green pepper between the cubes of meat.

Barbecue over a high heat, turning after 2 minutes, brushing with remaining marinade before and after turning. Kebabs are cooked as soon as pork feels firm, and a cube is no longer pink in its centre. Test after 4 minutes.

Porky Parcels

I hope that you will try this minced pork recipe, served as suggested, in lettuce leaf packages.

If you think that lettuce packages are not for you, put the mixture on little pancakes, baked potato halves, toasted hamburger buns, or in split pita breads or mini taco shells. All of these are good for an outdoor summer meal.

For 4 servings:
500 g (1 lb) minced pork
1 large onion, finely chopped
2 cloves garlic
2 Tbsp tomato sauce
1 Tbsp dark soya sauce
1 Tbsp wine or cider vinegar
½ –1 tsp five spice powder
about 1 tsp hot pepper sauce
½ cup (125 ml/4 fl oz) water
2 tsp cornflour
1 tsp instant chicken stock
½ cup (125 ml/4 fl oz) water
salt
3 or 4 spring onions
chopped coriander leaf, if available

Heat a large, preferably non-stick pan, and add to it the pork mince and the finely chopped onion. Stir constantly over a high heat, breaking the minced meat into small pieces and browning the onion in the pork fat.

Chop the garlic finely, add to the browned meat and stir for about 1 minute before adding the tomato sauce, soya sauce, vinegar, five spice powder and hot pepper sauce.

Add the first measure of water, cover and simmer for 5–10 minutes to cook the meat and onion. Stir together the cornflour, instant stock and second measure of water and stir into the mixture. Cook for a few minutes longer then taste and add more of any of the above flavourings to reach the flavour balance you like. After you have done this, add salt.

Heat, uncovered, until the mixture is dry enough to spoon into a lettuce leaf without dripping.

Serve immediately, or reheat when required.

Just before serving, stir the chopped spring onion and coriander (if used) into the mixture, or sprinkle it on top, or serve each ingredient in a small bowl, so diners can add what they like.

Porky Parcels

To serve lettuce packages:
Wash and remove the leaves from any loose-leafed lettuce. Serve the lettuce leaves on a large flat plate or shallow bowl, beside the hot meat.

Each diner should take a lettuce leaf, put a dessert-spoon of pork in the centre of it, fold the stem end over the meat, the sides over this, then roll up the rest of the leaf.

Hold the roll firmly while eating it, with a plate or paper serviette underneath, to stop dribbles. Make more rolls as required.

Note:
Five spice powder is a mixture of spices used in Chinese cooking. It contains star anise which gives the meat an interesting aniseed flavour. You will find it in some supermarkets or at Oriental food suppliers. It is a pity to leave it out of this recipe.

Coriander leaf, cilantro or Chinese parsley looks rather like parsley but tastes quite different. Look for it at stores which stock Indian or Chinese foods, or grow it yourself. It makes all the difference to a recipe like this.

Variations:
Add other seasonings, if preferred.
Use minced beef, if desired.

Barbecued Ham Steaks

Ham steaks are already cooked, and need only to be heated through, with a glaze to add a little sweetness. You can use pre-cut ham steaks for this recipe, or cut thick slices from a boneless pressed ham and cook them the same way.

For 4 servings:
4 ham steaks
pineapple rings (optional)

Glaze
¼ cup (60 ml/2 fl oz) pineapple juice
1 Tbsp tomato or barbecue sauce
1 tsp smooth mixed mustard
1 tsp cornflour
1 tsp light soya sauce
1 Tbsp maple syrup or brown sugar

Mix the glaze ingredients. Heat until boiling, stirring until mixture is thick and clear. Snip the edges of each steak in four to six places, so they will not curl up as they cook. Pour glaze over ham steaks in an unpunctured plastic bag, or in a shallow dish. Make sure that all ham surfaces are coated. Leave for at least 15 minutes.

Remove from bag and barbecue over a high heat on a hot plate or oiled grilling rack until steaks are hot and lightly browned on both sides, about 3–5 minutes per side. Do not overcook.

Barbecue canned pineapple rings to serve with each steak if desired. Place on an oiled heated plate or in a hinged wire basket, since they break easily when turned. If barbecuing fresh pineapple, sprinkle slices or cubes lightly with sugar first.

Quick Tangy Pork

Quick Tangy Pork

This is one of my favourite pork fillet recipes. It is quick, has a wonderful flavour and if care is taken with the cooking time, should be very tender.

For 2 servings:
1 small pork fillet (250 g/9 oz)
1 tsp dark soya sauce
1 tsp sesame oil
1 tsp sherry
1 clove garlic, chopped

Sauce
2 tsp cornflour
1 tsp instant chicken stock
¼ cup (60 ml/2 fl oz) plum jam
¼ cup (60 ml/2 fl oz) dry sherry
½ cup (125 ml/4 fl oz) water
1 clove garlic, chopped

Cut fillet into pieces about 5 mm (¼ in) thick. Mix the next four ingredients together, pour over the sliced pork and leave to stand for at least 10 minutes.

Microwave at Full power for 2–3 minutes, stirring after each minute, or stir-fry in a large non-stick pan, stirring constantly, for 3–4 minutes.

Cook until meat is no longer pink, but do not overcook! (Fillet cooks in a very short time.)

Combine sauce ingredients. Microwave or simmer, stirring occasionally, until smooth and clear. Stir the meat into the cooked sauce and serve over rice with Tender-Crisp Zucchini (see page 127).

Super Snarlers

SEE PHOTOGRAPH ON PAGE 82

Gas barbecues make a good job of cooking sausages because well-regulated heat is very important if you want to produce a good result. Nobody wants sausages which are charred on the outside and raw in the middle, yet many barbecued sausages finish up like this. There are several ways of coping with this problem.

Start with uncooked sausages of regular thickness, turn the heat to low, and move and rotate the sausages regularly, so that they heat through slowly, and the centres cook before the outsides darken too much.

Buy precooked sausages, or precook your own sausages before you take them outside to barbecue. In the precooking, the important thing is to cook the centre of the sausages. The outside will brown well on the barbecue, later. You can precook sausages just before you barbecue them, or cook them in advance, then refrigerate them. Simmer the sausages gently in a large covered pan with a little beer or water until they feel firm, about 20 minutes, then pour away and discard any fatty liquid. For larger numbers of sausages, bake in a covered roasting pan with a little added liquid for about 30 minutes at 150°C (300°F). To precook sausages in the microwave oven, put them in one layer in an oven bag or covered container and allow about 15 minutes at Medium (50% power) for 500 g (1 lb 2 oz) of sausages.

Barbecue your sausages on a solid plate or on a grilling rack. Both give good results. For ease of turning a large number of small sausages, put them in a double-sided wire basket.

Avoid fatty uncooked sausages, since these tend to drip a lot and produce a lot of fat which burns and chars the surface of the sausages. Precooked sausages generally produce much less fat as they brown and heat through.

Remember that all sausages are not created equal! There are many types of sausages available. Some are unmemorable but inexpensive, and need good sauces, relishes, breads and salads to turn them into an interesting meal, while at the other end of the sausage market are 'designer' sausages that you can serve to anyone with pride.

Family Burgers

This economical recipe uses 500 g (1 lb 2 oz) of inexpensive sausage meat to make eight generous burgers.

Before you start mixing, assemble all the ingredients since apple and potato may brown if left standing too long before mixing and cooking.

For 8 burgers:
1 egg
1 Tbsp Worcestershire sauce
1 tsp curry powder
1 large onion, grated
1 apple

2 medium-sized potatoes
500 g (1 lb 2 oz) sausage meat
oil
hamburger buns

Using a food processor, process briefly to just chop and mix the egg, sauce, curry powder, grated onion, apple (unpeeled and cut into large chunks) and the scrubbed and roughly chopped potatoes.

Add the sausage meat, in two batches if necessary, and mix to combine. Or grate the ingredients and mix by hand in a large bowl.

Using wet hands, divide the mixture into eight patties.

Cook in a pan with a little oil, over a moderate heat, for about 5 minutes per side.

Serve on toasted halved hamburger buns with your favourite hamburger accompaniments, or top with sautéed pineapple rings.

Savoury Sausages with Pineapple

Here is a down-to-earth, good, practical casserole which can be prepared with the minimum of mess and cooked in your oven with little attention. It fills the house with the most inviting aromas, and is especially welcoming on a cold night.

For 4–6 servings:
1 Tbsp cornflour
2 Tbsp brown sugar
1 Tbsp mixed mustard
½ cup (125 ml/4 fl oz) tomato sauce
1½ Tbsp dark soya sauce
½ tsp dried sage
1 cup (250 ml/8 fl oz) diluted pineapple juice
  (from can)
1 large onion, chopped
1 red pepper, chopped (optional)
1 green pepper or 1 or 2 stalks celery, chopped
8–12 sausages
1 (400 g/14 oz) can pineapple chunks in syrup,
  drained

Select a casserole dish big enough to hold the sausages in one layer. Add the ingredients in the order listed. Stir together the cornflour and sugar, then add the next four ingredients, and stir again. Drain the liquid from the pineapple, make it up to a cup with water, and stir it into the casserole dish, then add the chopped vegetables, and top with the sausages, pricked about eight times each to prevent bursting. Cover tightly and put in a cold oven. Heat oven to 180–200°C (350–400°F) and cook for 1–1½ hours, until the sausages are cooked and the liquid is clear and thick. Add a little hot water if the casserole lid is not tight-fitting and the sauce thickens too much. Stir the pineapple pieces through the cooked casserole and serve.

Savoury Sausages with Pineapple

Sausage Meat Roll and Marinated Florence Fennel

Sausage Meat Roll

A roll like this looks exciting and tastes good but is made of humble ingredients!

For 6 servings:
350 g (12 oz) flaky or puff pastry
250 g (8 oz) minced beef
250 g (8 oz) sausage meat
1–2 slices bacon, chopped
1 egg, beaten
1 cup (100 g/3½ oz) fresh breadcrumbs
1 cup finely chopped celery
2 Tbsp chopped parsley
2 Tbsp Worcestershire sauce

Roll pastry thinly to about 25×35 cm (10×15 inches).

Combine remaining ingredients, reserving a little egg. Form into a sausage about 25 cm (10 inches) long. Lay on pastry. Fold ends first, then sides over meat. Place on a baking dish with the joins underneath. Decorate with pastry leaves if desired. Brush with remaining beaten egg. Cut several steam vents.

Bake at 200°C (400°F) for about 30 minutes.

Slice when cold and serve with Marinated Florence Fennel (see page 122).

Pork Pie

I find that a pork pie made in a long, narrow loaf tin goes a long way. It is great for special summer picnics and lunches, and will last for several days.

For about 8 servings:
Pastry:
2 cups (250 g/8 oz) flour
125 g (4½ oz) butter
¼ cup (60 ml/2 fl oz) water

Filling
4 hard-boiled eggs
500 g (1 lb 2 oz) pork mince
4 rashers bacon
½ tsp allspice
½ tsp nutmeg
½ tsp cinnamon
¼ tsp ground cloves
½ tsp salt
black pepper
1 onion, finely chopped

Glaze
2 tsp gelatine
½ cup (125 ml/4 fl oz) cold water
1 tsp Kikkoman soya sauce
1 tsp instant green herbs stock
1 Tbsp sherry

To make the pastry, put the flour and cold cubed butter in a food processor fitted with the metal chopping blade. Add the water in a thin stream while chopping the butter into the flour. Add only enough water to make the dough particles stick together. This stage will be reached while the mixture still looks crumbly, so test at intervals. Do not over-process.

Press dough into a ball and refrigerate while making the filling, then roll out to line and top a loaf tin of six cup capacity (this is normal size). Line the bottom and long sides of the tin with non-stick or baking paper to ensure easy removal later on.

To make the filling, peel the hard-boiled eggs and place to one side. Take the minced pork from the refrigerator. Chop the refrigerated bacon into chunks and put into the unwashed food processor bowl with the seasonings. Process briefly to chop, then add the quartered onion and chop it with the bacon. Add the minced pork and combine, with brief bursts, taking care not to turn the mixture into sausage meat by over-processing.

To assemble the pie, put about a third of the pork in a layer on the bottom of the uncooked crust. Put the eggs on it in a row, then press the rest of the pork around and over them. Mound the top. Put the pastry top on the pie, crimping the edges to seal it. Glaze crimped edge and top with beaten egg if you want a good shiny surface.

Make one fairly large central hole in the centre of the pie crust. Form a square of greaseproof paper or foil into a cone and put it into the hole, so that it keeps it open.

Bake at 200°C (400°F) for 30 minutes, then at 170°C (325°F) for 1 hour.

After about 30 minutes, liquid needs to be sucked from the hole in the top with a basting syringe every 15 minutes. It stops dribbling out in the last 15–30 minutes of cooking. (It is easier to deal with this liquid if you have one hole rather than several holes.)

Cool the cooked pie. Check that you can lift it from its tin, but do not take it out permanently, since the glaze mixture must be poured in between the pork and the pastry when the pie is cool.

For the glaze, sprinkle the gelatine over the cold water. Leave to stand for 5 minutes, then add the soya sauce, instant stock and sherry, and warm until the gelatine and instant stock dissolve. Cool until syrupy before pouring down the cone into the pie. Refrigerate until set.

The flavour of this pie is best after it is one or two days old. Make sure you keep it really cold for easy cutting, and to prevent the growth of bacteria.

Sausage Combo

Sausage Combo

This inexpensive and quick recipe contains ingredients that complement each other.

For 4 servings:
about 600 g (1 lb 6 oz) sausages or sausage meat
2 apples, sliced
2 onions, sliced
1 (425 g/15 oz) can baked beans
about ½ cup (125 ml/4 fl oz) water
pinch dried sage or thyme

Brown the sausages or pieces of sausage meat in a pan, then remove, and cook the apple and onion in the pan until tender and lightly browned. Slice sausages and replace in pan with the baked beans and water. Add a pinch of sage or thyme, simmer for 10 minutes, then adjust seasonings, thin with more water if necessary, and serve on rice.

Variation:
Add a second can of baked beans to the pan if you are feeding people with large appetites!

Oriental Tofu and Noodles

SEE PHOTOGRAPH ON PAGE 94

This is a very quick and simple recipe as long as you can buy ready-fried tofu. Deep-fried tofu is golden brown, crisp, and chewy — quite different in appearance and texture from plain tofu.

For 4 servings:
200 g (7 oz) instant noodles
3–4 spring onions
3 cups (750 ml/24 fl oz) boiling water
2 Tbsp dark soya sauce
1 Tbsp dark sesame oil
½ tsp brown sugar
½ tsp salt
¼ tsp garlic powder

about 300 g (10 oz) deep-fried tofu
1 (385 g/14 oz) can whole mushrooms in brine
½ cup roasted cashew nuts

1 Tbsp cornflour
2 Tbsp sherry
2 tsp dark soya sauce
1 tsp brown sugar
¼ tsp ground ginger
¼ tsp garlic powder
½ cup (125 ml/4 fl oz) water
liquid from mushrooms

Break the blocks of noodles into a large saucepan. Chop the spring onions over them. Combine the next six ingredients in a jug or bowl, pour over the noodles, then heat the saucepan until the liquid boils. Cover, turn off the heat, and stir occasionally while preparing the rest of the recipe.

Cut the pre-fried tofu into slices about 1 cm (½ inch) thick. Open and drain the mushrooms, reserving the liquid, and halve or quarter the mushrooms. Mix together the tofu, mushrooms, and nuts.

Combine the remaining ingredients in a small saucepan, then bring to the boil, stirring constantly, to make a lightly thickened glaze. Thin down with extra water if necessary, then gently stir in the tofu, mushrooms and nuts.

Arrange the prepared noodles (which should have absorbed all the liquid) in a shallow serving dish, top with the glazed tofu mixture, heat if necessary, and serve.

Note:
The instant noodles used in this recipe are available in stores supplying Asian foods. They do not have sachets of dried stock enclosed.

Variations:
Mix stir-fried beansprouts, celery, etc., through the noodles or with the tofu mixture.
Replace salt with 1 teaspoon instant chicken stock and replace tofu with about 300 g (10½ oz) cooked chicken meat.

Pasta with Summer Sauce

This mixture is a cross between a salad and a pasta sauce. You make the uncooked sauce, then pour the hot drained pasta over it, stir, and leave it to stand. Serve it hot, warm, room temperature, or reheated, later.

For 6–8 servings:
250 g (9 oz) large pasta spirals
2 spring onions, chopped
1 large clove garlic, chopped
4–6 sprigs basil leaves
about a cup of loose parsley sprigs
3–4 anchovy fillets, chopped
1 Tbsp drained capers
1 Tbsp caper liquid
¼ cup (60 ml/2 fl oz) olive or other oil
1 tsp sugar
¼–½ tsp chilli powder
½ tsp salt
about 6 ripe red tomatoes
6 black olives, chopped

Cook the pasta in plenty of boiling, lightly salted water for about 10 minutes, until just tender. Chop the next six ingredients, by hand or in a food processor. Add the liquids and seasonings, and tip into the serving bowl. Next halve the tomatoes and discard their seeds by squeezing and shaking them. Chop finely, using a sharp knife or food processor, and add to the rest of the sauce ingredients with the chopped olives.

Drain the hot cooked pasta, and tip into the dressing. The pasta will soak up most of the dressing as it stands, over the next 15 minutes.

Note:
If the tomatoes do not have a lot of flavour, add a tablespoon of tomato paste.

Summer Spirals

This is an easy recipe which children love. It is good by itself, or it may be served alongside plainly grilled or barbecued lean meat.

For 1 large or 2 small servings:
100 g (3–4 oz) pasta spirals
½ tsp instant chicken stock
1 tsp cornflour
½ tsp sugar
¼ cup (60 ml/2 fl oz) water
1 tsp butter
¼ cup chopped parsley
basil or other fresh herbs
1 cup finely cubed tomato

Cook the pasta in about 4 cups (1 litre/32 fl oz) of lightly salted boiling water for about 10 minutes, or until just tender. Stir together in a small pan the instant stock, cornflour, and sugar, then add the water and butter and bring to the boil. Remove from the heat and stir in the parsley, with a few leaves of finely

Tortellini in Herbed Sauce

chopped basil or another herb, if you have any. Chop the tomato into tiny cubes. Drain the cooked pasta, bring the sauce with the added tomato to the boil, then stir the two mixtures together. Leave to stand for 2–3 minutes before eating.

Tortellini in Herbed Sauce

This is one of the quick, easy pasta dishes that I cook and serve with a salad when I do not have fast-cooking meat in the refrigerator and I am in a hurry.

I like it best when it is made with a noodle of con-voluted shape, which will hold a lot of the delicious sauce. Tortellini look like little turbans. They hold a lot of sauce in their folds, and are particularly satisfying to eat.

For 2 large or 3 medium servings:
250 g (9 oz) tortellini or other pasta
butter or oil for pasta
2 cloves garlic
1 Tbsp butter
¼ cup (60 ml/2 fl oz) white wine
½ cup (25 ml/4 fl oz) double cream or sour cream
1 cup grated cheese
1 Tbsp flour

¼–½ cup finely chopped fresh mixed herbs
salt to taste
hot pepper sauce (optional)

About 15 minutes before you want to eat, add the pasta to boiling, lightly salted water and cook until tender, then drain and toss with a little melted butter or oil.

While the pasta cooks, chop the garlic and heat it in the tablespoon of butter in a fairly large microwave dish, for about 30 seconds. Add the wine, cream, and the grated cheese which has been tossed in the flour, and microwave on Full power until the sauce bubbles vigorously around the edges. Stir well. If the sauce does not become smooth in a few seconds, cook it a little longer, and stir again. Stir the herbs and salt into the smooth sauce.

Just before serving fold the sauce and pasta together, reheat if either has cooled down, taste and add extra salt and a little hot pepper sauce if desired, and serve straight away.

Note:
Use whatever fresh herbs you have. I use a mixture of parsley, chives, thyme, marjoram, sage, and spring onions. Use only parsley and spring onions if these are all you can get.

Variation:
Stir small cubes of tomato through the sauced pasta.

Economical Lasagne

Most lasagne recipes call for precooking of the pasta, a slowly simmered meat and tomato sauce, and cheesy sauce topping. This easy recipe eliminates all pre-cooking but still produces a product with a good flavour and texture. What's more, you can make a small amount of meat feed four or five people if necessary.

For 4–5 servings:
250–400 g (8–14 oz) minced beef
1 (300 g/10 oz) can tomato purée
1 (440 g/15 oz) can tomato soup
2 cloves garlic, chopped
1 tsp instant beef stock
1 tsp each dried basil and oreganum
1 cup (250 ml/8 fl oz) boiling water
125 g (4–5 oz) uncooked lasagne noodles
1½ cups (150 g/6 oz) grated cheese

Use as much mince as you like. Mix together the mince, purée, soup, garlic, instant stock, herbs and boiling water and stir well.

Butter or spray a fairly shallow microwave or oven-proof dish of at least 8 cup (2 litres/64 fl oz) capacity.

Make layers of a third of the meat mixture, then half the noodles, then a third of the cheese. Repeat with more meat, noodles and cheese, finally topping with the remaining meat mixture.

Microwave, covered loosely, on Full power for 30 minutes, sprinkle with the remaining cheese and micro-wave for 1 minute to melt it.

Or cover and bake at 180°C (350°F) for 45 minutes, adding the cheese and cooking uncovered for the last 5 minutes.

Leave to stand for at least 15 minutes before serving.

Variations:
Add 200–400 g (about 8–12 oz) sliced, sautéed mush-rooms to the minced beef and tomato mixture.

Replace the minced beef with 2–3 cups thoroughly cooked, drained brown lentils.

If you are baking rather than microwaving the lasagne, after 40 minutes add the remaining cheese, then pour over it a mixture made by beating two eggs with 1 cup of milk. This sets to make a cheese custard when the lasagne is baked, uncovered, for about 15 minutes (instead of the 5 minutes suggested to melt the cheese).

Spinach and Mushroom Lasagne

This vegetarian lasagne is interesting, full of flavour, and substantial.

For 4–6 servings:
1 Tbsp butter
2 cloves garlic, chopped
2 Tbsp flour
½ cup (125 ml/4 fl oz) white wine
¾ cup (185 ml/6 fl oz) extra wine or vegetable
*   liquid*

¼ cup (60 g/2 oz) cream cheese
300 g (10 oz) firm button mushrooms, sliced

500 g (1 lb 2 oz) spinach
1 large onion, chopped
1 Tbsp oil
1 tsp grated nutmeg
½ tsp salt
1 tsp sugar
½ tsp oreganum
½ cup (125 g/4 oz) cottage cheese

¾ cup (180 g/6 oz) cream cheese
½ cup (125 ml/4 fl oz) milk
1 cup (100 g/3 oz) grated cheese

about 200 g (7 oz) fresh spinach lasagne sheets
paprika (optional)

Melt the butter in a medium-sized pan and cook the garlic gently for about a minute, then stir in the flour. Add the first measure of wine and bring to the boil, stirring constantly. Add the remaining wine or vege-table liquid (from spinach etc.) and boil again, stir-ring well. Stir in the first measure of cream cheese and remove from the heat, lift out and reserve half a cup (125 ml/4 fl oz) of the sauce, then stir the mushrooms into the remaining sauce. This is for the bottom layer.

Wash the spinach, then cook it with no added liquid, until it is wilted, but bright green. Drain, but do not squeeze or chop finely. Sauté the chopped onion in the oil, then add a tablespoon of water, cover the pan and cook until tender. Stir in the nutmeg, salt, sugar, oreganum, cottage cheese, cooked spinach and half the reserved sauce. This mixture is for the middle layer.

For the top layer, mix the remaining reserved sauce, the cream cheese, milk and grated cheese.

Assemble the lasagne in a baking dish about 25 cm (10 inches) square. Butter or spray the pan, then cover the bottom with one layer of lasagne. Spread mush-room mixture over it, then top with another lasagne layer. Spread spinach over this, then cover with a third layer of lasagne. Spread the cheese mixture over this.

Cover with a lid or foil, and bake at 180°C (350°F) for 45 minutes, then uncover and bake for 10 minutes longer. Sprinkle with paprika if light coloured. Leave to stand for at least 15 minutes before cutting and serving.

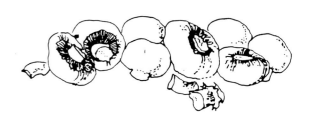

Economical Lasagne

Beany Pie

This is a great picnic pie! Make it just before you leave home and transport it uncovered. Don't leave out the seasonings — they make all the difference.

For 6–8 servings:
Pastry
100 g (3½ oz) cold butter, grated
1½ cups (185 g/6 oz) flour
6–8 Tbsp cold water

Mix the grated butter into the flour, then add enough water, slowly, to make a firm dough. Roll out thinly into two 30 cm (12 inch) circles. Ease one circle into a 20 cm (8 inch) round cake tin.

Filling
2 large onions, chopped
2 apples, sliced
1–2 Tbsp oil
1 tsp ground cumin
1 tsp oreganum
½ tsp chilli powder
1 (440 g/1 lb) can baked beans
1 cup (100 g/4 oz) grated tasty cheese

Cook the onions and apples in the oil until browned and tender. Take off the heat and stir in the seasonings, baked beans and cheese. Turn into uncooked crust.

Dampen edges of the remaining pastry with water and place over filling, sealing edges. Cut off excess pastry and use to decorate the top of the pie. Fold the edges double and pinch attractively. (For best appearance, brush surface with a little beaten egg.)

Bake at 220°C (425°F) for 20 minutes or until golden brown, then at 180°C (350°F) for 20 minutes longer. Serve warm.

Bacon, Corn and Rice

This is a lovely easy mixture that you can serve hot, or cold, tossed in dressing.

For 2 servings:
1–2 rashers lean bacon
2 tsp oil
½ cup (90 g/3 oz) Basmati rice
¼ cup (45 g/2 oz) red lentils
liquid from canned corn
water
¼ tsp salt
1–2 spring onions, chopped
about 1 cup drained, canned corn
fresh herbs — parsley, basil, dill or oreganum
(optional)

Chop the bacon into small pieces and heat in the oil until lightly browned. Stir in the rice and lentils, cook for about a minute, then add the liquid from the corn,

Beany Pie

made up to 2 cups (500 ml/16 fl oz) with water, and the salt.

Bring to the boil over a high heat, then cover and simmer gently for 15 minutes, or until the rice and lentils are tender and the liquid evaporated.

Stir in the finely chopped spring onions and the drained corn, and add the chopped herbs if using them.

Note:
I use a 440 g (1 lb) can of whole kernel corn for this recipe, but you can use a smaller can if you like. I sometimes add a finely chopped red pepper just before the rice is cooked.

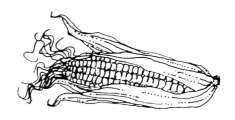

Grainy Mix

Serve this as a meal by itself, or alongside a small portion of lean meat. Top it with a thickened tomato sauce or Parmesan cheese if you like.

For 4 servings:
2 Tbsp oil
1 onion, finely chopped
2 stalks celery, chopped
1 carrot, diced
1 clove garlic, chopped
1 tsp ground cumin
1 tsp oreganum
1 tsp salt
2 small dried chillies
½ cup (90 g/3 oz) brown rice
¼ cup (45 g/2 oz) pearl barley
¼ cup (45 g/2 oz) brown lentils
3 cups (750 ml/24 fl oz) water
½ cup chopped parsley and other herbs

In a heavy lidded pan, heat the oil. Add, as you prepare them, the onion, celery, carrot and garlic. Stir in the seasonings then add the brown rice, pearl barley, brown lentils, and water.

Bring to the boil, cover tightly, and simmer until the grains and lentils are tender, for about 45 minutes. Remove from heat, stir in chopped parsley and other herbs. Leave to stand for 5–10 minutes before serving.

Variation:
Add other quick-cooking vegetables to the grains etc. 10–15 minutes before the end of the cooking time. Cauliflower, cabbage, spinach, corn, green beans or peas, peppers, and mushrooms are all suitable.

Use a different combination of grains and lentils. Brown rice, kibbled wheat and rye, pearl barley, brown lentils and moong dahl are some of the grains and pulses that cook in the same time. Wholegrain wheat (wheat berries) does not.

Brown Rice

Brown rice is used as you use regular long-grain white rice. It has a lovely nutty flavour, and requires at least twice the cooking time of white rice. If you serve undercooked brown rice, you are likely to put your family off it for life. Experiment until you get the cooking time and amount of water needed exactly right. Short-grain brown rice often cooks more quickly than long-grain brown rice. The grains do not stick together during cooking as white rice grains do, until the rice is very well cooked.

Try brown rice, baked in a covered dish while you cook other food in your oven. Put 1 cup (185 g/6 oz) of brown rice, 1 teaspoon salt and 3 cups (750 ml/24 fl oz) of water in a casserole dish with a tight-fitting lid. Put this in a cold oven, turn it on to 180°C (350°F), and cook for 45 minutes to 1 hour, until it is as tender as you like. If you find that it is as soft as you like it after say 40 minutes, and all the water is not absorbed, drain it through a colander, and use less water next time.

Or lift out with a slotted spoon the brown rice that you plan to eat straight away, and leave the rest to cook for 15 or so minutes longer, in the remaining water. It will swell and soften, and is delicious served as brown rice porridge the next morning.

Brown Lentil Pasta Sauce

For this recipe, you make a well-flavoured, easy sauce while the lentils cook, then combine the two mixtures.

For 6 servings:
1½ cups (285 g/10 oz) brown lentils
1 bay leaf
4 cups (1 litre/32 fl oz) water
2 Tbsp oil
2 large onions, chopped
2 or 3 garlic cloves, chopped
1 red pepper, chopped (optional)
1 (440 g/1 lb) can cream of pumpkin soup
1 (425 g/15 oz) can Mexican spiced tomatoes
cornflour if necessary

Simmer the brown lentils and the bay leaf in the water in a covered saucepan until the lentils are tender, about 45 minutes.

In another saucepan sauté in the oil until lightly browned the onion, garlic and red pepper. Add the pumpkin soup and Mexican tomatoes and simmer, breaking up the tomatoes, for about 10 minutes. Put aside until the lentils are tender, then add them, with as much of their cooking liquid as you need for a good sauce consistency.

If sauce is too thin, boil down until it thickens, or add a little cornflour paste.

Taste the sauce just before serving, and add a little sugar, salt, and pepper to balance the flavours if necessary. Spoon sauce over boiled drained pasta, or over brown rice. Serve with a salad if desired.

Big Bean Burgers

My son, Simon, a keen vegetarian cook, introduced me to the idea of grinding up dried beans etc. to make burgers. Odd though it may sound, it works!

Ironically, however, to make these nutritious, really inexpensive burgers, you need a piece of rather expensive machinery. A coffee grinder, free-standing, or as an attachment to a food processor, is needed to pulverise the mixture. Once you have it to this stage, you can take it backpacking etc., feeling confident that you can produce a nutritious meal which needs only a few minutes cooking.

For 8 10 cm (4 inch) burgers:
½ cup (95 g/3½ oz) black-eyed beans or any white beans
½ cup (95 g/3½ oz) brown lentils
½ cup (80 g/2½ oz) kibbled wheat or bulgar
½ cup (70 g/2½ oz) sunflower or pumpkin seeds
½ cup (45 g/1½ oz) rolled oats
¼ cup (30 g/1 oz) toasted sesame seeds
½ cup (40 g/1½ oz) wheatgerm
1 Tbsp cumin seeds
1 Tbsp dried oreganum
2–3 tsp garlic salt
¼–½ tsp chilli powder

In a coffee grinder grind to the consistency of fine dried breadcrumbs, one after another, the beans, lentils, kibbled wheat, sunflower or pumpkin seeds, rolled oats and toasted sesame seeds. Pile these in a large bowl, add the wheatgerm, then grind together the cumin seeds, oreganum, garlic salt and chilli powder. Use the larger amounts of garlic salt and chilli powder if you intend mixing grated carrot into the burgers when you make them.

Mix thoroughly and store for up to a month in an airtight jar.

To make one large burger, stir the mixture well, put ½ cup of it in a small bowl with ½ cup finely grated carrot, a chopped spring onion, and ¼ cup (60 ml/2 fl oz) water. Leave to stand for 15–30 minutes. The dry mix will firm up a little as it stands.

Cook in 1–2 tablespoons oil, over a low to moderate heat in a covered pan, for about 5 minutes per side.

Variation:
Mix ½ cup of the dry burger mix with a little more than ¼ cup water, with no grated carrot or spring onion. When mixed like this, the cooked burgers will be saltier and 'hotter'.

When you mix beans, grains and seeds, you get a good balance of nutrients. This is especially important for anyone 'eating vegetarian'.

The burgers above have a good balance of two different pulses, two types of grain, and two seeds. These ingredients are excellent value for money.

Big Bean Burger

Potatoes

Potatoes are always popular. Serve them as the main part of a light meal, or as an interesting accompaniment for a main meal.

Because they are an important part of a healthy diet, and are such good value for money nutritionally, it is worth paying a little more and buying the best quality potatoes you can find. Look for evenly shaped and sized potatoes, with clean, unblemished skins and a good flavour.

Save yourself time and money by scrubbing rather than peeling potatoes before you cook them. You get more flavour, and more nutrients.

Swiss Potato Cake

Recently, in Switzerland, my husband and I wandered along trails on the top of a mountain above a small town. We had asked the receptionist at our small hotel if we would be able to find any place to eat an evening meal. He looked surprised. 'Of course,' he said, 'Every fifteen minutes.' We puzzled about this answer. We found out that he meant exactly what he said. There were old farmhouses along the paths, each about fifteen minutes walk away from the next.

On the ground floor lived the cows, on the next, the family, and above this was the restaurant. The diners were walkers in summer, and skiers in winter.

We sat outdoors on a balcony, admired the nearby sunflowers, window boxes and apple trees, and ordered two different variations of Swiss potato cakes. I have eaten these before, and I love them, but they never tasted as good as they did in those surroundings!

I am sure that my untraditional version would horrify a traditional Swiss cook, but it works, is easy, and tastes very good.

For 1 serving:
2 scrubbed potatoes, grated
about 25 g (1 oz) butter, melted
½ cup (50 g/2 oz) grated cheese
2 tsp finely chopped herbs
½ cup sautéed mushrooms (see page 127)

Scrub the potatoes well so they need no peeling, then shred them with a sharp cutter, e.g. the blade of a food processor which makes long shreds.

Plunge them into cold water, leave to stand for at least 5 minutes, then drain them in a colander and pat them dry on a paper towel or teatowel. Melt the butter in a fairly large pan or bowl, then toss the potato in it, lightly coating as many pieces as possible.

Melt about a teaspoon of butter in the small, preferably non-stick pan in which the potato cake will cook. Rub it round the warm pan, then add the potato, pressing it down quite firmly. Put the lid lightly on the pan, and cook the cake over a moderate heat for 10–15 minutes, until it is golden brown. Slide the potato cake out of the pan on to the lid or a plate, then flip it back into the pan, so the uncooked side is down.

Cook the second side for about 10 minutes, again with the lid ajar. During the last 3 minutes put the grated cheese mixed with whatever fresh, chopped herbs you have and like, over the central part, top with the sautéed mushrooms, and let the cheese melt slightly. Slide the potato cake on to a plate and serve as soon as possible.

Swiss Potato Cake

Potato Pan Pizza

Potato lightens the base of this pizza, and adds bulk to its topping.

For 3–4 servings:
Base
1 cup (125 g/4 oz) self-raising flour
1 cooked potato
50 g (2 oz) butter
¼ tsp dried oreganum

Topping
2 cups altogether of cubed raw tomato,
 chopped red or green pepper,
 chopped mushrooms
1–2 rashers bacon
¼ tsp basil
¼ tsp marjoram
1 cup cubed, cooked potato
1½ cups (150 g/5½ oz) grated or cubed cheese

Mix together with a food processor or finger tips the self-raising flour, cooked potato, room temperature butter and the oreganum.

Press the resulting dough into a well sprayed 20 cm (8 inch) loose-bottomed cake tin. Measure all topping ingredients into a bowl and mix well.

Press topping quite firmly on to the uncooked base and top with extra cheese if desired.

Bake at 200°C (400°F) for 25 minutes. When cooked, lift pizza on its base, away from the sides of the pan. Serve hot or warm.

Potato Pan Pizza

Cottage Cheese Potato Pie

This is an unusual way to serve potatoes as part of a buffet meal or the main part of a luncheon, with a salad.

Doubled, this quantity makes a 25 cm (10 inch) flan or a deeper 23 cm (9 inch) pie.

For 4–5 servings:
200 g (7 oz) flaky pastry
1 cup (250 g/9 oz) cottage cheese
1 egg, beaten
¼ cup (60 g/2 oz) sour cream
1 tsp salt
3–4 spring onions, finely chopped
1 cup mashed potatoes
Parmesan cheese

Line a 20 cm (8 inch) flan tin or pie plate with flaky pastry. Press the cottage cheese through a sieve into a bowl containing the beaten egg, sour cream, salt, finely chopped spring onions and the mashed potato. Mix together thoroughly (or combine unsieved cottage cheese and other ingredients in a food processor).

Pour into the unbaked pie shell, sprinkle the surface with grated Parmesan cheese and bake at 220°C (425°F) for 30–40 minutes (45–50 minutes for a double quantity pie) until the pastry is cooked and the top is golden brown.

Gourmet Baked Potato

A little self-indulgence is not a bad thing! I have a short list of foods that I buy and prepare for myself whenever I am going to be the only person home for dinner.

Here is a quickly prepared, satisfying vegetable meal that I always enjoy. Its quantities need not be measured carefully.

Bake a large, scrubbed potato in the microwave oven until it will 'give' when pressed. Cut it open about two-thirds of the way up, and scoop the flesh into a shallow bowl. Add a chopped spring onion or chives, a little milk, salt, hot pepper sauce, some small cubes of your favourite cheese and mash with a fork. Then chop in a quarter to half of an avocado. Mash briefly, so that some of the avocado remains in chunks, heap all this back into the potato shell, then reheat for about a minute, until warm but not hot.

Baked Pizza Potatoes

Baked potatoes, stuffed with toppings often used on pizzas, can form the main part of a meal. One large potato serves one or two people depending on their appetites!

For 1–2 servings:
1 large potato
1 cup (100 g/3½ oz) grated cheese
2 spring onions, chopped
1 bacon rasher, chopped
¼ cup (20 g/¾ oz) chopped mushrooms or red or
  green peppers
¼ tsp dried oreganum
1 large tomato or 1 Tbsp tomato paste
milk or sour cream to thin

Scrub then bake potato in the microwave at Full power for 4½–5 minutes, turning once, or at 200°C (400°F) for 1–1¼ hours. While potato cooks mix together in a bowl the cheese, spring onions, mushrooms or peppers and the seasoning. Add the tomato cut into small cubes, or the tomato paste, and mix to combine.

When the potato is cooked, cut in half and scoop out the cooked flesh. Mash with the other ingredients, adding the milk or sour cream if the mixture is dry.

Pile filling into potato halves. Garnish with more of any of the filling ingredients, olives, or anchovies if you like.

Reheat in the microwave for 3–4 minutes, or in the oven for 15–20 minutes. Serve alone or with a side salad.

Baked Pizza Potatoes

Surprise Packages

Filo pastry makes a glamorous coating for potatoes!

This pastry may be kept refrigerated for several weeks if carefully wrapped to prevent drying out.

For 2 servings:
3 sheets filo pastry
2 medium-sized cooked potatoes
2–3 Tbsp sour cream
fresh herbs
garlic salt
freshly ground black pepper
butter (optional)

Cut the cooked potatoes into 5 mm (¼ inch) cubes. Mix with sour cream, chopped fresh herbs, garlic salt and pepper.

Cut the filo pastry sheets in half using three half sheets for each package. Brush each sheet lightly with melted butter and place two pieces on the third so the corners lie randomly.

Pile the potato mixture in the centre of each filo arrangement, gather the pastry around the potato, fanning out edges. Tie packages with a chive leaf for an edible 'string' or with thread.

Place on a buttered oven tray, brush with butter if desired, and bake at 190°C (375°F) for 10–15 minutes or until pastry is golden brown.

Surprise Packages

Easy Raclette

Cheese and potatoes are popular partners. Try this updated version of a traditional Swiss idea.

Heat an easily melted type of cheese and serve it on boiled potatoes, with pickled cucumbers as a complete meal.

I use New Zealand-made Raclette cheese which has the texture and aroma, when heated, of cheese used to make Raclette in Switzerland.

I heat slices of this cheese in small shallow microwave dishes until soft and bubbly at the edges. Use amounts to suit yourself.

I sometimes boil the potatoes conventionally or microwave them before the cheese.

To microwave new or main-crop potatoes:
Cut 500 g (1 lb 2 oz) scrubbed, scraped or peeled potatoes into even-sized pieces. (Smaller pieces cook more quickly.) Microwave at Full power in a covered dish with ½ cup (125 ml/4 fl oz) water for new potatoes, ¼ cup (60 ml/2 fl oz) for main-crop potatoes, for 6–8 minutes. Allow 2–3 minutes standing time. (If potatoes shrivel they have been overcooked.)

Note:
Cook more potatoes and more cheese than you think you will need as they are very popular! Heat cheese in a hot oven or under a grill if preferred.

Easy Raclette

109

Sautéed Potato Balls

Cut potato balls using a melon-ball cutter (or cut cubes).

Sauté in oil with 2 crushed garlic cloves for about 15 minutes, or until evenly browned and tender.

Remove the garlic as soon as it browns.

Garlic Roast Potatoes

These are roast potatoes with a difference — in flavour and appearance.

Allow 1 or 2 small potatoes per serving. Peel and boil in salted water to cover, for 5 minutes, then drain and stand aside till cool enough to handle.

Squash, but do not break up completely, one or two garlic cloves. Put in a shallow baking or roasting pan big enough to hold potatoes with about ½ cup (125 ml/4 fl oz) oil.

Slice potatoes nearly to base.

Turn them in the oil and bake, uncovered at 200°C (400°F) for about an hour, spooning oil over potatoes occasionally, and removing garlic from pan before it blackens.

Note:
Garlic potatoes cooked at a lower temperature (for a longer time) may be browned under the grill before serving.

Duchesse Potatoes

These look festive and can be prepared ahead and reheated when needed. (They can be frozen before or after browning, too.)

For best results use floury potatoes. For four servings boil 500 g (1 lb 2 oz) peeled potatoes cut into evenly sized pieces. When tender but not mushy, press through a sieve or potato ricer then mash with 25 g (1 oz) butter and a large beaten egg (and extra egg yolk if possible). Keep mixture firm. Season to taste then pipe rosettes on to a greased or sprayed baking tray using a forcer bag with a star nozzle.

Bake at 200°C (400°F) for 20 minutes or until edges turn brown. Rosettes spread a little when baked.

Variation:
Pipe rings instead of rosettes. After browning fill with mushrooms, peas, etc.

Garlic Roast Potatoes (above) and Duchesse Potatoes

Barbecued Potatoes

Barbecue Packs

It always takes a while to get a barbecue fire to the right stage for cooking meat over hot embers. Before this stage is reached you can start cooking Barbecue Packs because of their double aluminium foil coating. The packs are delicious and take 30–45 minutes to cook, depending on the heat of the fire.

For each pack tear off a piece of foil about 30 cm (12 inches) long. Fold in half so it is 15 cm (6 inches) wide. Smear a teaspoon of butter over central part of foil.

Scrub then slice 1 or 2 new potatoes. Overlap the slices on the top half of the foil, leaving the edges clear. Sprinkle with salt, or onion or celery salt, then add a pinch of basil and marjoram (or other herbs).

Put a few small pieces of butter on top then fold the foil over the potatoes, squeeze to push out most of the air, then turn the edges several times to seal the packages.

Place on a rack over the barbecue fire. Turn every few minutes for the first 15 minutes, then turn occasionally. Open a pack after 30 minutes to see whether potatoes are cooked. If not, reseal carefully.

Serve hot, warm or cool (but not chilled).

Variation:
Add chopped bacon if desired.

Barbecued Potatoes

When you barbecue precooked potatoes, all you have to do is brown and crisp the outside and heat them through.

Scrub large potatoes, simmer until just tender or microwave them as follows: scrub and quarter lengthways 8 fairly large potatoes, (about 1.5 kg/ 3 lb 6 oz). Put them in an oven bag with 25 g (1 oz) butter and 2 tablespoons water. Fasten bag with a rubber band, leaving a finger-sized opening. Microwave at Full power for 12–20 minutes, repositioning potatoes in the bag twice, until potatoes are barely tender. Leave potatoes in the bag until you want to barbecue them. Put the quarters on a preheated, oiled grill rack or plate, and turn to brown all sides evenly, brushing with flavoured butter or oil only if they burn.

Barbecue time is likely to be 6–15 minutes, depending on conditions.

Barbecued New Potatoes

Microwave 750 g (1 lb 11 oz) small potatoes with 1 tablespoon butter, 2 mint sprigs and 2 tablespoons water in an oven bag (see previous recipe) for about 8 minutes. Thread them alone or with other vegetables on skewers. Brush with melted butter or Garlic Herb Butter (see page 55) before cooking on an oiled grill rack until nicely browned.

Portuguese Potatoes

Portuguese Potatoes

These potatoes cook very quickly and taste delicious.

For success you must put the potatoes into very hot oil so they do not stick and cover them tightly during cooking. At these high temperatures the potatoes absorb little oil — you pour off the extra before serving.

For 2 servings:
2–3 Tbsp oil (preferably olive oil)
2 large new potatoes
2 cloves garlic, chopped
finely chopped parsley
salt

Heat the oil over a fairly high heat in a small non-stick frypan with a close-fitting lid, until it starts to smoke.

Scrub the potatoes and cut each into four to six slices, and then into strips the size of small chips. Pat dry on a paper towel. Drop the chips gently into the hot oil, shaking the pan to make sure they do not stick.

Sprinkle the chopped garlic over the potatoes, turning gently. Cover the pan, lower the heat and cook for 6–8 minutes, turning once or twice during this time. The potatoes should turn golden brown but not dark brown.

Drain off remaining oil and sprinkle with parsley and a little salt before serving.

Special Scalloped Potatoes

SEE PHOTOGRAPH ON PAGE 104
This recipe starts with cooked rather than raw potatoes. As a result its cooking time is reduced. The flavour is particularly good, because a packet of soup is added.

For 6 servings:
1 kg (about 2 lb) cooked potatoes
1 packet onion soup mix
2 cups (50 ml/16 fl oz) milk
½ cup (50 g/2 oz) grated cheese

Precook the potatoes if necessary, by boiling or microwaving them in a large covered container with ½ cup (125 ml/4 fl oz) water. (This quantity of potatoes should cook in the microwave in about 10 minutes.)

Slice the potatoes and arrange them in layers in a large, shallow ovenware dish about 23 cm (9 inches) in diameter, which has been buttered or sprayed with non-stick spray. Sprinkle the dry packet soup over each layer, using it all. Pour the milk over the potatoes, dampening the soup mix, but do not worry if the milk does not cover the potatoes. If the underside of the top layer is above the milk, add up to half a cup water.

Sprinkle the grated cheese over the potatoes, then cover loosely with aluminium foil and bake at 200°C (400°F) for 15 minutes, then remove the foil and bake uncovered for 15–30 minutes, until the potatoes on top are golden brown.

Notes:
If you are in a hurry, brown the top under a grill after a total of 30 minutes in the oven.

If sauce looks too thick before potatoes are browned, add up to half a cup (125 ml/4 fl oz) boiling water.

Creamy Mashed Potatoes

Mashed potatoes taste so good with many meat dishes that you should make them often.

Get perfect results each time by remembering these pointers:

For preference, use a pan which is not made of aluminium, since potatoes may discolour if mashed in an aluminium container.

Cut peeled potatoes into evenly sized pieces and drop into a small amount of boiling salted water. Cover and cook over a moderate (not high) heat until soft in the middle. Drain and let pan stand over very low heat with lid ajar for 2–3 minutes, to dry out potatoes.

Add 1 teaspoon butter for each serving then mash with a potato masher. Then beat mashed potatoes with a fork (not a spoon), adding as much milk as you need for a creamy consistency. Add extra seasoning if necessary and serve as soon as possible.

Speedy Spicy Spuds

Potato Salad with Peanut Dressing

The peanutty dressing makes this salad substantial enough to serve for a light meal.

For 6 servings:
1 onion, finely chopped
2 cloves garlic, chopped
2 Tbsp oil
2 tsp brown sugar
2 tsp soya sauce
1 Tbsp lemon juice
¼ cup peanut butter
coconut cream and water
hot pepper sauce or chilli powder
8 medium-sized cooked, waxy potatoes
about 250 g (9 oz) barely cooked green beans
4 spring onions, chopped
lettuce
2–4 hard-boiled eggs
cucumber

Cook the chopped onion and garlic in the oil in a covered pan or microwave oven until tender but not browned. Mix in the brown sugar, soya sauce, lemon juice and peanut butter and heat until the mixture bubbles.

Add water and coconut cream about 2 tablespoons at a time, heating between additions, until the sauce is the consistency of cream. Add hot pepper sauce or chilli powder to taste.

Arrange room temperature potatoes, beans and spring onions on lettuce leaves on a platter or in individual plates, pour over the warm dressing and garnish with spring onions, quartered hard-boiled eggs and cubes of cucumber.

Speedy Spicy Spuds

A microwave oven cooks potatoes easily and quickly, but without browning or crisping them.

If you use a preheated browning dish, and carefully selected seasonings, however, you can produce microwaved potatoes which are slightly crisp, well-coloured and have an interesting flavour.

For 2 servings:
2 large potatoes
1 Tbsp flour
1 tsp garlic salt
1 tsp paprika
1 tsp ground cumin
½ tsp oreganum
½ tsp curry powder
1 Tbsp oil

Preheat browning dish for 6 minutes.

Scrub or peel the potatoes and cut into small (1 cm/½ inch) cubes, then pat dry on a paper towel. Shake in a plastic bag with the next six ingredients, to coat evenly.

Add the oil to the heated browning dish. Quickly spread the coated potatoes on to the hot surface.

Microwave, uncovered at High power for 3 minutes. Turn then cook for 2–3 minutes longer, or until tender.

Creamy Mashed Potatoes

Main Course Salads

When the weather is warm and summery, or when you wish that winter would finish, a salad meal can be just what you want.

The salads of today are truly exciting. There are many light, interesting, well-flavoured dressings that complement the flavours of salad ingredients instead of masking them. We have a wonderful range of foods to use in our salads, and we have become open-minded about what foods are served warm, cold or hot, and what can be cooked at some times, and served raw at others.

The range of ready-prepared salads at gourmet food shops and supermarkets has grown enormously, as the demand for 'Take Home' food has increased. Salads that would have been regarded as unusual a few years ago are now regarded as quite acceptable!

The enthusiastic but busy cook can prepare and serve some very interesting and practical salads, knowing that these fit in with the nutritional goals of today, as well as being easy and practical.

Although, ideally, you might like to cook all your salad foods 'from scratch', you will probably find it practical to keep a selection of carefully chosen cans, bottles and packets handy, to add to your raw or home-cooked ingredients.

Take special care with the appearance of your salads. Aim for casual arrangements of quite large chunks, rather than formal patterns, and tiny pieces.

By all means use leftovers, but make sure that they have not been waiting around in your refrigerator too long. Make sure that fresh ingredients are in peak condition.

Different rules apply to different foods. Some ingredients will be improved by standing in a well-flavoured dressing or marinade. Other foods, like pasta, for example, soak up dressings if left to stand in them too long, and taste best if some more dressing is added just before serving.

Most lettuce-like salad greens wilt if dressed too soon. They should be tossed with dressing just before serving, or even dressed on the diner's own plate, if they are part of a buffet where the food will stand over some time. Some cabbage salads, on the other hand, are meant to be dressed ahead, so that their texture is changed.

For main dish salads which are filling, but not high in fat, use something starchy, like cooked pasta, rice,

Main Course Salads

potatoes, kumara (sweet potato), bulgar, or beans, as the main component.

Take smaller amounts of lean cooked chicken, lamb, beef, ham, cheese, eggs or fish, and cut into easily managed slices, strips, or chunks.

Choose a dressing which will complement what you have chosen, then add fruit and/or vegetables of contrasting flavours, colours and textures.

Add small amounts or 'highlights' of distinct or strongly flavoured foods, olives, anchovies, capers, and herbs, if you feel they are needed.

Combine salad ingredients attractively, if possible, just before serving.

Hints for dressings:

- Thin down thick mayonnaise-type dressings with citrus juice, white wine, or oil and vinegar dressings, so they will coat foods thinly.
- When you mix oil and vinegar dressings, season them well, since they will be used sparsely, with their flavour diluted.
- Try using less oil than many dressing recipes call for, keeping other quantities the same.
- Use small quantities of highly flavoured oils such as sesame or nut oils, to add interest to simple oil and vinegar dressings.
- Be very fussy about the vinegar you use in dressings, especially if the salads are to be eaten soon after the dressing is made. Wine vinegars are milder than other vinegars. Experiment with herb-flavoured vinegars.
- If you are adding raw garlic to a dressing, leave it to stand for at least an hour to mellow its flavour.
- Make good use of Dijon, and similar mild, tangy mustards in dressings. These add good flavours to dressings, and stop them separating so quickly.
- Use just enough dressing to coat the salad ingredients, without forming puddles at the bottom of the container.

Canned Vegetable Salads

It pays to keep some canned vegetables on hand so that you can turn them into 'instant' salads when you do not have a ready supply of fresh vegetables.

Ways to use cans:

- Mix drained whole-kernel corn with chopped red and green peppers, with any oil and vinegar dressing, or a Mexican dressing.
- Sprinkle canned asparagus with lemon juice and herbs of your choice.
- Serve beetroot in a sweet-sour dressing, or cube it and mix with unpeeled cubed raw apples, and top with thinned mayonnaise.
- Combine drained canned kidney beans, corn, and canned pimento with an oil and vinegar dressing flavoured with cumin, oreganum and chilli powder.
- Slice canned new potatoes and mix with a mustard-flavoured oil and vinegar dressing, or with curry-flavoured mayonnaise. Sprinkle generously with chopped parsley or other fresh herbs.

Cooked Vegetable Salads

For a change, or when raw vegetables are not available, serve salads made from cooked vegetables which have been left to stand for at least 15 minutes in a well-flavoured oil and vinegar dressing. You can make your own dressings, or keep several good bought dressings on hand, to use alternately. Look for Mexican, Italian, bacon-flavoured dressings, etc.

Vegetables to try:

- Florence fennel (finocchi) quartered lengthways, simmered until tender, then left to stand in French or Italian dressing.
- Globe artichokes covered in water and boiled until the petals pull off easily, then served with mayonnaise for the petals to be dipped into. The soft part of the petal is scraped off with the teeth.
- Whole young beans boiled until barely tender, then turned in enough of any garlic-flavoured dressing to coat them.
- Cooked carrots, whole, sliced lengthways or in rounds, turned in a mixture of lemon juice, oil, salt, sugar and mustard, with lots of chopped parsley.
- Asparagus, cooked until barely tender, with plain or orange-flavoured mayonnaise for dipping.
- Zucchini, chopped and boiled until tender-crisp, coated with (olive) oil, freshly ground black pepper, and a little lemon juice.
- Beans, cauliflower, zucchini, celery, carrots etc cooked 'à la Grecque', and served at room temperature, in their cooking liquid.

Rice, Potato and Pasta Salads

Salads based on rice, potatoes or pasta are substantial and may be prepared ahead, then dressed a short time before your meal.

Good additions to cold cooked rice are cooked peas, corn, beans and red or brown lentils. Raw vegetables include celery, radishes, red and green peppers, firm tomatoes, and small cauliflower florets. Add fresh herbs and spring onions for extra flavour, and moisten with well-flavoured dressing about 10 minutes before serving.

Potato salads are especially good when made with new potatoes that have had dressing poured over them straight after cooking. Add cooked peas and toss with a mustardy French dressing or thinned mayonnaise about 15 minutes before serving. Sprinkle generously with parsley and/or chives.

Pasta made from hard flour should be used in pasta salads. As long as this is not overcooked it will not lose its bounce and slightly chewy texture. Lightly cooked vegetables such as broccoli, canned corn, and fresh herbs are good additions. Toss lightly with well-flavoured French, Italian or Mexican dressing 15–30 minutes before serving.

Any of these salads in this last group will become bland and flavourless if left to stand too long after the dressings are added.

117

Greek Summer Salad

SEE PHOTOGRAPH ON PAGE 114

This salad goes well with barbecued or grilled lamb kebabs, but it is almost substantial enough for a main meal on a hot night, especially if you serve it with interesting, crusty bread rolls.

For 2 servings:
telegraph cucumber about 20 cm (8 inches) long
4 large tomatoes
1 small red onion
dried oreganum
about 50 g (2 oz) Feta cheese
about 10 black olives
olive oil
black pepper
lemon wedges (optional)

Cut the cucumber in half lengthways and scoop out the seedy area using a teaspoon. Cut into 1 cm (½ inch) chunks, and divide between the two plates. Top with thickly sliced, cubed or whole small tomatoes, then with onion rings made by slicing the red onion and separating the slices into rings.

Sprinkle the surface of the salad with dried oreganum, then add small cubes or thin slices of Feta cheese, and toss the black olives over the top.

Dribble olive oil over the salad, and add black pepper to taste.

Squeeze the lemon wedge over the salad if you like. Beware of adding salt until you have eaten some of the rather salty Feta cheese and the black olives in between mouthfuls of the other vegetables.

Note:
As the seasons change use other vegetables as the Greeks do. Replace the cucumber with chopped lettuce or light-coloured cabbage heart, and add green and red peppers, if they are of good quality and plentiful.

Cumin Bean Salad

SEE PHOTOGRAPH ON PAGE 114

This is a salad which may be kept in a covered container in the refrigerator for a week and served as the main part of a dinner or a light meal whenever you want something quick and easy.

For 6 servings:
4 cups cooked drained dried beans or drained
* canned beans*
1 cup chopped cooked green beans
½–1 cup diced green peppers
1 cup diced celery
about 1 cup diced tomato
Cumin Dressing (see below)

To prepare the salad using dried beans soak 1½ cups of dried beans (in hot water) for several hours or overnight, then drain and boil in unsalted water for 1–2 hours or until very tender.

To test for this, the beans should be easily squashed

between the thumb and index finger, or against the roof of the mouth with the tongue!

Put the drained beans, peppers and celery in a large covered container. Add the dressing and mix to coat. Cover and refrigerate for at least 2 hours before serving.

When required, bring to room temperature, add tomato to the amount you want to serve, and toss to mix.

Cumin Dressing
½ cup (125 ml/4 fl oz) corn or soya oil
¼ cup (60 ml/2 fl oz) wine or cider vinegar
2 tsp ground cumin
1–2 tsp onion powder
¾ tsp salt
2 tsp dried oreganum
½–1 tsp garlic powder
black pepper and hot pepper sauce to taste

Place all the dressing ingredients in a screw-topped jar. Shake well.

Note:
It is very important that the cumin is fresh, and has a pungent, definite flavour. If necessary, grind whole cumin seeds, toasting them lightly first if desired. Without the cumin flavouring, the salad will not be interesting.

Shredded Carrot Salad

I find this salad is especially popular with children.

For 2 servings:
200 g (7 oz) carrots
1 Tbsp oil
1 Tbsp lemon or orange juice
1 Tbsp very finely chopped parsley, spring onions,
* basil, dill or other herbs*
sugar and salt to taste

Shred carrots, making long matchstick-like shreds if you have the right sort of cutter. Toss carrot with oil, juice and herbs. Taste, add a sprinkling of sugar and salt, and taste again. When you have the balance of flavours right, refrigerate for 30 minutes before tossing again, draining off any liquid, and serving.

Red Pepper Salad

When red peppers are grilled to remove their skins, they develop an interesting flavour and a 'meaty' texture, and make excellent salads.

Char skins of red peppers by turning over a gas flame or under a hot grill. Remove skins under a cold tap. Slice flesh into olive or other oil flavoured with a garlic clove crushed with a little salt.

Serve at room temperature.

Undressed Salads

Undressed Salads

I realised, recently, that I could simplify some of my meal preparation and prevent wastage if I let my family do a little more for themselves at the table.

For maximum vitamin retention, leafy vegetables should be washed briefly but carefully, shaken dry, and stored so that they do not dry out and wilt.

I have recently started to let some leafy salad vegetables sit in this state in my salad bowl, rather than in the vegetable crisper of the refrigerator.

I wash, shake dry, and arrange in my salad bowl the salad leaves that I think I will use for the meal, at any time of the day that suits me. A short time before the meal I add chopped peppers, cucumber, radishes, carrot, spring onions, etc. I keep the bowl containing these salad foods covered with a lid, plate or plastic cling wrap in the refrigerator.

The salad is then ready to go on to the table whenever I like, with no additions. People can serve themselves, and add whatever dressing they like, in whatever amounts they want. The undressed salad remains crisp, and any which is unused can be covered and refrigerated until the next time it is needed.

Mushroom Salad

Make this salad only when particularly good quality mushrooms are available.

4–6 servings:
2 Tbsp red or white wine vinegar or lemon juice
¼ cup (60 ml/2 fl oz) salad oil
½ tsp each salt, sugar, and freshly ground black pepper
2 tsp Dijon mustard
2 Tbsp finely chopped parsley
200–300 g (7–10.5 oz) clean button mushrooms

Shake together or food process all ingredients except the mushrooms. Just before serving, slice the mushrooms and toss with enough dressing to coat them. Serve in bowl lined with lettuce leaves.

Tomato and Pasta Salad

Tomato and Pasta Salad

Serve this mixture warm or cold, with barbecued meat or picnic food. The hot pasta soaks up the delicious, easy dressing.

For 4 servings:
250 g (9 oz) pasta, spirals or macaroni
1 (520 g/15 oz) can diced tomatoes
2 spring onions, chopped
¼ cup (60 ml/2 fl oz) oil
1 Tbsp wine vinegar
1 tsp cumin
1 tsp oreganum
1 tsp sugar
1 tsp celery salt

Cook the pasta in a large saucepan of boiling, lightly salted water for about 10 minutes, or until tender. While the pasta cooks, put the diced tomatoes, their liquid and all the remaining ingredients in a serving bowl. Tip the hot drained pasta on to this, mix gently but thoroughly, and serve warm or cold.

Potato Salads

You can make 101 versions of potato salad, all of which are likely to be popular!

Slice or cube cooked, waxy or new potatoes, making sure that you allow up to twice as much as you allow for a normal serving.

Mix with chopped chives or spring onions, chopped parsley, basil and/or oreganum, or chopped dill leaf.

Add chopped or sliced hard-boiled egg if you like.

For dressing, thin down mayonnaise with mild vinegar or use French or Mustard Cream Dressing (see page 122) or any other thin dressing.

Fold the dressing through the sliced potato, trying not to break up the pieces. Arrange in a serving dish and leave to stand for at least 15 minutes.

Garnish with more herbs, or egg etc. Serve with extra dressing if desired.

Rice Salad

Be generous with the vegetables in this salad. Leftovers keep well for later use, but may need a little extra dressing added just before serving.

1 cup (185 g/6 oz) long-grain (Basmati) rice
2½ cups (625 ml/20 fl oz) water
½ tsp salt
1 Tbsp Dijon mustard
2 Tbsp wine vinegar
3 Tbsp olive or other oil
2–3 stalks celery
about 4 spring onions
4–8 radishes
½ cup drained whole-kernel canned corn
about ¼ cup chopped parsley

Put rice, water and salt in a heavy pan with a tight-fitting lid. Bring to the boil, then lower the heat and cook very gently, without stirring, until the rice is tender and nearly all water absorbed. Watch carefully during the last few minutes. Drain if necessary.

Mix the mustard, vinegar and oil, and stir into the warm or cold drained rice with a fork. Chop the raw vegetables into rice-sized pieces, and toss them, the corn, and the chopped parsley through the salad. Serve in lettuce cups or in a bowl lined with lettuce leaves.

Spinach Salad

This extra-special salad is worth a little effort! I like it so much that I always serve it as a separate course, so its flavour and texture can be fully appreciated.

For 4 servings:
300–400 g (10½–14 oz) best quality spinach
2–3 rashers lean side bacon
3 Tbsp oil
¼ tsp salt
2 tsp mixed mustard
2 Tbsp wine vinegar
100–200 g (3½–7 oz) firm, white button
  mushrooms

Wash the spinach very carefully, shake as dry as possible, then break into large bite-sized pieces, removing stems. Spread on a clean teatowel or on a long piece of paper towel and roll up to dry leaves thoroughly. (Dressing sticks better to dry leaves.)

Remote the rind from the bacon then cook it in a fairly large pan, with 2 tablespoons of the oil until crisp. Lift the bacon from the pan, chop, and put aside for garnishing. Add to the pan drippings the remaining oil, salt, mustard and vinegar. Taste, and adjust seasonings if necessary.

When you are ready to serve, put the dry, crisp spinach in a big plastic bag, slice and add the mushrooms, pour the luke-warm dressing into the bag, close bag so plenty of air is enclosed, then tilt and toss carefully but thoroughly, without bruising the leaves. Serve immediately, sprinkled with the bacon.

Quick Vegetable Salad with Cumin Dressing

This is a salad that you can put together in a few minutes, with ingredients from your store cupboard. The dressing brings the vegetables to life!

For 6 servings:
1 (425 g/15 oz) can sliced green beans
1 (440 g/15½ oz) can whole-kernel corn
1 cup diced celery
½–1 diced red pepper

Cumin Dressing
(See page 118)

Quick Vegetable Salad with Cumin Dressing

Marinated Florence Fennel

Florence fennel looks rather like celery with a swollen base and feathery leaves. It can be sliced like celery and used in salads, but it tastes particularly good when cooked, left to stand in an oil and vinegar dressing, and served warm, or at room temperature.

Trim the feathery side leaves. Remove any tough or discoloured outer leaves, then cut the fennel in half from top to bottom. Cut each half into two, three, or four lengthways wedges, depending on its size. Lay wedges in a covered pan with about a cup of water and a little salt. Simmer until the outer stalks are fairly tender, 5–20 minutes, depending on age, then drain off half the water, add ¼ cup (60 ml/2 fl oz) white wine vinegar, and ¼ cup (60 ml/2 fl oz) of your favourite salad oil. Add half a teaspoon of sugar, then adjust other seasonings to taste. Sprinkle generously with chopped parsley, then cover and leave until required. Serve at room temperature.

Jellied Beetroot

When you make this old favourite you don't get spots on the tablecloth or on your clothes. At home or taken on a picnic it is always popular.

For 6 servings:
1 (425 g/15 oz) can sliced beetroot
2 Tbsp vinegar
1 packet raspberry jelly crystals
1 tsp gelatine

Drain the liquid from the beetroot. Add the vinegar and bring to the boil. Mix the jelly crystals and gelatine. Stir into the hot liquid until the crystals dissolve. Continue heating if necessary. Add the beetroot, chopped if desired, and pour into a mould.

Unmould or cut into squares, when set. Serve as cold as possible.

French Dressing

The name of this dressing is loosely given to dressings of oil and vinegar in proportions of three parts oil shaken with one part mild vinegar. Mustard is added for extra flavour and to stop the two main ingredients from separating immediately.

Season this dressing fairly strongly, and use it in very small amounts to coat salad greens. (If you use a lot of dressing, reduce the amount of seasoning.)

You can mix small amounts of this dressing, by guesswork, in the bottom of a salad bowl, and combine it with a whisk or fork, before tossing it with the salad ingredients, or you can mix larger amounts and keep it in a jar, to be shaken and applied over a period of several days.

You can change the character of the dressing by adding one or more of the optional ingredients. It is worth experimenting with one at a time.

2 Tbsp olive or corn or soya oil
2 Tbsp corn or soya oil
2 Tbsp wine or cider vinegar
1–2 tsp Dijon mustard
¼–½ tsp salt
freshly ground black pepper
hot pepper sauce

Optional
chopped capers
chopped fresh herbs
chopped spring onions
finely chopped garlic
about 1 Tbsp cream
1–2 tsp tomato paste
½–1 tsp sugar

Combine the ingredients of your choice in a screw-top jar, blender or food processor. Shake or process, and use as required.

Blender Mayonnaise

This is an extremely useful and delicious mayonnaise.

1 egg
½ tsp salt
½ tsp sugar
1 tsp Dijon mustard
2 Tbsp wine vinegar
1 cup (250 ml/8 fl oz) corn or olive oil

Measure the first five ingredients into a blender or food processor. Turn on, and pour in the oil in a thin stream until the mayonnaise is as thick as you like.

Store in a covered container in the refrigerator for up to 2–3 weeks.

Mustard Cream Dressing

This is one of my favourite salad dressings. I like to dribble it over mixed salad greens in a large bowl just before serving, then turn the greens gently until all the leaves are completely coated. Use so little that you hardly see the whitish coating.

¼ cup (60 ml/2 fl oz) cream
1 Tbsp Dijon mustard
2 Tbsp lemon juice or 1 Tbsp wine vinegar

Measure the ingredients, in the order given, into a jar with a screw-topped lid. Shake well.

Thin the dressing with a little extra water or white wine, if you think it is too thick.

Alter the flavour by adding horseradish, chopped capers, chopped chives, spring onions, or other fresh herbs, if desired. Depending on the mustard used, you may want to add salt or sugar, too, although I do not.

Use small quantities of dressing to coat salad greens, as above, or pour over tomatoes, etc., without thinning it.

Marinated Florence Fennel

Cooked Vegetables

The vegetables on your dinner plate are just as important as the other foods alongside them.

We are lucky to have so many interesting and delicious vegetables available fresh, at different times of the year, and when these are out of season we have good quality canned and frozen vegetables to fall back on.

Roughly, vegetables fall into the categories of green leafy vegetables, root vegetables, and seeds and seed containers.

To make sure that we get a good balance of nutrients we should eat several different vegetables a day from different categories. If we do this, we can enjoy the many flavours, textures and colours of our choices.

We should also aim towards a balance of cooked and raw vegetables. When we eat freshly harvested uncooked vegetables we get the benefit of nearly all the nutrients in them. During cooking some nutrients disappear. Some are destroyed by heat, and others leach into the cooking liquid.

Prepare vegetables just before cooking, and cook as briefly as possible, in a covered container in as little liquid as necessary. Eat as soon as possible.

I try to add just enough water to cook the vegetable, with no liquid to pour off before the vegetable is served. For this I am dependent on pots and pans with a non-stick finish, and good heat regulation. I cook the vegetable at fairly high heat, and remove the lid and raise the heat to evaporate the last few spoonfuls of liquid. When you cook vegetables like this, you need very little or sometimes no salt.

Carefully cooked vegetables do not need to be covered in a heavy blanket of rich sauce to taste good. Make creamy, buttery sauces the exception rather than the rule, and look at interesting Asian vegetable recipes, rather than rich European ones. There are some light and lovely sauces and glazes based on reduced stock, lemon juice, and herbs. A little cornflour will often thicken juices enough to keep them on the vegetable rather than running off it. A small amount of butter, added to a sauce or glaze like this, will give the vegetable an excellent flavour.

Barbecued Vegetables

Vegetables are easy to barbecue if you remember two things:
- Because they are naturally low in fat, vegetables need to be brushed with oil or butter mixtures, before and during cooking.
- For speed, precook long-cooking vegetables by microwaving or briefly boiling them before you take them outside to barbecue.

Barbecued Mushrooms
Mushrooms barbecue well without precooking. Toss in, or brush with Garlic Herb Butter or mayonnaise, or any oil-based dressing you like, thread on soaked bamboo skewers and cook over a grill rack, or cook directly on the preheated hot plate. For interesting vegetable kebabs, thread mushrooms with quick-cooking vegetables like cherry tomatoes, or with precooked vegetables like new potatoes, cubed cooked kumara (sweet potato), lightly precooked red, yellow and green peppers, etc. Brush with Garlic Herb or plain butter before barbecuing.

Cooked Vegetable Kebabs
Vegetables cut into 2 cm (¾ inch) chunks and precooked by brief boiling or microwaving can be threaded on soaked bamboo or metal kebab skewers, brushed with butter, oil, or any flavoured butter, and browned lightly over a barbecue grill rack. Make colourful combinations of carrot, cauliflower, green, red or yellow peppers, parsnip, pumpkin, kumara, zucchini and other summer squash, small whole onions or larger quartered onions. Brush your favourite glaze over kebabs just before serving if you like.

Barbecued Tomatoes
Small cherry tomatoes and quartered firm tomatoes may be skewered and barbecued with other quick-cooking vegetables. Large 'meaty' halved tomatoes cook quickly on a heated plate or on a grill rack. Watch all tomatoes carefully, since they become very soft if barbecued too long.

Barbecued Corn Cobs
Young corn cobs may be barbecued in their green husks. Pull back husk, remove silk, brush with garlic or plain butter, rewrap in husk, cover with a 10 cm (4 inch) wide band of aluminium foil if liked. Barbecue, turning frequently until all sides are very hot and exposed husks char, about 5–10 minutes.

Don't barbecue very mature corn. Middle-aged cobs may be de-husked, brushed with butter and sealed in foil packages, and turned frequently on grill rack until grains are cooked. If preferred, precook cobs, butter, foil-wrap and reheat on barbecue.

Barbecued Aubergine
Thick slices or cubes threaded on a skewer may be brushed with any well-flavoured oil and vinegar dressing, and barbecued until tender and browned. These may take longer than expected, and need frequent basting, so it is best to cook them alone, rather than on kebabs with quicker cooking vegetables. Well-cooked aubergine has an interesting, meaty texture.

Potato Cakes

Mix 2 cups mashed potato with seasonings and about 1 cup self-raising flour to make a firm mixture. Shape into patties and cook immediately on a hot, well-oiled solid plate. (Uncooked mixture softens on prolonged standing.)

Barbecued Vegetables

Savoury Cabbage

For 2 servings:
½ rasher lean bacon
1 clove garlic, chopped
few drops oil or ¼ tsp butter
200 g (7 oz) shredded cabbage
freshly ground black pepper
cornflour (optional)

Remove rind and chop bacon thinly. Put in a saucepan with garlic and oil or butter. Heat gently until bacon starts to sizzle, then add shredded cabbage with some of the water in which it was washed still clinging to the leaves. Add a grinding of black pepper, cover the pan, raise the heat, and toss the contents occasionally until they come to the boil.

Lower the heat, and cook until the cabbage is tender-crisp. It should still be bright green at this stage. The actual cooking time will depend on the tenderness of the cabbage, but it may be as short as 3 minutes. Raise the heat and evaporate the liquid on the bottom of the pan, or thicken it with a little cornflour and cold water paste. Toss the cabbage in the thickened liquid, and serve straight away.

Carrot and Parsnip Purée

Slice carrots then parsnips into a pan with a tight-fitting lid. In a small amount of water, cook until tender, then drain, reserving the liquid for gravy etc.

Purée the vegetables in a food processor, or push through a food mill, seasoning to taste with a little butter, salt, sugar, nutmeg and pepper.

Savoury Cabbage

Garlic Cucumber

Thinly peel or slice about 75 g (3 oz) telegraph cucumber, discarding the seeds.

Melt 1 teaspoon butter with 1 sliced garlic clove. Add the cucumber, cover and microwave for 1 minute at Full power or cook in a saucepan on the stove top for about 3 minutes.

Sweet Potato Cakes

For 2 servings:
300g (10½ fl oz) kumara (sweet potatoes)
1 egg
2 spring onions, finely chopped
1 tsp ground cumin
1 tsp dried oreganum
½ tsp salt
2 Tbsp flour

Scrub, trim off thin ends, then lightly oil sweet potatoes. Bake at 200°C (400°F) until the flesh gives when pressed, as a baked potato does when cooked. Chop into fairly small pieces. The quantity given should fill a 2 cup measure when tightly packed.

In a medium-sized bowl beat together with a fork the egg, spring onions, ground cumin, dried oreganum, and salt. Add the cooked sweet potato, and mash it into the egg mixture with the fork, then beat in flour. Form mixture into eight flat cakes or patties, heat a little oil in a non-stick pan, and cook the patties over a moderate heat, until golden brown on both sides, and heated through to the middle.

Serve with coleslaw or a lettuce-based salad, as a complete meal for two, or serve with pork, for four.

Mushroom-Filled Filo Triangles

Savoury mushrooms wrapped in filo pastry can be served as a lunch dish or as a vegetable at a main meal.

For 4 servings:
8 sheets filo pastry
about 25 g (1 oz) butter
2 cloves garlic
200 g (7 oz) mushrooms, quartered or chopped
2 rashers ham
parsley, tarragon, thyme, etc.
2–3 spring onions, chopped
1 slice bread, crumbled
1–2 Tbsp sour cream
black pepper to taste

For this recipe you need eight sheets of filo pastry from a packet. Do not open packet until the mushroom filling is cooked, as sheets must be fresh and pliable or parcels will be hard to shape. Rewrap unused filo immediately.

Put 1 tablespoon butter in a pan with the finely chopped garlic, cook gently for a few minutes, then add the quartered or chopped mushrooms. Raise heat, add a few tablespoons water and cover pan to wilt mushrooms, then raise heat even further and remove lid so that mushrooms are nearly dry by the time they are cooked (about 2–3 minutes altogether). Add the chopped ham and herbs to taste, and the chopped spring onions. Cook until onions have heated through. Taste, season well, then add the bread (crumbed in a food processor), and the sour cream to bind the mixture, and black pepper to taste.

To prepare the filo packages melt the remaining butter, then paint some of it over half of one sheet, using no more than ½ teaspoon per sheet. Fold the unbuttered half over the buttered side (folding short sides to each other). Repeat with remaining sheets.

Put two folded sheets on top of each other on a perfectly dry surface. Cut in two to make two long strips.

Place an eighth of the filling close to one end of the strip, then fold the filo so the bottom of the strip is folded against the side, and the filling is covered by the resulting triangle of pastry. Keep folding, making more layers around the triangle. Repeat with the remaining strips.

Place with joins down on an oven tray, brush lightly with more butter, then cook at 200°C (400°F) for 5–10 minutes, until golden brown.

Tender-Crisp Zucchini

Halve very small zucchini lengthways or quarter large ones. Use 125–150 g (4 oz–5 oz) for 2 servings.

Cook with a little butter and water in a covered pan for about 4 minutes or microwave in a covered dish at Full power for about 2 minutes. Season to taste before serving.

Serve with Quick Tangy Pork (see page 89).

Sautéed Mushrooms

Sautéed mushrooms are delicious, but they can absorb a great deal of butter before they soften and cook. You can get very good results with a small amount of butter by heating a finely chopped garlic clove in a teaspoon of butter per serving, then adding the whole, halved, quartered or sliced mushrooms, with about a tablespoon of dry white wine per serving. Cover and cook over a high heat, adding more wine if the pan looks dry before the mushrooms soften and produce liquid. Add about 2 teaspoons chopped parsley per serving, and pepper as you like it. When the mushrooms are wilted, lightly thicken the pan liquid with cornflour paste, and stir the mushrooms until they are coated with it. Raise the heat to evaporate excess liquid in the pan. Add a little salt to taste, if necessary.

Variation:
Add a little fresh or dried thyme with the parsley. It is particularly good with mushrooms.

Roast Yams

SEE PHOTOGRAPH ON PAGE 58
Little pink yams roast nicely, but you have to watch they are not undercooked, or they have an after-taste, nor overcooked or they collapse. You should watch them carefully, removing them from the oven before the meat is cooked if necessary.

The cooking time is dependent on their size and maturity.

Scrub, dry and coat with a film of the pan drippings. Bake uncovered for 20–45 minutes. Unfortunately their pink colour fades during cooking, whatever you do.

Sweet and Sour Yams

This is an unusual but delicious way to prepare yams.

For about 6 servings:
400–500 g (about 1 lb) little pink yams
1 Tbsp butter
2 Tbsp honey
2 Tbsp wine vinegar

Slice scrubbed yams about 1 cm (½ inch) thick, diagonally. Cook in a covered pan in a little lightly salted water for about 15 minutes or until they feel soft when pierced. Drain, keeping the liquid, then add the remaining ingredients to the pan. Cook uncovered until the liquid has thickened. If they dry out, add a little of the reserved liquid, and heat a little longer.

Sauces for Vegetables

When it comes to vegetable cooking, I think that you have two options. You can either cook the vegetables in an interesting way so that by the time they are cooked they have plenty of flavour exactly as they are, or you can cook them more plainly, and serve them with a sauce.

The sauce can be very simple. A knob of butter, with a squeeze of lemon juice, a grinding of pepper, and a sprinkling of chopped herbs makes a sauce which will coat the vegetables lightly and be very hard to beat.

When I was cooking for children, I often made cheese, parsley, and fresh tomato sauces. I found that vegetables which were not very popular would be eaten with more enthusiasm if they were cloaked with one of these.

These sauces are thickened with flour. It is not easy to make sauces which are thickened by boiling down and/or beating in butter when you are cooking for four or six.

When you are cooking for one or two and do not have children's palates to worry about, you can widen your range of sauces.

Here are three sauces which are flavoured with white wine, butter, and/or cream. I make them in a little non-stick pan, allow small quantities per serving, and like the way they bring out the flavour of the vegetables.

Wine and Tomato Sauce

This sauce is nice with anything savoury. Try it with cauliflower, batons of zucchini, as photographed, or on a poached or peeled soft boiled egg on spinach.

For 4 servings:
½ small onion, finely chopped
2 tsp butter
½ tsp flour
2 large tomatoes
¼ cup (60 ml/2 fl oz) white wine
1 tsp finely chopped basil, if available
1 tsp chopped parsley
⅛ tsp salt
1–2 tsp butter

Cook the chopped onion and first measure of butter gently in a small covered frypan for 5 minutes then stir in the small amount of flour. Pour boiling water over the tomatoes, leave to stand for 30 seconds, then remove their skins. Halve, shake out and discard most of the seeds, then cube the rest finely. Add to the pan with the wine, basil and parsley, and cook over a moderate heat for another 5 minutes, then add the salt, and beat in the first teaspoon of the second measure of butter.

You should find that the sauce tastes good like this, if the tomatoes are well-flavoured and ripe, but if not, beat in the last teaspoon of butter, with a little extra seasoning if necessary.

Mustard Sauce

I like this sauce with carrots, cauliflower, and lightly cooked, 'teenage' zucchini, as well as with boiled cured meat. Made with butter beaten in at the end, it has a stronger flavour than it does when cream is added at this stage.

For 2 servings:
2 tsp butter
1 Tbsp finely chopped onion or shallot
½ tsp Dijon mustard
½ tsp grainy mustard
¼ cup (60 ml/2 fl oz) white wine
¼ cup (60 ml/2 fl oz) water
2–3 tsp extra butter or 2 Tbsp cream

Melt the butter in a small, preferably non-stick pan with a lid. Add the very finely chopped onion or shallot, cover pan, and cook gently for 5 minutes or until the onion is tender.

Stir in both mustards, then add the wine and water and boil briskly, stirring often, until reduced to half its volume. Beat in teaspoon lots of the second measure of butter with a whisk, stopping when the sauce is smooth and thick enough to coat the vegetable on which you plan to serve it, or add the cream and boil down further, until sauce is of coating consistency.

Herbed Wine Sauce

This is another sauce which makes anything savoury taste better. It seems to bring out the flavour of the food it is poured over, without taking over itself. Make it with any one fresh herb that you grow, or with several herbs. Take the time to chop the herbs very finely. Tarragon is especially nice in it.

1 clove garlic
1 tsp butter
¼ cup (60 ml/2 fl oz) white wine
1 tsp chopped tarragon, etc
1 tsp chopped parsley, etc
¼ cup (60 ml/2 fl oz) cream
1 small tomato, cubed

Chop the garlic very finely and cook gently in the butter in a small non-stick pan, without browning, for 2–3 minutes. Add the wine and herbs and cook rapidly until the sauce is reduced to half its volume. Add the cream and bring to the boil. If using fairly thin cream, boil to reduce this a little, too, then add the finely cubed, skinned tomato, without its seeds, simmer for about a minute, and serve.

Variations:
Add green peppercorns or chopped capers, and a little of their liquid, to either of the last two sauces if desired. Change proportions of ingredients to suit your taste.

Clockwise from left: zucchini with Wine and Tomato Sauce, leeks and carrots with Mustard Sauce, Brussels sprouts with Herbed Wine Sauce

Layered Vegetable Casserole

This casserole needs a long baking time, so that it can compact. It is good served with steak or chops or sausages which do not have a sauce with them, and with baked or mashed potatoes.

For 4 servings:
3 large onions
25 g (1 oz) butter
3 or 4 apples
about 8 tomatoes
½ tsp salt
2 tsp sugar
sage or thyme
4 slices bread, crumbed
½ cup (50 g/2 oz) finely grated cheese or 2 tsp
    extra butter

Slice the onions 5 mm (¼ inch) thick, and lightly brown in the butter in a covered pan for about 10 minutes, turning at intervals. Slice the peeled apples and the

Layered Vegetable Casserole

tomatoes and assemble the seasonings. Crumb the bread, using a grater, blender or food processor.

Put a third of the browned onions in a buttered or sprayed casserole dish big enough to hold the food you have prepared. On top, put half the sliced apple, half the tomatoes, and half the crumbs. Sprinkle half the seasonings over this. Repeat the onion, apple and tomato layers, sprinkle with the remaining seasonings, then put the last of the onions over this. Toss the remaining crumbs with the grated cheese or melted butter, and sprinkle evenly over the surface.

Cover with a lid if you will be able to remove it after 30–40 minutes, or lie a piece of flat aluminium foil or greaseproof paper on top if you cannot, and bake at 180°C (350°F) for 60–75 minutes, until the top is golden brown and the casserole compacted. If you use a shallow dish, watch to check the casserole's moistness, pouring a little water down the side of the dish if it looks dry towards the end of the cooking time.

Mediterranean Vegetable Stew

In late summer the overflowing bins of vegetables in markets and supermarkets look almost too good to be real.

At this time of year I make this vegetable stew.

For 4 main or 6 side servings:
1 small aubergine, 200–300 g (7–10½ oz)
1 large onion
1 Tbsp butter or oil
2–3 cloves garlic
1 red pepper
1 green pepper
2 zucchini
6 ripe red tomatoes
  or 1 (425 g/15 oz) can diced tomatoes in juice
  or 1 (400 g/14 oz) can whole tomatoes in juice
  or 1 (425 g/15 oz) can savoury tomatoes
fresh or dried basil and oreganum
salt, sugar, and pepper
cornflour (optional)
chopped parsley

Pierce the skin of the small aubergine in several places and microwave at Full power in a shallow uncovered dish for 3–4 minutes or until it loses its uncooked, slightly spongy feel, turning once or twice. The skin may brown during this cooking.

Cut the onion into 1 cm (½ inch) chunks and brown lightly but evenly in a small amount of butter or oil in a large frypan. Add the chopped garlic. Cut the aubergine into 1 cm (½ inch) thick slices, using a serrated knife, then cut these into cubes and add to the onion in the pan. Raise the heat and add a little more butter or oil if necessary, and stir regularly for a few minutes, then add the cubed peppers, sliced zucchini, and cook a little longer, until the peppers have lost their raw look and texture.

Cube and add the tomatoes, or add one of the canned tomato products if this suits you better. Adjust the heat so that the whole mixture simmers in the tomato juice for 5–10 minutes. During this time add the herbs and seasonings in quantities to suit your taste. Keep tasting, since the flavourings added at this stage are very important to the final flavour. Add extra water or tomato if it seems too dry. If it is to be served hot, the mixture may be thickened slightly with cornflour if you like. If it is served at room temperature, you should use oil not butter for the cooking, and you may like to add a little more oil and some lemon juice.

Sprinkle with chopped parsley before serving.

Mediterranean Vegetable Stew

Apple Cream Pie

SEE PHOTOGRAPH ON PAGE 132

Everybody likes apple pie! This particular version has always been very popular in our house, probably because we like the contrast of the firm pastry, the creamy mixture that surrounds the apple and, of course, the apple itself.

For a 23–25 cm (9–10 inch) flan:
2 cups (250 g/9 oz) wholemeal flour
125 g (4½ oz) cold butter
1 Tbsp lemon juice
about ½ cup (125 ml/4 fl oz) cold water
3 large apples
2 eggs
½ cup (125 g/4 oz) sugar
1 Tbsp cornflour
¼ cup (60 ml/2 fl oz) cream or evaporated milk
beaten egg (optional)

Spoon the flour lightly into the cup measure. Cut the butter into cubes. Rub or cut the cold butter into the flour until crumbly, then mix the lemon juice and water and add to the flour mixture a few drops at a time, tossing with a fork until the dough particles stick together.

Chill for 10 minutes, then roll out in two rounds. Use one to line a 23–25 cm (9–10 inch) flan tin, and cut the other into strips about 15 cm (6 inches) wide.

Shred the cored but unpeeled apples into a bowl. Add the eggs, sugar, cornflour and cream and stir with a fork until evenly blended.

Push ends down over edge of flan tin so they are cut off. Brush lattice with beaten egg if desired.

Bake at 200°C (400°F) for 30 minutes, until pastry is golden brown. Dust with icing sugar and serve warm, with lightly whipped cream, or ice-cream.

Feijoa Crumble Pie

Aromatic feijoas make an interesting pie. Replace coconut with extra rolled oats if desired.

For 4–6 servings:
Pastry
1 cup (125 g/4½ oz) flour
75 g (2½ oz) cold butter
about ¼ cup (60 ml/2 fl oz) cold water

Filling
400–500 g (14 oz–1 lb 2 oz) feijoas

Topping
¼ cup (30 g/1 oz) flour
¼ cup (25 g/1 oz) coconut
¼ cup (20 g/¾ oz) rolled oats
¼ cup (50 g/2 oz) brown sugar
50 g (2 oz) cold butter

For pastry, cut butter into flour. Add cold water drop by drop, stirring with a fork, until dough particles can be pressed together in a firm dough. Chill for 10 minutes then roll out to fit a 23 cm (9 inch) flan tin.

Prepare topping before preparing fruit. Mix dry ingredients together, then cut in butter until mixture is crumbly.

Peel feijoas thinly. Slice about 5 mm (¼ inch) thick. Work quickly to prevent browning. Place half the prepared fruit in uncooked pastry shell.

Sprinkle with quarter of a cup of the topping mixture. Cover with remaining fruit then spread rest of topping evenly over fruit.

Bake at 200°C (400°F) for 20 minutes or until pastry browns lightly, then at 180°C (350°F) for 15–20 minutes longer.

Serve warm with ice-cream or whipped cream.

Swiss-Style Rhubarb Tart

The cream in this tart 'softens' the acidity of the rhubarb with delicious results!

For 6–8 servings:
Pastry
¾ cup (95 g/3½ oz) flour
½ tsp baking powder
60 g (2¼ oz) cold butter
¼ cup (60 ml/2 fl oz) milk
½ tsp wine vinegar

Filling
2–3 cups finely sliced rhubarb
2 eggs
½ cup (125 g/4 oz) sugar
¼ cup (60 ml/2 fl oz) cream or sour cream

Sift or toss well together the flour and baking powder. Cut the butter into cubes, using either a food processor or the coarsest blade on the grater. Do not chop too finely if using the food processor.

Sour the milk with the vinegar then add most of it to the flour. Mix it in, using enough to make a dough which is a little moister than normal short pastry, but is firm enough to roll out easily.

Roll out thinly, using just enough flour to stop sticking. Line a well-sprayed 23 cm (9 inch) pie plate with the pastry, easing it carefully into the sides of the plate. Trim the edge 15 mm (¾ inch) beyond the edge of the pie plate and brush with water. Fold the edge of the pastry inwards, a little more than 1 cm (½ inch). Press evenly and firmly. Decorate the edge of the pie by pinching firmly at intervals, and push pinched section down against pastry sides.

Cut the rhubarb into 5 mm (¼ inch) slices and place in the uncooked pastry shell.

In a food processor or bowl, combine the eggs, sugar and cream or sour cream until smooth. Pour the creamy mixture over the fruit and bake at 220°C (425°F) for 15–20 minutes until golden brown, then at 180°C (350°F) until set in the middle and the fruit is tender. Serve hot or warm sprinkled with icing sugar.

Swiss-Style Rhubarb Tart

Caramel Peach Shortcake

These delicious individual peach shortcakes can be
made with fresh or canned peaches.

1 large (820 g/1 lb 13 oz) can peach halves, or 10–12
*   fresh peaches*
50 g (2 oz) butter
¾ cup (185 g/6 oz) sugar
1¼ cups (155 g/5½ oz) flour
½ cup (55 g/2 oz) icing sugar
100 g (3½ oz) butter
1 egg

Drain the canned peaches, or peel fresh peaches. Cut
cooked halves or raw peaches into chunks.

Heat the butter and sugar in a pan, until the sugar
caramelises, then pour it into six individual pie plates.

Process the flour and icing sugar with the cold cubed
butter until the butter is finely chopped, then break
in the egg, and process again until a ball of dough
forms.

Arrange the drained peach chunks on the caramel.

Caramel Peach Shortcake

Roll the dough into a cylinder, then cut in six even pieces. Pat each piece out to form a circle big enough to fit over the peaches. Dough should just touch edges of tin when in place.

Bake at 200°C (400°F) for about 15 minutes, until the shortcakes feel firm. They do not brown very much. It is a good idea to place a large shallow dish under the cooking shortcakes, to stop bubbling syrup from burning on the bottom of the oven.

Leave shortcakes in pans until they are almost cold. Heat bases of pans for a short time before turning out on to plates. Serve with apricot yoghurt or lightly whipped cream.

Note:
Line pans with circles of baking paper as a precaution against sticking.

Make one large shortcake if desired. Liquid from this may need to be poured off into a frypan before the shortcake is inverted (and later concentrated over low heat).

Baked Rhubarb Custard Pudding

When we can buy an exciting array of fruit all year round, it is difficult to realise how hard our grandmothers had to work to serve fruit to their families regularly, especially in winter. How they must have welcomed the first spring rhubarb, using it in a variety of delicious desserts.

If you know that you are settled in the same dwelling for a few years, think seriously about planting a few rhubarb crowns in a forgotten corner of your garden. You don't need to be a dedicated gardener to grow rhubarb, but you shouldn't expect big crops until the plants have established themselves.

For about 6 servings:
1 cup (125 g/4½ oz) flour
¼ cup (50 g/2 oz) soft brown sugar
50 g (2 oz) cold butter
1 tangelo or orange
½ cup (100 g/3½ oz) soft brown sugar
500 g (1 lb 2 oz) rhubarb
2 eggs
1 cup (250 ml/8 fl oz) evaporated milk or cream

Rub together the flour, first measure of sugar, cold butter, and half the grated rind of the tangelo or orange. (If you have a food processor, use it for the job, peeling the rind with a potato peeler, then chopping it into the other ingredients with the metal chopping blade.)

Spray with non-stick spray, or butter a 23 cm (9 inch) round cake tin or pie plate. Press the crumb mixture firmly and evenly into the tin.

Bake at 200°C (400°F) for 10 minutes, or at 180°C (350°F) for about 15 minutes, if you have the oven on at this temperature to cook something else. While it cooks prepare the topping.

Grate (or peel) the skin from the rest of the tangelo or orange, and mix (or food-process) it with the second measure of sugar.

Chop the rhubarb into 1 cm (½ inch) lengths, and heat it with the sugar, peel and tangelo juice, in a saucepan or microwave dish, without cooking it enough to break it up.

Beat or food-process the eggs and your chosen liquid until the two are combined, then add them to the hot rhubarb mixture. Pour all this over the hot base.

Bake for 30–40 minutes, until the custard is set in the middle. Dust with icing sugar and serve warm, in wedges.

Note:
If desired, replace the milk or cream with sour, dairy, double, or plain cream, or yoghurt.

Berry Buckle

I love the interesting names of some desserts!

Blackberry Grunt, Blueberry Buckle, Apple Cobbler, Peach Crumble and the like all promise to be homely, warming everyday recipes that are served often because they are practical, as well as popular.

Berry Buckle is nice even if you have only a handful of berries to scatter over its surface. I make it with the first side-of-the-road blackberries that are brought home by keen foragers, with blueberries and other bought berries, and with raw cubed peaches and nectarines.

It reheats well, so I always make what I think will be enough for several meals. This does not always prove to be the case, however!

For 6–9 servings:
50 g (2 oz) butter
½ cup (100 g/3½ oz) soft brown sugar
1 egg
1 cup (125 g/4½ oz) flour
1½ tsp baking powder
½ tsp cinnamon
¼ cup (60 ml/2 fl oz) milk
1–3 cups berries or cubed fruit

Topping
½ cup (60 g/2 oz) flour
¼ cup (50 g/2 oz) brown sugar
½ tsp cinnamon
50 g (2 oz) cold butter

Melt the butter until barely liquid. Add the sugar and egg and beat until creamy. Sift in the dry ingredients, then tip in the milk, and fold all together until blended, without overmixing. Spread thinly over a buttered tin about 23 cm (9 inches) across.

Sprinkle the cleaned berries or cubed fruit evenly over the surface.

Using a food processor or pastry blender, cut or rub the topping ingredients together to make a crumbly mixture. Sprinkle this over the fruit layer, covering the complete surface as evenly as possible.

Bake at 180°C (350°F) for 45–60 minutes, or until firm in the middle.

Dust with icing sugar and serve warm or reheated, with lightly whipped cream or ice-cream.

Peachy Ginger Steamed Pudding

Steamed puddings cook remarkably quickly if you cook them in an uncovered ring mould, in a covered pot!

For 6 servings:
2 Tbsp butter, melted
4 Tbsp golden syrup
2 tsp custard powder
2 Tbsp peach syrup (from canned peaches)
4 canned peach halves
50 g (2 oz) butter
½ cup (125 g/4 oz) sugar
1 egg
1½ cups (190 g/6½ oz) flour
2 tsp baking powder
2 tsp ginger
¾ cup (185 ml/6 fl oz) milk

Melt the first measure of butter and the golden syrup together in a saucepan. (Measure the golden syrup using rounded household spoons.) Add the custard powder that has been mixed with the peach syrup. Stir over a low heat until just boiling and thickened. Spread evenly in a buttered ring mould (use a plastic microwave or metal ring pan) and cut each peach half in two and place, rounded surface down, in the sauce.

Melt the second measure of butter in a pan. Remove from heat, add the sugar and egg and beat with a rotary beater until well mixed. Sift in all the dry ingredients, add the milk and fold mixture together until combined. Spoon evenly over the fruit in ring mould.

Steam on a rock or upturned saucer in a large pan with a tight-fitting lid for about 45 minutes, adding more boiling water if necessary, so the pan does not boil dry. The pudding inside the pan should not be covered. Do not let the water stop boiling, and do not take the lid off the pan for the first 30 minutes unless really necessary.

Peach Crisp with Sauce

This is a cross between a shortcake and a crumble. It is very quick and easy to assemble and mix.

For about 6 servings:
1 (820 g/1 lb 13 oz) can sliced peaches, drained
1 egg
1 Tbsp oil
1 tsp vanilla essence
1¼ cups (155 g/5½ oz) self-raising flour
½ cup (125 g/4 oz) sugar

peach syrup from canned peaches
orange juice or white wine
2 Tbsp cornflour
2 Tbsp sherry
2 rounded dessertspoons golden syrup

Spray or butter an ovenware dish, about 23 cm (9 inches) in diameter, and place the drained peaches in it.
Beat the egg, oil and vanilla in a medium-sized bowl

until blended, then tip in the self-raising flour and sugar and toss with a fork until evenly dampened. Sprinkle this mixture over the peaches, without smoothing the surface at all, and bake at 180°C (350°F) for about 30 minutes, or until top is evenly crisp and lightly browned.

Peach Sauce
Make the syrup up to 1½ cups (375 ml/12 fl oz) with orange juice or white wine. In a saucepan mix cornflour and sherry to a thin paste, then add golden syrup and the juice mixture. Stir over a moderate heat until clear and thick. Taste, adjust flavourings if desired, then cover and put aside until required.

Serve warm sauce over individual servings of Peach Crisp. Save any extra sauce to pour over ice-cream on another occasion.

Variations:
Replace peaches with 2 cups (500 ml/16 fl oz) of any other drained, cooked fruit.

Bread and Butter Pudding

Even though you may have childhood memories of rather boring bread and butter puddings, you should make this one. It is a pudding for special occasions, and the combination of the rum sauce with the warm custard is wonderful!

For 4–6 servings:
50 g (2 oz) stale white bread or stale bread rolls
3 eggs
1½ cups (375 ml/12 fl oz) milk
½ cup (125 ml/4 fl oz) cream
3 Tbsp brown sugar
1 tsp vanilla essence

apricot jam

50 g (2 oz) butter, melted
¾ cup (80 g/3 oz) icing sugar
3–4 Tbsp rum

Cut the bread or bread rolls into slices and lay them in an oval or rectangular buttered baking dish that holds 4–5 cups (1–1¼ litres/32–40 fl oz) liquid.

Break the eggs into a bowl, putting aside one yolk for later use. Mix with remaining eggs the milk, cream, sugar and vanilla. Pour over bread, leave to stand for 10 minutes, then bake, at 180°C (350°F), standing dish in a roasting pan of hot water, for 30–45 minutes, until the custard under the bread is set in the middle.

Lift dish out of roasting pan. Gently brush surface with heated apricot jam, and serve warm, with a sauce made by heating together in a bowl over boiling water the melted butter, the reserved egg yolk, and the icing sugar. When this mixture is very hot, lift away from the heat, cool for a few minutes, and stir in the rum.

Bread and Butter Pudding

Chocolate Pear Custard

Pears and chocolate seem to be made to go together! This easy pudding is very popular with children.

For 4–6 servings:
2 Tbsp custard powder
3 Tbsp cocoa
3 Tbsp sugar
1 egg
1½ cups (375 ml/12 fl oz) milk
1 (425 g/15 oz) can pears
1 Tbsp butter
½ tsp vanilla essence.

Mix the custard powder, cocoa and sugar together thoroughly in a medium-sized pan, so you will not get a lumpy mixture later. Add the egg, mix well, then stir in the milk and the juice drained from the can of pears.

Bring to the boil, stirring all the time. As soon as the mixture is hot, add the butter and vanilla and keep stirring and heating until the pudding is dark, thick and bubbling around the edges.

Remove from heat and, while the pudding cools, chop the pears into smaller pieces. Put into four to six individual dishes and pour the pudding on top, or put the pudding into the dishes and put the pears on top.

Serve plain or top with a little runny cream or whipped cream and decorate with chopped nuts.

Lemon Meringue Pie

Ask your friends if they would like a lemon meringue pie for dessert. I have been amazed at the enthusiastic responses I have received to this question. Lemon meringue pie is something which obviously does not go out of fashion! This recipe has several short cuts to make it easier.

For a 20 cm (8 inch) pie:
Pastry
1 cup (125 g/4½ oz) flour
70 g (2½ oz) cold butter
about ¼ cup (60 ml/2 fl oz) cold water

Filling
1 cup (200 g/7 oz) sugar
rind and juice of 2 large or 3 small lemons
½ cup (60 g/2 oz) cornflour or custard powder
1½ cups (375 ml/12 fl oz) water
2 Tbsp butter
3 egg yolks

Topping
3 egg whites
pinch of salt
¼ cup (50 g/1¾ oz) castor sugar)

First make and cook the pastry shell. Put the flour and the cubed cold butter in a food processor and add just enough water to make the dough particles stick together, processing briefly, in bursts. Take care not to overmix or add too much water. Chill pastry for 5 minutes, then roll out and shape over the outside of an upturned 20 cm (8 inch) pie plate. Trim, dampen and fold back the edges, and prick all over so it will not puff up as it cooks. Bake, still upturned, at 230°C (450°F) for about 10 minutes, or until lightly browned. Cool until you can lift the cooked shell off the tin then stand it right side up in a bigger pie plate or on a flat plate.

For the filling, put the sugar in the unwashed processor bowl with the rind of the lemons, removed with a potato peeler. Chop very finely, then mix in the cornflour or custard powder. Tip into a microwave dish, mix with water and microwave at Full power until clear and evenly thick, stirring every 2 minutes. Do not hurry this step. Stir in the butter and egg yolks, mix well and heat again until it bubbles and thickens even more. Do not overcook at this stage. Stir in lemon juice (squeezed with food processor attachment) but do not cook again. Pour into cooked shell.

Beat the egg whites and salt with an electric or rotary beater until their peaks turn over, then add the sugar and beat again until the peaks are stiffer, turning over only a small amount at the top. Pile on to the filling in the pie shell. Swirl attractively, making sure that meringue is touching the shell at the edges, then bake at 190°C (375°F) for 5–10 minutes, until tips of meringue are lightly browned. Do not overcook.

Serve warm, or at room temperature.

Baked Fruity Sago

Old-fashioned sago makes a delicious and interesting fruity pudding which can bake alongside a casserole or other baked food.

For about 6 servings:
½ cup (60 g/2 oz) sago
3 cups (750 ml/24 fl oz) hot water
½ cup (60 g/2 oz) dried apricots, chopped finely
pinch of salt
3–4 Tbsp golden syrup
about ¼ cup (60 ml/2 fl oz) passionfruit pulp
2 bananas, chopped

Butter or spray a casserole, and measure into it the sago, hot tap water, the dried apricots cut into small pieces with a sharp knife or kitchen scissors, and the salt.

Bake uncovered, at 180–200°C (350–400°F), for 30–45 minutes, or until the sago is clear and thick. Take out of the oven and stir in the golden syrup. Taste after adding three tablespoons and add more if you like. Stir in bottled, fresh, or frozen passionfruit pulp and leave to cool to lukewarm. Stir the sliced bananas into the pudding·just before serving it.

Serve the pudding lukewarm, mounded in stemmed glass dishes, with a dribble of cold, runny cream.

Chocolate Pear Custard

Crème Caramel

This very rich custard should be made and enjoyed by custard-lovers at infrequent intervals only! Its velvety texture is due to the rich ingredients from which it is made.

It is not an easy task for an inexperienced cook, since it requires judgment as well as some attention to detail, but it is worth the effort.

2 cups (500 ml/16 fl oz) cream
2 Tbsp sugar
1 vanilla pod
4 egg yolks
3–4 Tbsp castor sugar

Heat the cream or cream mixture with the sugar and the vanilla pod until it bubbles around the edge of the pan, then pour it over the egg yolks in a metal rounded base bowl that can be heated over a pan of boiling water. Heat, stirring constantly, until the custard thickens enough to coat the back of a metal spoon. Pour into a fairly shallow 15 cm (6 inch) diameter flame-proof baking dish that holds about 3 cups (750 ml/24 fl oz).

Stand this in a roasting pan, pour very hot water around it to the level of the custard, and bake uncovered at 150°C (300°F) for 15 minutes. Leave to stand in the hot water for 5–10 minutes, then cool in a container of iced water, or in the refrigerator.

Sprinkle the surface of the custard evenly with the castor sugar and put it under a preheated grill, with the surface about 8 cm (3 inches) from the heat, until the sugar caramelises and turns golden brown. Remove from the heat and leave this topping to cool and set.

Berry Ice-Cream

When serving, you cut through the set toffee layer on top, to the soft custard underneath.

To serve the Crème Caramel with strawberries, put the custard in the centre of a flat plate or basket lined with leaves. Pile strawberries on the leaves, around the custard.

Note:
You do not need heavy cream for this custard, so you can dilute double or high-fat creams with milk, or mix unsweetened evaporated milk and cream.

Berry Ice-Cream

Summer berries make excellent ice-cream. Use whatever berries are available fresh, or freeze your favourite berries so that you can enjoy your ice-cream all year round. Ice-cream made from evaporated milk is economical and has a low fat content.

For about 8 servings:
1 cup (250 ml/8 fl oz) well-chilled evaporated milk
3 level tsp gelatine
3 Tbsp cold water
½ tsp vanilla essence
1 cup (125 g/4 oz) icing sugar
about 2 cups (200 g/7 oz) fresh or frozen berries

Evaporated milk will not beat up light and fluffy unless it is well chilled. Either keep a can in the refrigerator, or put one in the coldest part of the freezer for about 30 minutes.

Mix the gelatine and water in a small container, leave to stand until it is swollen and solid, 2–3 minutes, then warm over low heat or in a microwave until the gelatine dissolves.

Beat the chilled milk until it is thick and fluffy. Add the vanilla and icing sugar, beat again, then add the dissolved gelatine gradually, beating well all the time.

Mash the berries with a fork, and stir or beat them in, to get a total mix or a ripple effect.

Spoon the ice-cream into a 2 litre (8 cup/64 fl oz) container, cover, and freeze as quickly as possible in the coldest part of the freezer.

If the ice-cream is frozen too hard to scoop, stand it in the refrigerator to soften a little while the main course is being eaten.

Serve with a scoop or spoon which has been heated by dipping in hot water.

Variation:

For a richer ice-cream, replace the evaporated milk with cream. Take care not to overbeat. The volume will not be so great, and the ice-cream will be very rich. Because of its higher fat content it will withstand long freezing without going hard and icy.

Note:

500 ml (16 fl oz) carton = 2 cups evaporated milk
375 ml (12 fl oz) can = 1½ cups evaporated milk

Peachy Mincemeat Topping

This is a good way to give a Christmas flavour to a festive pudding which can be served in warm or cold weather.

For 6 servings:
1 Tbsp custard powder
¼–½ cup (55–110 g/2–4 oz) sugar
½ cup (70 g/2.5 oz) mixed dried fruit
½ tsp cinnamon
½ tsp mixed spice
¼ tsp ground cloves
1 Tbsp cider vinegar
1 (425 g/15 oz) can sliced peaches
¼ cup (60 ml/2 fl oz) sherry, white wine or water

Mix the custard powder and sugar thoroughly in a medium-sized pan. Add chopped dried fruit and spices, then stir in the vinegar, all the juice from the peaches and the sherry, wine or water. Bring to the boil, stirring all the time, then add the drained peaches. Serve slightly warm over ice-cream or over a half (unfilled) sponge that has been split, filled with ice-cream and replaced in the freezer till needed.

Peachy Mincemeat Topping

Chocolate Fondue

There is something very satisfying about a group of people sitting round a communal pot, dipping into it. I first started to make fondues 20 years ago, when we lived in California for a couple of years. In the early seventies many families experimented with fondue meals.

After some time, however, fondues died a quiet death, and my pots gathered dust at the back of my cupboards, like many others!

When microwave ovens appeared, however, my interest in fondues returned. Now a fondue can be cooked in a glass, plastic or ceramic dish, served in it or transferred to another more decorative but still microwavable dish, then popped back in the microwave for reheating when required. This means that there is no need for candles and other burners, and the pots themselves do not have to be balanced precariously on long-legged burners.

Start a new tradition at Christmas, or for birthdays or other family celebrations. You can always pass mince pies around if you feel that you will miss more traditional fare.

200–250 g (7–9 oz) dark, milk, or cooking chocolate
½ cup (125 ml/4 fl oz) cream
grated rind of 1 orange
or 1–2 Tbsp brandy, rum or liqueur

Break the chocolate into squares or small pieces and place in a flat-bottomed microwave casserole dish. Pour the cream over the chocolate, then grate the coloured peel of an orange into the mixture. (Do not add spirits at this stage.)

Microwave at Full power for 2 minutes, leave to stand for 1 minute, then stir until the chocolate and cream are evenly mixed. If there are any remaining lumps, microwave again in 20-second bursts, until these disappear when stirred. If adding spirits, stir them into the cooked mixture.

Pour the warm mixture into the serving dish, or put aside for later reheating and serving.

Pile bite-sized pieces of fruit on a flat plate around the hot chocolate dip. Prepare the fruit ahead and refrigerate it in plastic bags until required, if desired.

Suitable fruits include:

apples	*nashi*
apricots	*pawpaw*
bananas	*peaches*
cherries	*pears*
grapes	*pineapple*
kiwi fruit	*strawberries*
melons	

Variations:

Include cubes of plain sponge, or marshmallows.

Offer an alternative dip of fruit-flavoured yoghurt.

Zabaglione

Zabaglione is an interesting light and frothy special dessert, more suitable for adults than children. Serve it over strawberries, or by itself, with crisp biscuits.

4 egg yolks
¼ cup (60 g/2 oz) sugar
¼ cup (60 ml/2 fl oz) Marsala or 2 Tbsp sweetish sherry mixed with 2 Tbsp water
¼ cup (60 ml/2 fl oz) dry white wine

Combine the egg yolks and sugar in a round metal bowl, place it over a pot of boiling water, and beat with a whisk until combined. Add the Marsala or the sherry and water, and the white wine. Beat with the whisk for about 10 minutes, until the mixture heats up and gradually thickens. The mixture will increase in volume while it cooks. (It will resemble well-beaten eggs and sugar as they look when you make a sponge cake.)

If you stop beating, the mixture will set on the sides of the bowl, and form a type of scrambled eggs!

When the mixture is thick enough to pile up, stop beating it. If you want to serve it cold or warm, keep beating it until it cools down, over a container of cold water. Once it is cool you can leave it untended.

Serve it hot, warm, or cold, by itself, in stemmed glasses, or spoon it over strawberries in stemmed dishes or small bowls.

Citrus Syllabub

This quickly made, rich dessert is best eaten very cold, but not frozen solid. It should be the consistency of partly thawed ice-cream when you eat it.

For 6 servings:
2 lemons
1 tangelo or orange
½ cup (125 g/4 oz) sugar
1½ cups (375 ml/12 fl oz) cream

Very finely grate all the coloured peel from the lemons and tangelo or orange. Place in a pan with the sugar and juice squeezed from both fruit, then place over a moderate heat until sugar dissolves.

Stand pan in iced water to cool liquid to room temperature quickly, then mix with the cream and whip until floppy, very soft peaks form. Do not over-beat. Place in freezer until very thick, but not solid. If syllabub freezes, refrigerate until it softens. Serve in small glasses, with crisp wafers.

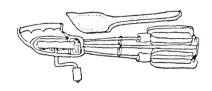

Chocolate Fondue

BREAD, SCONES
& MUFFINS

Banana Muffins

SEE PHOTOGRAPH ON PAGE 146

These muffins have a very good flavour and texture. They should be eaten while warm from the oven.

For 12–24 muffins:
50 g (2 oz) butter, melted
¾ cup (150 g/5 oz) brown sugar
1 egg
1½ cups mashed banana (3–4 bananas)
1 tsp vanilla
¾ cup (95 g/3½ oz) flour
¾ cup (100 g/4 oz) wholemeal flour
½ cup (25 g/¾ oz) bran
2 tsp baking powder
2 tsp cinnamon
½ cup chopped walnuts (optional)
½ cup sultanas (optional)
milk

Melt the butter until liquid. Stir in the brown sugar and egg, and mix well with a fork. Add the banana and vanilla and mix again.

In a fairly large bowl, measure all the dry ingredients in the order given. Add the walnuts and the sultanas, mixing them with dry ingredients by tossing lightly with a fork.

Add the liquid mixture all at once. Fold carefully into the dry mixture, taking care not to overmix. All the flour should be dampened, but the mixture should not be smooth. If firm bananas are used, 2–3 tablespoons of milk may be needed.

Spoon the mixture into muffin or patty pans which have been well buttered or sprayed. The mixture will fill 12–15 large, deep muffin pans, or 24 smaller patty pans. Bake at 200°C (400°F) for about 20 minutes, or until the centres spring back when pressed.

Orange Honey Muffins

Muffins like these are really appreciated! They have a good flavour, and are lovely, moist and tender.

Thaw or warm them for a weekend breakfast, serve them with tea or coffee for a mid-morning or mid-afternoon break, team them with cheese and a salad at lunch time, include them in a packed lunch, or serve with fresh fruit for dessert.

For 12–15 large muffins:
2 cups (250 g/9 oz) flour
4 tsp baking powder
¼ cup (55 g/2 oz) sugar
rind of 2 oranges
75 g (2½ oz) butter, melted
¼ cup (60 ml/2 fl oz) honey
1 egg
¾ cup (185 ml/6 fl oz) orange juice/milk

Measure the flour and baking powder into a fairly large bowl. Toss lightly with a fork to mix thoroughly.

Mix the sugar and finely grated rind with the dry ingredients.

In another bowl or saucepan, melt the butter. Add the honey, and heat again. In both cases, use as little heat as necessary. Break the egg into the mixture, and beat with a fork to mix. Squeeze the oranges and measure the volume of juice. Stir the juice through the liquid. Measure out enough milk to make the total amount of combined juice and liquid up to ¾ cup (185 ml/6 fl oz), but do not tip it into the other liquid.

Without stirring, pour the milk and the other liquid on to the dry ingredients. Fold the three together, stirring only enough to combine them. The dry ingredients should be dampened, but the final mixture should look lumpy, rather than smooth.

Stirring as little as possible, spoon the mixture into well-buttered or sprayed non-stick muffin pans, filling each no more than three quarters full.

Bake at 200°C (400°F) for 10 minutes, or until the centres spring back when lightly pressed.

Cool for 3–5 minutes before twisting gently to loosen, and removing from the pans.

Serve warm or reheated if possible.

Blueberry Muffins

These muffins may be made right through the year using different fruits and berries in season. Blueberries make especially good muffins because they are not sour when cooked.

For about 12 muffins:
2 cups (250 g/9 oz) flour
4 tsp baking powder
½ tsp salt
½ cup (100 g/3½ oz) castor sugar
100 g (3½ oz) butter
1 cup milk
1 egg
1–2 cups fresh or thawed blueberries
1 Tbsp sugar
½ tsp cinnamon

Sieve the first three dry ingredients into a fairly large bowl. Add the castor sugar. In another container melt the butter, remove from the heat and then add the milk and egg, and beat to combine these three.

Prepare the blueberries, then tip the milk mixture and (drained) fruit into the bowl with the dry ingredients. Fold everything together, taking great care not to overmix. The flour should be dampened, but the mixture should not be smooth.

Butter or oil 12 deep muffin pans thoroughly. Place spoonfuls of mixture into pans, filling each half to three-quarters full.

Combine the second measure of sugar with the cinnamon and sprinkle over the muffins before baking. Bake at 220°C (425°F) for about 12–15 minutes, until muffins spring back when pressed in the centre.

Remove from the oven, stand for 2–3 minutes, then twist muffins carefully before lifting them out.

Blueberry Muffins

Oaty Fruit Pancakes

Oaty Fruit Pancakes

When you want a weekend treat, serve these pancakes as a complete breakfast with the drink of your choice.

For 4 servings:
1 (400 g/14 oz) can sliced peaches in juice or
*   syrup*
½ cup (125 ml/4 fl oz) milk
¾ cup (68 g/2¼ oz) rolled oats
1 egg
2–3 Tbsp sugar
½ tsp salt
½ cup (60 g/2 oz) flour
1 tsp baking powder
25 g (1 oz) butter, melted

Drain the peaches, reserving the juice. Chop ½ cup of the peaches. Put chopped peaches and ¼ cup (60 ml/2 fl oz) of juice in a bowl with the milk, rolled oats, egg, sugar and salt. Beat with a fork to mix thoroughly. Sift the dry ingredients on to this, add melted butter and mix only enough to combine.

Cook spoonfuls like pikelets, on a preheated, lightly buttered surface. Turn when bubbles burst on the surface, then lightly brown second side.

Serve immediately with peach slices and golden syrup or syrup made by boiling together remaining juice, 2 tablespoons golden syrup, ½ teaspoon vanilla essence and 1 teaspoon cornflour.

Scones, Plain or Fancy

One of the easiest things to mix and bake, when you need something to serve with tea or coffee, is a batch of scones.

If you feel that your scones leave a little to be desired, do not make plain scones, where every imperfection shows, but make an interesting variation.

Try twists or pinwheels, using fillings based on brown sugar, cinnamon and butter. Vary the fillings, adding coconut, currants, sultanas or nuts.

The food processor is useful when it comes to making these scones, but do not actually mix the scone dough with it, because it is easy to overmix and toughen the dough.

Basic dough
2 cups (250 g/9 oz) self-raising plain or wholemeal
*   flour*
25 g (1 oz) butter
about ¾ cup (185 ml/6 fl oz) milk

Filling
¼ cup (50 g/1½ oz) brown sugar
1 tsp cinnamon
1 Tbsp cold butter
¼ cup (25 g/1 oz) coconut

Measure the flour into the bowl of a food processor. Add the butter, cut into cubes, and process until chopped into small pieces.

Tip into a bowl, and add the measured milk, all at once. Cut and stir the liquid into the dry ingredients.

Add a little more milk or flour if the mixture seems too dry or too wet. The dough should be as soft as you can handle, to roll out on a floured bench. The scones will rise better if the mixture has been lightly kneaded with your fingertips before it is rolled out.

For plain scones pat or roll the scone dough out, 20–25 cm (8–10 inches) square. Cut into nine squares with a sharp, lightly floured knife. Place on a baking tray, about 1 cm (½ inch) apart.

For pinwheels or twists, roll the dough out to make a long thin rectangle, about 40×20 cm (16×8 inches). Make the filling by combining the filling ingredients in the unwashed food processor bowl. Process just enough to combine the ingredients. (Overmixing turns them into a paste.)

To shape pinwheels:
Spread the filling mixture evenly over the uncooked dough, leaving 1 cm (½ inch) clear on the long edge farthest away from you. Dampen this edge, then roll up the dough to form a long, thin sausage, rolling the dampened edge last. Cut the roll into pieces about 1 cm (½ inch) thick, and place each piece on a lightly buttered baking tray, allowing space for spreading.

To shape twists:
Spread the filling in a long strip on the half of the dough farthest away from you, leaving the outside 1 cm (½ inch) uncovered. Dampen the uncovered strip, then fold the uncovered half over the covered section. Press firmly together, then cut into 1 cm (½ inch) strips, crosswise. Twist each strip twice, then place on a lightly buttered baking tray and press the ends down firmly.

Bake at 200°C (400°F) for 10–15 minutes, until lightly browned. Serve plain or buttered soon after cooking.

Variations:
For savoury scones add a little grated cheese (about ½ cup/50 g/2 oz) and some fresh herbs to the dough. Try making savoury pinwheels or twists using this dough and 1–1½ cups of savoury filling. Grated cheese with tomato relish or grated cheese with creamed corn are good fillings. Use your imagination and whatever you have on hand to create your own favourites.

Easy Barbecue Scones

2 cups (250 g/9 oz) self-raising flour
2 tsp sugar
2 Tbsp oil
about ¾ cup (185 ml/6 fl oz) milk

Measure the flour and sugar into a mixing bowl. Add the oil and enough milk to make a soft dough just firm enough to form a ball. Coat with a little more flour and pat out to form a 20–23 cm (8–9 inch) circle.

Thoroughly butter the bottom and lower sides of a 20–23 cm (8–9 inch) frypan with a lid, put the circle of dough in it, pat it out further if necessary, so that it covers the whole base, then mark it into eighths with a floured knife. Put the lid on the pan and take it outside to stand until it is needed, up to an hour.

Place the covered pan on the barbecue, and cook over a fairly high heat until the pan heats up. It should take about 6 minutes for the bottom to become light brown, and for the scone to cook through to the centre. Turn the gas higher or lower to achieve this if necessary. Turn the segments of scone with a spatula or fish slice, and cook the remaining side for about 4–5 minutes, or until similarly browned. Have pan lid ajar while the second side cooks. Serve soon after cooking.

Variations:
For savoury scones, add about 2 tablespoons Parmesan cheese, and about ¼ cup chopped fresh herbs.

Spiral Scones:
For scone spirals take a walnut-sized ball of scone dough and roll it to pencil width on a floured board. Roll each piece around a buttered metal skewer, leaving the point of the skewer uncovered. Brush with melted butter and cook on the grilling rack for about 5 minutes altogether, turning until fairly evenly browned. Pull off the skewer, and dip in jam or golden syrup. (Use freshly cut twigs of non-poisonous wood if metal skewers are not available.)

Brown Sultana Tea Bread

1 cup (160 g/6 oz) sultanas
1¼ cups (315 ml/10 fl oz) hot tea
¼ cup chopped nuts (optional)
2 tsp mixed spice or cinnamon
¼ tsp salt
¾ cup (150 g/5 oz) brown sugar
2 Tbsp oil
2 cups (280 g/10 oz) self-raising wholemeal flour
¼ cup (60 ml/2 fl oz) sherry (optional, but nice!)

Measure the sultanas into a large mixing bowl. Pour the hot freshly brewed tea over them. The flour cannot be added until the mixture is cool, but all the other ingredients can be added, in the order given, to the cooling mixture. Stir to mix.

When the mixture has cooled to room temperature, add the flour and stir just enough to dampen it. Spoon into a loaf tin that holds about 6 cups, that has been lined across the bottom and long sides with a piece of folded baking paper.

Bake at 180°C (350°F), for about 45 minutes, until a skewer inserted in the centre of the loaf comes out clean. For a lovely flavour and extra moistness, drizzle about ¼ cup (60 ml/2 fl oz) sherry over the top of the loaf as soon as you take it from the oven. Leave to stand for 10 minutes before removing from the tin. Cool on a rack before slicing.

Note:
If you replace the wholemeal self-raising flour with white self-raising flour, use 1 cup (250 ml/8 fl oz) of tea instead of the larger amount.

Hot Cross Buns

At Easter many people who would not dream of making bread and buns at any other time of the year feel the urge to get into the kitchen and start mixing and kneading.

When I was young we baked (or bought) and ate Hot Cross Buns only on Good Friday. Now, however, we are aware of the spicy smell of these buns on sale long before Easter.

In this, my favourite recipe, the spices are added after the yeast mixture has risen once, and the flavour of the buns seems better for it.

Hot Cross Buns

When baking these buns, remember that they rise because of the yeast in them. If the mixture is too cold, the rising will be very slow. If, on the other hand, you heat the mixture too much, the yeast will be killed, and the buns will never rise. When you work with yeast mixtures you have to use your judgment, rather than follow an exact formula.

For about 24 buns:
1 cup (250 ml/8 fl oz) milk
½ cup (125 ml/4 fl oz) hot water
2 Tbsp sugar

152

1 Tbsp dried yeast granules
2 cups (250 g/9 oz) flour
100 g (3½ oz) butter
½ cup (100 g/3½ oz) soft brown sugar
1 egg
1 tsp salt
1½ Tbsp mixed spice
1 tsp grated nutmeg
1 tsp vanilla essence
about 1 cup mixed dried fruit
2–3 cups (250–375 g/9–13 oz) flour

60 g (2 oz) cold butter
1 cup (125 g/4½ oz) flour
water
milk or beaten egg

2 Tbsp golden syrup
1 Tbsp water

Measure the milk, hot water and sugar into a bowl, saucepan or food processor. Warm or cool to body temperature if necessary, then sprinkle the yeast granules on. Stir to mix, or process briefly with the metal chopping blade of the food processor. Stir in the first measure of flour, cover, and leave to rise in the sun or a sink of warm water while you prepare the next mixture. (A food processor is a good place to rise this mixture.)

In a large bowl, cream together the warmed butter and the soft brown sugar. Beat in the egg, salt, spices, vanilla and dried fruit. When the yeast mixture is at least twice its original volume, tip it into the creamed mixture with 2 cups (250 g/9 oz) of the second measure of flour. Mix well. Stir in enough extra flour to make a dough that is firm enough to turn out on a board or benchtop and knead.

To knead, push the dough firmly away from you with the heel of one hand, and collect it towards you with your other hand. At first the dough will be sticky and difficult to work with, and you may need to add some extra flour to stop it sticking, but after a few minutes it will become easy to handle. Knead until the dough feels satiny but does not stick on the board, and springs back when poked with a finger. Put it on a lightly floured board and cut it into four quarters. Cut each of these into six. Shape each piece into a ball, rolling it on the board, flattening it, then tucking the edges underneath to produce a ball with a smoothly stretched top.

Arrange the balls in buttered cake tins, leaving space the width of an unrisen bun between each, to allow for rising. Cover the tins with plastic cling wrap, or put each tin into a large plastic bag and tie the end. Leave in a warm place to rise to twice their size, from 15 to 45 minutes, depending on the temperature, the freshness of the yeast, and the consistency of the dough.

Rub the cold butter into the second measure of flour, then add water to form a stiff dough. Roll out thinly on a floured board, and cut into strips to make crosses for the tops of the buns. Brush with milk or beaten egg to make them stick, then lie them gently over the risen buns.

Bake uncovered, at 225°C (435°F) for 10–12 minutes, until lightly browned.

Warm the golden syrup with 1 tablespoon water. Brush this over the buns as soon as they are taken from the oven.

Tip out of tins after 3–5 minutes. Serve warm.

Bread

Bread made of wholemeal flour is an excellent food. If you eat reasonably large amounts of bread made from ground whole grains, it will satisfy your appetite, give you the energy you need to function well and efficiently, and make your weight control effortless.

Many interesting wholegrain breads are available. Try different ones, and enjoy their nutty flavours. Notice, too, how much more satisfying wholegrain breads are to eat than light white bread.

Remember that, although it is important to eat more wholegrain, complex carbohydrate foods, it is also important to cut down on fat. If you are concerned about losing or regulating weight, use high-fat spreads with great restraint.

It is not difficult to make good bread yourself. The bread you make will cost about half the price of commercially made bread. It will stale more quickly, but it is unlikely to get the chance to sit around, because it tastes so good the day it is made, especially when you serve it warm from the oven. Even if you have never baked with yeast, give it a try! It is remarkably satisfying, the dough is fun to work with, and everyone will appreciate the wonderful smells that fill the house while your bread cooks.

Sesame Bread Sticks

Make up half the recipe for quick yeast bread, adding to the dry ingredients:

3 Tbsp grated Parmesan cheese
¼ cup (30 g/1 oz) toasted sesame seeds
1 tsp sesame oil
beaten egg
coarse salt
extra sesame seeds

Mix and knead dough as for the bread. Cut the kneaded dough into 12 pieces, then roll each one out with your fingers to form a 30 cm (12 inch) stick, starting with your hands in the centre of each stick, moving them out towards the ends, and opening your fingers as you roll.

As each stick is ready, put it on a well-buttered or sprayed oven tray, leaving a little space between the sticks. When the tray is filled, brush over lightly with beaten egg, then sprinkle with coarse salt and more toasted sesame seeds. Bake at 200°C (400°F) for 10 minutes, or until golden brown. If sticks do not feel dry and crisp when cold, dry out at 150°C (300°F) for 15–20 minutes longer or leave to stand in a turned-off oven.

153

Brown Bread

For 16 bread rolls, or a 750 gram (1 lb 9 oz) loaf:
2 tsp dried yeast granules
1 Tbsp sugar
½ cup (125 ml/4 fl oz) warm water
25 g (1 oz) butter
1 cup (250 ml/8 fl oz) low-fat milk or water
1–1½ tsp salt
1 Tbsp lemon juice
1½ cups (190 g/6½ oz) white flour
2 or more cups (280 g/10 oz) wholemeal flour

Put the yeast granules, sugar and lukewarm water in a large bowl, and stand in a warm place. In a saucepan over a low heat, melt the butter, then stir in the milk or water and salt, and mix thoroughly. Try to finish up with the buttery liquid at blood heat, too.

When you can see small bubbles in the yeast mixture, or see it frothing, or smell a definite yeasty smell, add the buttery mixture to the yeast mixture, stir in the lemon juice and all the white flour, then beat well until the thin mixture is smooth.

Cover and stand the bowl in a sink of blood-heat water or in a sunny draught-free place, until it rises to about twice its original size. Stir in as much wholemeal flour as you need to make a dough which is firm enough to turn out on a board and knead. Knead until dough feels smooth and satiny, does not stick to the work bench, and springs back when a finger is poked into it. (Never add more flour than you need to when mixing, kneading or shaping.)

To shape a loaf:
Roll out to form a circle about the same size as the length of the tin you will bake it in, then roll up the circle of dough to form a sausage, and place it in the buttered tin, with joins down. (Use a tin that holds about 6 cups (1.5 litres/48 fl oz) of water.) Leave the dough to rise in a warm, draught-free place until it is twice its bulk, then bake at 190°C (375°F) for 30–45 minutes, or until the crust is brown, firm, a skewer pushed deeply into the centre comes out clean, and the loaf sounds quite hollow when turned upside down, out of its tin, and tapped. Cool on a rack.

To shape rolls:
To shape round rolls, cut the dough into 16 even pieces, and roll each one into a smooth ball. For rosettes or knots, shape dough into long pencil shapes, then knot these, turning ends over twice for rosettes. Place shaped rolls on an oiled baking tray with plenty of space between rolls so they can rise to double their bulk.

For Fan-tans:
Roll dough about 3 mm (¼ inch) thick. Brush lightly with melted butter. Cut dough into 4 cm (1½ inch) squares with a sharp knife. Place four to six squares on top of each other. Place each little pile, cut edges uppermost, in an oiled muffin tin. Reroll scraps, and shape in the same way. Stand rolls in a warm place to rise to nearly twice their original bulk.

Bake rolls at 210°C (425°F) for about 10 minutes, or until lightly browned. For a more glazed appearance, brush gently with beaten egg just before baking. Sprinkle toasted sesame seeds, poppy seeds, etc. over the rolls after brushing with egg if you like.

Cool on racks. Store rolls which will not be eaten immediately in a plastic bag. Freeze rolls which will not be eaten the same day. Homemade bread stales more quickly than commercially made bread.

Note:
If you use stoneground wholemeal flour to make this bread, you will find that the dough requires less flour than it does if you use regular wholemeal flour. You get a slightly softer larger loaf when you use regular wholemeal flour.

Quick Yeast Rolls or Bread

This recipe seems to break all the bread-making rules. It works, though. The resulting buns do, however, stale quickly and should be eaten the day they are made.

¼ cups (315 ml/10 fl oz) warm water
3 Tbsp sugar
1 Tbsp dried yeast granules
1 Tbsp oil
1 tsp baking powder
1 tsp salt
3 cups (420 g/15 oz) wholemeal or white flour
  (375/13 oz) (or any combination of the two)
milk or beaten egg

Dissolve the sugar in the warm (blood-temperature) water, then sprinkle in the yeast granules. Add the oil and stir gently for a few seconds. Leave to stand for at least 5 minutes to allow the yeast to begin acting.

Once the yeast mixture has begun to bubble and looks slightly foamy, add the remaining dry ingredients, mixing the baking powder and the salt through the flour first.

Stir everything together until the dough begins to come away from the sides of the bowl and forms one large ball.

With oiled hands shape into rolls or into two long loaves. Stand the rolls or loaves on oiled oven trays, leaving space for rising. Brush tops with milk or beaten egg and top with grated cheese, poppyseeds or toasted sesame seeds if desired.

If you have the time, leave to rise for 5–15 minutes, although this is not strictly necessary.

Using a sharp (serrated) knife cut diagonal slashes in the loaves just before baking them.

Bake loaves at 200°C (400°F) for 20–25 minutes. Bake rolls at same temperature for about 15 minutes.

Variations:
Shape dough into two or three plaited loaves: cut each piece of dough into three, then roll into long strips. Plait, brush tops and add toppings as above.

Roll dough for individual rolls into long strips, then knot or twist these into interesting shapes. Brush tops as above.

Bran Bread

This recipe for a quickly made 'health' bread was popular in the early 1900s and was passed from friend to friend, just as we share our recipes today. Looking through old hand-written recipe books of this time, I found many variations of it.

Here is my version of this recipe. It makes a good, quick brown loaf, with an interesting flavour.

For fast-cooking and an attractive 'cottage' appearance I make the dough into two round loaves, cutting crosses in the tops before baking them.

2 cups (250 g/9 oz) white flour
1 cup (45 g/1½ oz) bran
2 Tbsp baking powder
¼–½ tsp salt
1 Tbsp golden syrup
¼ cup (60 ml/2 fl oz) hot water
½ cup (125 ml/4 fl oz) creamy milk

Stir the flour, bran, baking powder and salt together in a fairly large bowl until evenly mixed.

Measure the golden syrup using a household table-spoon which has been preheated in hot water. The

Quick Yeast Rolls and Fancy Scones
(fruity cinnamon pinwheels)

syrup should be rounded on the spoon, but you will find that, if you use too much, the loaf will be sweet.

Stir the syrup and hot water together to dissolve the syrup, then add this, with about three-quarters of the measured milk, into the dry ingredients. Stir with a fork or knife to form the mixture into a ball of dough.

Add a little more flour or bran, or more milk if necessary, to make a dough the consistency of scone dough. Rub the dough around the bowl to incorporate all the ingredients.

Turn the dough out on a lightly floured or bran-covered board and knead lightly four or five times, then shape as desired, e.g. into two round small loaves. Cut a cross about 1 cm (½ inch) deep in the top of the round loaves.

Bake loaves at 170°C (325°F) for 15–30 minutes, until brown on top and underneath, and until the bottoms sound fairly hollow when tapped. Cool on a wire rack to stop the bottom getting soggy.

Break into quarters while fresh and warm, and serve with butter and jam.

155

Gingernuts

Many of my friends regard gingernuts as part of their childhood, and remember that they tasted best when dipped in, or at least drunk with, a glass of cold milk.

I make tiny gingernuts. People with larger appetites know that they are allowed to take a handful. I vary the spices and add finely chopped walnuts if I have them.

The only difficult thing about this recipe is judging the amount of flour to use. If you do not use enough, your biscuits will spread too much. If you add too much, your biscuits will not spread into gingernut shape. I usually weigh the flour to prevent these deviations.

For 70–80 small biscuits:
100 g (3½ oz) butter
1 Tbsp golden syrup
1 cup (220 g/8 oz) sugar
2 tsp ground ginger
1 tsp mixed spice (optional)
1 egg
1 tsp baking soda
2 cups (250 g/8 oz) flour
¼ cup (25 g/1 oz) chopped walnuts

Melt the butter until liquid, but not hot. Stir in a rounded tablespoon of golden syrup, warming to soften it if necessary, then remove from the heat and add the sugar, spices and egg. Beat with a fork until well mixed, add the baking soda, and mix thoroughly.

Weigh the flour if possible, otherwise measure it by the cup, stirring it with a fork first, and measuring it without packing it down into the cup. Add to the biscuit mixture with the nuts. Stir to mix, then take a teaspoonful at a time and roll into balls with damp hands if mixture is firm enough. Place on lightly greased or sprayed oven trays, allowing room for spreading, and bake the first tray while shaping more biscuits.

Bake at 180°C (350°F) for 8–10 minutes, until golden brown. Cool on a rack, and store in airtight containers.

Gingernuts, Rock Cakes and Chocolate Crunchies

Rock Cakes

When I asked my husband which of his mother's recipes he remembered most fondly, it took him only a second to answer. Rock cakes! Elizabeth, our five-year-old grand-daughter was not impressed with the name. I assured her that they were not so hard that they could not be eaten, and the two of us retired to the kitchen to make some.

As we sat at her little table, shaping our cakes with two spoons each, I assured her that our rock cakes would taste good. I was right. The next morning, when we went in search of something to have with a cup of tea, we found that the jar was empty. Plain, old-fashioned baking, using good ingredients, does not lose its appeal.

For 30–40 rock cakes:
125 g (4½ oz) butter
½ cup (110 g/4 oz) sugar
½ tsp vanilla
1 egg
¾ cup (90 g/3 oz) self-raising flour
1 cup plain flour
1 cup currants, sultanas, or mixed fruit

Soften but do not melt the butter. Add the sugar and vanilla, beat or food process to combine, then add the egg and a tablespoon of the measured flour, and beat or food process until light coloured. Add the remaining flours, and mix just enough to combine. Add the dried fruit and stir or process very briefly.

Using two spoons, form into mounds on a non-stick Teflon-lined or lightly buttered oven tray, leaving a little space for spreading.

Bake at 180°C (350°F) for 10–15 minutes, until golden at the edges, and firm in the middle. Cool on a rack, then store in an airtight container.

Note:
For best results, sift flour with a fork before spooning it into the cup measures. Do not pack it into the cups. Rock cakes which spread a lot do not have quite enough flour, and those which stay exactly as shaped and do not flatten at all contain too much flour.

Instead of rolling out biscuit mixture thinly, then cutting it into shapes with cutters, roll the dough into a cylinder, chill it until firm, then cut it into thin slices.

The results may not be quite as neat as the cut biscuits, but they take a fraction of the time to shape, and are often crisper, since no extra flour is required during the rolling process.

Chocolate Crunchies

I enjoy reproducing the biscuits of my childhood as easily and quickly as I can. Afghans were always popular additions to our school lunches 40 years ago, so I worked out an easy version to please my own family.

For 50 biscuits:
100 g (3½ oz) butter, melted
¾ cup (165 g/6 oz) sugar
3 Tbsp cocoa
1 tsp vanilla
1 egg
¾ cup (105 g/3¾ oz) self-raising flour
½ cup (45 g/1½ oz) rolled oats
1 cup cornflakes
100 g (3½ oz) dark chocolate
50 walnut pieces or halves

Melt the butter and stir into it the sugar, cocoa, vanilla and egg. Mix well with a fork. Measure the flour and rolled oats on top of this. When measuring the cornflakes into the measuring cup, press them down firmly. Stir these additions into the chocolate mixture.

Form into about 50 small balls on lightly buttered oven slides, or on a non-stick Teflon liner. Flatten firmly using the heel of your hand.

Bake at 170°C (325°F) for 8–12 minutes, until biscuits look evenly cooked but have not darkened around the edges. Transfer to a cooling rack while warm.

Microwave or heat over a double boiler the broken chocolate pieces until barely melted. Stir until smooth. Spread on each biscuit, and top with a walnut. Leave in a cool place for chocolate to set. Store in an airtight tin.

Food Processor Fruit and Nut Balls

You can make delicious fruit and nut balls in a few minutes, if you have a food processor.

For 16–20 balls:
½ cup (60 g/2 oz) dried apricots
2 Tbsp orange juice or sherry
½ cup (40 g/1½ oz) walnuts or roasted peanuts
½ cup (80 g/3 oz) sultanas
½ cup (50 g/2 oz) coconut
extra coconut for rolling

With the metal chopping blade, process dried apricots with orange juice or sherry. When very fine add walnuts or roasted peanuts, sultanas, and coconut. Process until mixture is very fine (it becomes firmer as it gets finer), then roll into 16–20 balls, coat with extra coconut, then leave to stand, uncovered, in a cool place for an hour or more. Make replacements and add extra dried fruit and nuts according to availability.

159

Lacy Wafers

Lacy wafers are delicate little biscuits that are delicious served with ice-cream, or with a cup of after-dinner coffee.

For approx. 50 (7 cm/3 inch) wafers:
125 g (4½ oz) butter
1 cup (220 g/8 oz) sugar
1 cup (90 g/3 oz) rolled oats
1 egg
1 tsp vanilla
½ tsp almond essence

Melt the butter in a microwave dish or shallow saucepan. When it is liquid but not hot add the sugar, rolled oats, egg and essences, and beat with a fork until well mixed.

Cover a baking tray with a square of non-stick Teflon liner, or aluminium foil. Brush a thin film of soft butter across it.

Put level teaspoon lots of the uncooked mixture 10 cm (4 inches) apart on the Teflon or foil. Use an ordinary household teaspoon and make sure that it is not heaped.

Bake at 170–180°C (325–350°F) for 5–8 minutes. As they cook the biscuits first spread, then start to bubble, then brown. It does not matter if the outside rim is a little darker than the middle of each one, but if the outside darkens while the middle is still very pale, reduce the heat a little.

If the biscuits on the first tray run into each other, make them smaller or put them further apart on the next tray. Just like brandy snaps, the biscuits are too soft to handle when they come out from the oven. They harden as they cool. Peel the Teflon or foil away from the biscuits as soon as they are cool enough to work with.

If you can work fast enough and do not cook too many biscuits at once, you may be able to press them into shallow patty pans to form baskets, or lie them over a rolling pin so they are curved. Biscuits which harden too soon may be reheated briefly to soften them again.

As soon as biscuits are cold, store them in an airtight container.

Lacy Wafers

Economical Meringues

I like to save egg whites so that I can make these economical meringues.

They keep for months and months, and can be produced at very short notice.

As well as eating them sandwiched, I love meringues broken up roughly and folded into vanilla-flavoured whipped cream. After standing for 15 minutes or so, they turn marshmallowy, and the mixture makes an excellent accompaniment for summer berries.

For 75–100 small meringues:
2 egg whites
1½ cups (330 g/12 oz) sugar
2 tsp vanilla
2 tsp vinegar
¼ cup (60 ml/2 fl oz) boiling water

Place a fairly large bowl over a saucepan of just boiled water on a flat surface.

Measure the ingredients into the bowl in the order given, and beat with a hand-held electric beater or a strong rotary beater at high speed, until a smooth, stiff meringue forms.

Cover two oven trays with wetted baking paper, or squares of non-stick Teflon liner.

Using a forcer bag with a many-pointed star nozzle, a heavy plastic bag with the corner cut out, or two teaspoons, shape the mixture into 75–100 small meringues, leaving some space on the tray for expansion during cooking.

Bake at 130–140°C (250–275°F) for an hour, or until meringues are quite dry. To test, remove and cool a meringue. It is cooked when it is dry right through when broken.

As soon as the meringues are cool, store them in airtight jars or cannisters, or in unpunctured bags with the air sucked out, sealed with rubber bands.

Cherry and Almond Slice

I made this slice after tasting a similar one on the other side of the world and deciding that I could not live without it!

I use crystallised cherries and jam as a substitute for fresh or frozen (pitted) sour cherries.

Base
1½ cups (60 g/2 oz) flour
½ cup (110 g/4 oz) sugar
150 g (5 oz) cold butter

Filling
½ cup red jam
½ cup chopped crystallised cherries
½ tsp almond essence

Topping
2 cups (200 g/7 oz) coconut
1½ cups (330 g/12 oz) sugar
½ cup (60g/2 oz) flour
75 g (2½ oz) cold butter
3 eggs
1 tsp almond essence
½ cup flaked almonds (optional)

First make the base. Into a food processor fitted with a metal chopping blade put the flour, sugar and cold butter cut in about 20 small cubes. Process to form even, fine crumbs. Press them into a well-buttered or paper-lined sponge roll tin, about 24×35 cm (9×14 inches), using the back of a fish slice, or anything flat. Bake at 180°C (350°F) for 12 minutes.

While the base cooks, mix together the filling ingredients, then make the topping.

Briefly mix the first three topping ingredients in the unwashed food processor bowl. Cut the butter into cubes and add, processing until it is evenly cut through the mixture, then add the eggs and essence, and mix again.

Take the partly cooked base from the oven and spread the filling over it, then cover it with the topping, spreading it as evenly as possible over the cherry mixture. Sprinkle the almonds over the surface if desired.

Bake at 180°C (350°F) for 20–30 minutes, until evenly coloured and firm in the middle. Leave to stand for 15 minutes before cutting into 25×60 mm (1×2½ inch) fingers. Finish cooking on a rack. Store between layers of greaseproof paper in an airtight tin.

Yoghurt Cake

Our grandmothers knew that a pound cake was a good basic cake that they served plain, or with sweetened fruit. Few young cooks today make cakes like this, because they would consider them rather heavy and rich.

Here is a much lighter version of a plain cake that is delicious served with berries. I like to make the quantity given below. It makes two loaves. I use one of them straight away and freeze the other one.

For 2 loaves:
75 g (2½ oz) butter, melted
1 cup (220 g/8 oz) sugar
2 eggs
1 tsp vanilla
1½ cups flour
1 tsp baking soda
¼ tsp salt
300 g (5 oz) yoghurt

Melt butter until liquid but not hot. Measure sugar, eggs, and vanilla into a food processor bowl, add the melted butter and process to mix thoroughly.

Add the flour, baking soda and salt, then the yoghurt, and process very briefly, until combined. The mixture will be airy and puffy. Do not beat it or you will lose some of its lightness. Handle it as little and as gently as possible.

Turn mixture into two loaf tins, each lined with a strip of baking paper along their long sides and bottom.

Bake at 180°C (350°F) for 30 minutes, or until the centre springs back when pressed lightly, and a skewer comes out clean.

This cake is nicest eaten the same day as it is baked (or thawed), with the top dusted with icing sugar. Try slices topped with fresh berries, with extra yoghurt of the same flavour, or with cream.

Notes:
Use plain or flavoured, low fat or normal yoghurt.

Without a food processor, use a beater to combine the first four ingredients, then fold in the sifted dry ingredients and the yoghurt.

Eating Cake

In the years that followed the Second World War, my mother used to make a cake which she called a 'War Cake'. It was a large cake which she made in a roasting pan. It contained a lot of marmalade and, I suspect, not many eggs, nor too much butter. She made it often, and I loved it.

I suppose it was about 15 years later when I asked her for the recipe. To my surprise, she had no recollection of ever making the cake, nor did she have the recipe.

This cake, from the mother of one of my friends, has a similar flavour, although it has a different texture.

My father would have described it as a good 'eating cake'. Translated, this meant that it was not to be saved for special occasions.

For a 20 cm (8 inch) square or 23 cm (9 inch) round cake:
1 orange or 2 tangelos
125 g (4½ oz) butter
1 cup (220 g/8 oz) sugar
2 eggs
1 tsp baking soda
½ cup (125 ml/4 fl oz) water
1 tsp vanilla
2 cups (250 g/9 oz) flour
1 cup (160 g/5½ oz) sultanas

Halve the orange or tangelos and remove the seeds. Cut each half into quarters, then chop these finely, using the metal chopping blade of a food processor. Tip the pulp into another container.

Without washing the bowl or blade, add the butter which has been softened but not melted, the sugar and the eggs. Process for about 20 seconds.

Add to the bowl the baking soda dissolved in the water, the vanilla, the flour and the sultanas.

Using the pulse blade in brief bursts, mix in the orange pulp until everything is combined.

Turn mixture into a sprayed or paper-lined 20 cm (8 inch) square or 23 cm (9 inch) round cake tin.

Bake for 1–1¼ hours, or until the cake springs back when pressed lightly in the centre, and a skewer comes out clean.

Orange Cake

Make this cake by the conventional creaming method, or use a food processor. Serve it with coffee or tea at any time of the day, or dress it up! Produce it warm for dessert, in slices topped with drained mandarin segments and lightly whipped cream flavoured with orange liqueur.

Orange Cake

For a 23 cm (9 inch) ring cake:
1 large orange or two small oranges
1 cup (220 g/8 oz) sugar
125 g (4½ oz) butter
3 eggs
1 cup (125 g/4½ oz) self-raising flour
¾ cup (95 g/3½ oz) plain flour
water
1 Tbsp lemon juice

Thinly peel the orange with a floating-blade peeler. Put peel in food processor with the sugar and process with the metal chopping blade until very finely chopped. Add the softened but not melted butter and the eggs, and process until thoroughly mixed. Measure in the two different flours, then the juice from the orange(s) made up to ½ cup (125 ml/4 fl oz) with water, and the lemon juice. Process briefly, just enough to mix, then spoon into a well-buttered or sprayed ring pan that holds 7–8 cups (1¾ –2 litres).

Bake just below the middle of the oven (with or without fan) at 180°C (350°F) for 35–50 minutes, until skewer comes out clean. Leave to stand for 5–10 minutes, then remove from the pan. Invert on a rack, dust generously with icing sugar.

163

Apricot and Almond Cake

This is a wonderful cake. You may find yourself inventing a special occasion so you have an excuse to make it!

For a 20 cm (8 inch) ring cake:
140–150 g (5 oz) slivered almonds
2 tsp baking powder
20 (75 g/2½ oz) lightly salted crackers, e.g. Snax biscuits
½ cup (75 g/2½ oz) dried apricots
3 egg whites
1 cup (220 g/8 oz) sugar
1 tsp vanilla
whipped cream or Fromage Frais to decorate

Toast the almonds until evenly golden under a grill. Do not let them brown. Put aside about a table-spoonful for a garnish, later.

Put the rest of the nuts, the baking powder and biscuits in a plastic bag and bang the bag with a rolling pin until contents are broken into small pieces, but are not as fine as breadcrumbs. Wash the dried apricots and chop while wet into small pieces, using a sharp knife or kitchen scissors. Mix these with the crumbs, breaking up any clumps.

In a large, grease-free bowl, beat the egg whites until the peaks turn over when the beater is lifted out. Add the sugar and beat until the peaks stand up straight when the beater is removed. Fold the crumb mixture and the vanilla into the meringue.

Spoon the mixture into a ring tin which has had its sides well-buttered or sprayed with non-stick spray, and its bottom lined with a ring of baking paper or a non-stick Teflon liner.

Bake at 180°C (350°F) for 30 minutes, then run a knife around the tin and tip the cake carefully on to a rack. As soon as it is cold, turn it right side up again on to a flat serving plate.

Apricot and Almond Cake

Decorate with whipped cream or Fromage Frais, piling it on top, then sprinkle with the reserved nuts and a few extra chopped apricots if desired.

Notes:
Do not use a food processor to crumb the biscuits. If they are crushed into pieces which are too small the resulting cake will be dry and too firm.

You can bake this cake in a 20 cm (8 inch) tin without a central hole, but you may find that the centre drops a little. Cook until the centre springs back and feels as firm as the part nearer the edge. You do not notice the depression in the middle if you fill it with cream. Fromage Frais is best chilled, stirred with a fork until smooth, and piled on the cake (or on individual servings) just before serving.

Kiwi Layer Cake

SEE PHOTOGRAPH ON PAGE 156
This delicious cake is quite easy to make. It is best made the day before it is required. If this is not possible, make it two days ahead!

1 unfilled sponge sandwich
1 Tbsp instant coffee
¾ cup (165 g/6 oz) sugar
¼ cup (60 ml/2 fl oz) water
½ Tbsp rum or brandy
1–1½ cups (250–375 ml/8–12 fl oz) cream
6–8 kiwi fruit
½ cup slivered almonds
½ cup canned mandarins (optional)

Split each layer of sponge so you have four thin round layers. Put one of these aside for other use and place the other three side by side on a clean working surface.

Heat the coffee, sugar and water, stirring until the sugar dissolves, then boil without stirring until a drop between your thumb and forefinger forms a thread when these two fingers are moved a centimetre apart. Cool until you can put your hand on the bottom of the container, then stir in the rum or brandy.

Drizzle each of the three sponge layers with a third of the coffee syrup, covering the surface evenly.

Whip the cream stiffly, put a quarter on each of two layers, then cover with two thirds of the thickly sliced kiwi fruit. Stack these two layers on a flat serving plate, and cover with the remaining layer. Spread the remaining cream over the top and sides.

Toast the almonds under a grill until golden brown, and when they are cool press them into the cream on the sides of the cake, tilting it slightly, and rotating it. Cover lightly, and refrigerate for at least 12 hours before serving. The texture changes during this time.

Just before serving decorate the top with a ring of overlapping kiwi fruit slices. Pile drained mandarin segments in the centre of the cake if desired.

Note:
Refrigerate leftovers. The kiwi fruit between the layers will look good a day later, but the fruit on the top may need to be replaced.

Simnel Cake

As a child I preferred the Simnel Cake my mother made for Easter to the other fruit cakes that she made for birthdays and Christmas, because I loved the layer of almond icing baked in the middle of the cake.

In 1980 a friend gave me a recipe where the central mixture was semolina flavoured with almond essence. I prefer the flavour and texture of this (economical) version.

For a 20 cm (8 inch) round cake, 4 cm (1½ inches) high:
Filling
50 g (2 oz) butter
½ cup semolina
½ cup (110 g/4 oz) sugar
¼ cup (60 ml/2 fl oz) water
2 tsp almond essence

Cake
125 g (4½ oz) butter
½ cup (110 g/4 oz) sugar
2 eggs
1 tsp vanilla
¼ cup (22.5 g/¾ oz) rolled oats
½ cup (60 g/2 oz) flour
½ cup (60 g/2 oz) self-raising flour
1 tsp mixed spice
1 tsp cinnamon
3 cups (420 g/15 oz) mixed dried fruit
¼ cup (60 ml/2 fl oz) sherry

Make the almond-flavoured paste first. Melt the butter in a (non-stick) frypan, then stir in the semolina and cook over a moderate heat for about 2 minutes, without browning. Add sugar and water and cook, stirring frequently, until it leaves a wide band on the bottom of the pan when the spoon is pulled across it (about 4–5 minutes). Stir in essence, then stand pan in cold water to cool it.

Make the cake by the conventional creaming method, or use a short-cut method if you have a food processor. Cut butter into cubes and microwave it until soft but not melted. Put in food processor (fitted with plastic mixing blade) with sugar, eggs, vanilla, rolled oats and half the plain flour. Process only after adding all these. Add the remaining flours, and spices, process again until evenly blended, then add the dried fruit and mix briefly, using pulse action. If mixture is very thick, add 1–2 Tbsp sherry to make it easier to spread.

Line bottom and sides of a 20 cm (8 inch) round or square tin with baking paper or non-stick Teflon liner, and spread half the cake mixture over it. Spread the almond mixture over this. If fairly firm, flatten pieces with wet hands. If too wet to handle, put over the top in little blobs, and try to spread them evenly. Top with remaining cake mix, then bake at 150°C (300°F) for 1¾–2 hours, until the centre springs back, and a skewer comes out clean.

While still very hot, dribble the sherry over the cake, putting more round the sides than in the middle. Cool on a rack, then remove lining paper.

If desired, decorate with pale green icing and Easter eggs.

Christmas Mince Pies

The flavour of Christmas mincemeat improves on keeping. Make it at least a week before using it.

Mincemeat Filling
2 small apples
1 cup (160 g/5½ oz) sultanas
1 cup (140 g/5 oz) mixed dried fruit
1 lemon, rind and juice
rind of 1 orange
½ cup (100 g/3¼ oz) brown sugar
1 tsp mixed spice
1 tsp cinnamon
½ tsp salt
¼ tsp ground cloves
¼ cup (60 ml/2 fl oz) brandy, whisky or rum

If using a mincer to make this filling, mince the apple, dried fruit and the rinds together, then mix them with the remaining ingredients using your hand.

If using a food processor, first chop up the thinly peeled orange and lemon rinds with the sugar, then add the chunks of unpeeled apple, and process with the metal chopping blade into pieces the size of sultanas. Add the dried fruit and process until chopped as finely as desired. Add the remaining ingredients and process briefly to mix.

Spoon into sterilised jars, pour extra spirits over the surface, cover tightly and store in a cool place for up to 3 months. The jars may be kept in a refrigerator up to a year, if you stir in more spirits at intervals whenever the fruit seems dry. If you add more fruit juice, the mincemeat may ferment.

To make the mincemeat go further, mix grated raw apple and extra spices with it at the time when you are using it as a filling.

Pies:
125 g (4½ oz) butter
1 cup (110 g/4 oz) icing sugar
1 cup (125 g/4½ oz) flour
1 cup (125 g/4 oz) cornflour

Cream the softened butter and the icing sugar together. Add the flour and cornflour and mix well, adding a little water if necessary to mix to a soft dough. Chill until firm enough to roll out on a well-floured board.

Cut from the rolled pastry circles big enough to fit the bottom of well-buttered shallow patty tins. Spoon in sufficient mincemeat mixture to fill the pastry-lined tins. Cut tops from the pastry slightly smaller than the bottoms. Decorate as desired, and place carefully over the mincemeat filling, sealing the edges lightly.

Bake at 170–180°C (325–350°F) for 20–30 minutes, removing from the oven as soon as the edges start to colour. Cool for 2–3 minutes before carefully lifting from the patty tins.

Use within 48 hours, or freeze for longer storage. Warm in a cool oven (in patty tins) before serving.

Christmas Mince Pies

'Extra Fruity' Christmas Cake

This dark, rich, fruity cake has a wonderful flavour.
It is best made 2–4 weeks before it is to be cut.

For a 23 cm (9 inch) cake:
225 g (8 oz) butter
1 cup (220g/8 oz) sugar
1 tsp vanilla
½ tsp lemon essence
½ tsp orange essence
½ tsp almond essence
3 cups (375 g/13 oz) flour
6 large eggs
2 tsp cinnamon
2 tsp mixed spice
1 tsp ground cloves
1 Tbsp cocoa
1 kg (2 lb 3 oz) sultanas
500 g (1 lb 2 oz) raisins
300 g (10½ oz) currants
100 g (3½ oz) cherries
100 g (3½ oz) preserved ginger, chopped
1 (450 g/1 lb) can crushed pineapple (squeezed dry)
1 tsp baking soda
2–3 Tbsp rum, whisky or brandy

First line a 23 cm (9 inch) cake tin with one or two
layers of greaseproof paper. Make a paper collar about
10 cm (4 inches) high.

'Extra Fruity' Christmas Cake

Assemble all the fruit before starting mixing. Make
sure it is clean and dry before combining with other
ingredients.

Cream butter and sugar until light and smooth.

Add essences with a tablespoon of the measured
flour.

Add eggs one at a time, with a tablespoon of the
measured flour between additions if the mixture shows
any sign of curdling.

Mix spices and cocoa with remaining flour then mix
well with dried fruit.

In a very large bowl combine the creamed mixture,
floured fruit, the pineapple, squeezed dry in a cloth,
and the baking soda mixed with 1 tablespoon pineapple
juice or water. Add spirits. Press mixture into a lined
tin, slightly rounding the surface. Decorate with extra
cherries and almonds if desired. Bake at 150°C (300°F)
for 1 hour, then at 130°C (260°F) for 2–2½ hours, or
until a skewer comes out clean when inserted in the
middle of the cake.

Sprinkle edges of hot cake with an extra ¼ cup spirits
if desired.

Store at room temperature, loosely wrapped in
paper and a teatowel for up to a month. Refrigerate
or freeze in a plastic bag, aluminium foil, or other airtight container.

Orange and Lemon Drops

SEE PHOTOGRAPH ON PAGE 168
There is something very appealing about jars of different shapes and sizes, filled with different flavoured toffees, lined up on a counter.

These are not as difficult to make as you might think, although they are not the best sweets for young children or beginners, since the hot toffee must be quickly shaped by hand before it sets.

These orange and lemon drops are the closest thing I can get to old-fashioned acid drops. Don't be tempted to double the quantities — it is easier to work with small quantities.

½ cup (110 g/4 oz)
¼ cup (60 ml/2 fl oz) water
¼ cup (60 ml/2 fl oz) liquid glucose
1 tsp butter
¼ tsp powdered tartaric acid
¼ tsp orange or lemon flavouring

Bring the sugar, water, liquid glucose and butter gently to the boil. Stir only until the sugar is dissolved, then raise the heat a little, and stop stirring. Too high a temperature will make the toffee brown before its end point is reached.

Butter a shallow metal tin, and get out the tartaric acid and flavouring so that it is handy when you need it.

Test quarter teaspoonfuls of the toffee every minute or so, until it forms a hard ball when dropped in cold water. Turn off the heat, leave to stand for about a minute, then pour it on to the buttered surface. Sprinkle the tartaric acid and flavouring on to the surface of the cooling toffee, then pour the essence over it. As soon as the toffee is firm enough to lift at the edges, lift the edges over the central part, until the flavourings are covered. Keep moving the mixture around until the flavourings are mixed in, then take small pieces of the toffee, form it into balls, and, if there is a second person working with you, press the toffees with a meat hammer or something similar to make a pattern on them.

Wrap or store in an airtight bottle as soon as toffee is firm.

Note:
Liquid glucose is available from most chemists.

Barley Sugar

SEE PHOTOGRAPH ON PAGE 168
If you can keep the heat high enough to cook the toffee but low enough to stop it browning, you can make this old-fashioned favourite quite easily. Work with the small quantities rather than doubling the recipe.

½ cup (110 g/4 oz) sugar
2 Tbsp water
¼ cup (60 ml/2 fl oz) liquid glucose
1 Tbsp strained lemon juice
1 tsp butter
¼ tsp orange essence
¼ tsp lemon essence

Measure the sugar and water into a fairly small non-stick pan. Heat gently, stirring frequently, until the sugar crystals have dissolved.

Add the glucose, and stir gently until mixed, then add the lemon juice which has been strained through a sieve, stir again to mix, rub a spatula around the side of the pan to make sure that there are no sugar crystals there, then boil over a fairly high heat until a little of the mixture dropped in cold water forms a soft ball. Add the butter, stir it in, then boil more gently, to try to stop the mixture darkening too much.

Cook, without stirring, until a drop of the mixture in cold water is so hard that it breaks when bitten.

Remove from the heat and measure the flavourings into the pan. Swirl the pan around, then stir gently, to mix them in evenly.

Pour the hot mixture into a well-buttered sponge roll tin, and lift up the edges, and push them towards the middle until you can pick up the pieces of candy with buttered hands. Pull it, then put the ends together and pull again, until the barley sugar is lighter in colour and firm enough to twist into a rope, then roll to even thickness between your hands and the board. As soon as you have an even rope, cut it into short, 2–3 cm (1 inch) lengths with buttered kitchen scissors, and push the corners in so that they do not poke out. Repeat with the remaining barley sugar.

Store in an airtight container as soon as barley sugar is cold and hard.

Notes:
Different batches may vary in colour. The lighter ones will taste best.

Liquid glucose is available from most chemists.

Butterballs

½ cup (110 g/4 oz) sugar
2 tablespoons water
2 tablespoons honey
2 tablespoons butter
½ teaspoon rum essence

Put the sugar and water into a small pan and heat gently until the sugar dissolves. Add the honey and the butter and boil the mixture gently, without stirring.

Get a shallow container of cold water, and dip some of the mixture into it. As soon as the drops are hard, and break when you bite them, take the pan off the heat and leave it to cool a little.

While you wait, rub a fairly thick layer of butter on to a metal plate. Add the essence to the candy, stir it gently, and pour it on to the buttery plate. When it is cool enough to touch, push it into a lump with a buttery knife. Pick up the lump and twist it into a rope. Cut pieces off the rope using buttered kitchen scissors, and roll them into balls. When cold, store in an airtight jar.

Chocolate Log

This rich log makes a good gift.

200 g (7 oz) dark chocolate
¾ cup (185 ml/6 fl oz) caramelised condensed milk
½ tsp vanilla
½ tsp rum essence (optional)
1 cup toasted nuts
½ cup glacé cherries
½ cup sultanas or dried apricots
about ½ cup finely chopped nuts

Break chocolate into 5 mm (¼ inch) squares. Melt in microwave dish at Medium (50% power) for 2–3 minutes.

Warm caramelised condensed milk if necessary. Assemble remaining ingredients except chopped nuts. Combine chocolate, condensed milk and additions, working fairly quickly.

Tip the mixture on to a long strip of plastic cling wrap. Form a long sausage. Wrap and chill for 15 minutes. Unwrap, cut into shorter lengths and coat with chopped nuts. Refrigerate for up to 2 months. Slice as required.

Note:
To caramelise condensed milk simmer unopened can in a large pot full of water for 2–3 hours, making sure that the can is covered with water at all times.

Roasted Peanuts

Heat the oven to 180°C (350°F). Spread plain (uncooked, unsalted) peanuts one layer thick in a baking tin and bake them for 20–30 minutes or until their colour darkens slightly.

To skin the roasted peanuts, rub them between your hands. Stand outside in a breeze, and the skins will blow away. When the nuts are cold, store in an airtight jar.

Scroggin (roasted peanuts, sultanas and pieces of chocolate) is a good mixture to take tramping, or to school when you don't have time to make a packed lunch.

Note:
Remember not to give peanuts to small children since inhaled peanuts can cause serious trouble.

Curried Walnuts

Walnuts are particularly nice baked and salted or spiced. Curried walnuts, although they may sound rather odd, are really delicious and I notice that a dish of them is always emptied before other nuts are eaten. Walnuts which have been freshly shelled are best.

Boil the halved, shelled walnuts in water for three minutes before they are baked. Drain them and bake them in a shallow dish at 180°C (350°F) for 15–30 minutes until they start to turn brown.

As soon as they come out of the oven add a little butter and toss them in it, or brush them with melted butter, then sprinkle them with a mixture of ½ teaspoon curry powder to 1 teaspoon salt.

Leave to cool on absorbent paper and store in airtight tins when cold.

Salted Cashew Nuts

Wash and drain cashews and spread them out thinly, one or two layers deep, in a shallow roasting pan. Sprinkle with salt and add a little butter. For 500 g (1 lb 2 oz) nuts use ½ teaspoon salt and 2 teaspoons butter.

Bake them at 180°C (350°F) for 15–30 minutes shaking the pan or stirring occasionally after the butter melts to make sure the nuts are well coated.

When they turn golden brown remove them and leave them to cool on kitchen or other absorbent paper. They will become crisp as they cool.

Do not put them in tins until they are quite cold.

Spiced Almonds

Nuts can be coated with a sweet spicy mixture before they are baked.

Wash and drain the almonds to be used, then coat them with a little unbeaten egg white. Use 1–2 teaspoons egg white to 1 cup of almonds, mixing them together with your fingers in a small shallow basin or plate.

When they are coated, sprinkle them with a mixture of 2 tablespoons castor sugar and 2 teaspoons cinnamon or mixed spice.

When they are covered with this, spread them out on an oven tray or shallow pan so that they are not touching, and bake them at 150°C (300°F) for 20–30 minutes.

Cool, and store in airtight tins.

Peanut Toffee

¼ cup (55 g/2 oz) sugar
¼ cup (35 g/1¼ oz) roasted peanuts

Rub a metal tray or sponge roll tin with butter.

Sprinkle the sugar into a clean, dry frypan. Hold the pan over a medium heat until the sugar melts. Watch that the heat is not too hot, or the sugar will brown in some places before it melts in others. You can tilt the pan to move the sugar, but do not stir.

When the sugar is melted, and is light golden brown, tip in the roasted peanuts. Tilt the pan so the peanuts and toffee fall to one side. Tip the mixture on to the buttered tray.

Butter your fingers and some kitchen scissors. When the toffee is cool enough to touch, push and pull it into a bar. Cut the bar into pieces while it is warm, or break it into pieces when it is cold. Store in an airtight jar to stop it going sticky.

Ginger Fudge

Whenever I see a plateful of creamy fudge I think of the way my sweet-toothed sisters and I used to experiment, making ginger fudge on wet Sunday afternoons, when we were teenagers.

Fudge-making requires some practice. If you overcook the fudge, or overbeat it, you will finish up with hard, dry, grainy fudge. The use of a candy thermometer will help, but will not be the answer to all your problems.

2 cups (440 g/16 oz) sugar
½ cup (125 ml/4 fl oz) milk
50 g (2 oz) butter
½–1 tsp ground ginger
1 Tbsp golden syrup
½ tsp vanilla essence
2 Tbsp chopped walnuts

Measure the sugar, milk and butter into a medium-sized saucepan. Add the ground ginger and the golden syrup.

Bring to the boil over a medium heat, stirring occasionally, until the mixture starts to boil. Do not stir after the mixture starts boiling.

Boil until ¼ teaspoon of the mixture dropped into cold water forms a soft ball which keeps its roundish shape unless flattened by the fingers, or until a candy thermometer reads 235°F. (All candy thermometers seem to be calibrated in Fahrenheit.) The fudge is cooked at this stage. Remove from the heat and leave until the saucepan is cool enough to touch.

Add the vanilla and the chopped nuts and beat with a wooden spoon until the fudge shows signs of thickening.

Pour it quickly on to a buttered sponge roll tin, 'swirling' the top with a knife before it sets hard, if possible. Cut as soon as it is firm, in case you have overcooked it, in which case it will harden so it is difficult to cut neatly.

Peppermint Chews

These sweets have a 'different' texture and are from an old recipe. One of my friends has the recipe for them handwritten in an old cookbook, under the name Stick-jawettes! Take care not to let the mixture brown too much before it reaches its end point.

1 Tbsp butter
2 Tbsp sugar
¼ cup (60 ml/2 fl oz) golden syrup
¾–1 cup skim milk powder
1 tsp peppermint essence

Heat the butter, sugar and syrup gently, stirring only until the sugar has dissolved. Boil this mixture until ¼ teaspoonful dropped into a bowl of cold water forms a soft ball.

Take the pan off the heat, add ¾ cup of the milk powder and the essence and stir with a wooden spoon until it is thoroughly mixed and cool enough to touch. If the mixture seems very soft, add the rest of the milk powder.

Knead the mixture until it is smooth, then roll it into two or three long thin sausages. Cut the sausages into little pieces with greased kitchen scissors or a greased knife, or break off pieces with your fingers, roll them into balls, then squeeze the balls between your finger and thumb.

When cool, store in a screw-topped jar.

Candied Mandarin Peel

It is easy and quick to candy mandarin peel — you can use this either as a sweet, or for chopping up for baking. Chocolate-dipped peel makes a special treat.

peel from 8–10 mandarins
water to cover
about ½ cup (110 g/4 oz) sugar
¼ tsp citric acid
1 tsp water
extra sugar for coating
about 100 g (3½ oz) easy-to-melt cooking chocolate

Refrigerate mandarin peel in a plastic bag until you have enough to candy.

Cover the pieces of peel with water and simmer for about 30 minutes, until they are very tender. Pour off and measure the liquid, then add the same volume of sugar — i.e. ½ cup liquid needs ½ cup sugar.

Boil gently, uncovered, until a small amount dropped in cold water forms a soft ball.

Remove from heat and add the citric acid dissolved in the water. Work fast after you do this, because the liquid sets like marmalade when the acid is added.

Pick out the pieces of peel and turn each one in sugar. Leave the sugar-coated peel sitting on the sugar until it is cool and fairly firm.

Before it has completely cooled cut the pieces into strips, and make sure the cut edges are sugar-coated.

Leave peel to stand, uncovered, until it is fairly firm.

If you are going to use it for cooking, store it in an airtight container in the freezer.

If you are going to coat it with chocolate, melt the chocolate in a small bowl over hot water.

Stir the chocolate until it is liquid. Nestlé's easy-to-melt chocolate does not need anything added, but other chocolate may need a little solid white vegetable fat to make it liquid enough to work with. Dip one side of each strip of mandarin peel into the chocolate, then put it on a piece of plastic. If you like, you can dip each end, instead of one side of the strips.

Refrigerate the chocolate-coated strips on the plastic until the chocolate solidifies, then lift them off. Store in a cool, dry place until required.

Note:

If you boil the syrup too long the peel will be hard. If you don't boil it enough it will be soft and sticky.

Ginger Fudge and Peppermint Chews

Yoghurt Smoothy

Using a food processor or blender, purée the fruit and liquid from any can of fruit. (Sieve boysenberries to remove seeds, if desired.) Add unsweetened or sweetened plain or fruited yoghurt and process to mix. Use about ¾ cup (200 ml/6 fl oz) yoghurt to a 450 g (1 lb) can of fruit.

Variation:

For a hot weather treat, freeze the fruit and liquid after removing from the can. Break up and process until slushy, then add the chilled yoghurt.

Soya Milk

It is not difficult to make an inexpensive and nutritious 'milk' from soya beans. One cup of dried beans yields six cups of liquid which may be used for drinking 'straight', making flavoured cold drinks, hot chocolate drinks, in baking, and even for milk puddings.

The flavour is not the same as cows' milk but it is an acceptable alternative to many people.

(Soya milk needs added calcium and vitamin B12 to give it a nutritive value similar to that of cows' milk. See the note at the end of the recipe.)

Follow the instructions exactly, since the milk will have a strong flavour if boiling water is not used during the grinding.

For about 6 cups:
1 cup (1.5 litres/48 fl oz) dried soya beans
4 cups (1 litre/32 fl oz) warm water
7 cups (1.75 litre/56 fl oz) boiling water

Flavourings:
2–3 Tbsp honey, malt or brown sugar
1 tsp vanilla essence
about ½ tsp salt

Pour the lukewarm water over the soya beans and leave to stand for 2–4 hours, or until the beans have softened right through. Change the water, and rub the beans to halve them if you are in a hurry. Leave the beans to soak for longer if this suits you.

When you are ready to grind the beans, drain them and pour 1 cup (250 ml/8 fl oz) boiling water over them. Rinse out a food processor with hot water, then discard the bean water and the rinsing water.

Put half the drained beans in the food processor. Process to chop finely then add 2 cups (500 ml/16 fl oz) boiling water and process until very finely chopped. Pour mixture into a large sieve lined with a clean cloth over a large bowl. Repeat with remaining beans.

Tip the beans from the cloth back into the processor, process again to chop as finely as possible, then add the remaining 2 cups (500 ml/16 fl oz) of boiling water, and process for about a minute longer. Pour into the cloth-lined sieve. Squeeze and twist the bag to get out as much liquid as possible, then heat all the strained

Yoghurt Smoothy

liquid, in a microwave oven until liquid boils, or in a covered bowl over boiling water for 30 minutes. Remove from heat.

Add extra boiling water to make up to 6 cups (1.5 litres/48 fl oz), if necessary, then stir in flavourings, varying quantities to taste. Store in a covered container in the refrigerator for up to 4 days.

Note:
To fortify soya milk so that it is about the same composition as cows' milk, add to the warm liquid above, at the same time as the flavourings:

2 Tbsp oil
1 Tbsp (about 2 g) powdered calcium carbonate
1 (25 microgram) tablet Vitamin B12, crushed

Get the powdered calcium carbonate and vitamin B12 from a chemist.

Shake the bottle of soya milk before using it.

Tofu-Shakes

Here's a nutritious meal in a glass that is almost as quick to make as it is to drink!

For 2 medium shakes:
about 125 g (4½ oz) tofu
1 banana
2 Tbsp brown sugar
1 cup (250 ml/8 fl oz) orange juice or milk
½ tsp vanilla essence

Put the tofu and pieces of banana in a blender or food processor and process until well mixed.

Add the sugar, orange juice or milk and vanilla. Process again until the mixture is smooth and creamy.

Pour into two medium-sized glasses. Serve with thick straws and/or long handled spoons.

Economical Orange Drink for Children

When you want to make a small amount of orange juice go a long way, try this quick mixture. It makes a pleasant drink that children enjoy.

1 cup (250 ml/8 fl oz) orange juice
1 cup (220 g/8 oz) sugar
1½ tsp citric acid
2 litres (8 cups/64 fl oz) water

Use any flavoured fruit juice that you have. Measure the sugar and citric acid into a 1 litre container and add enough hot water to dissolve it. Fill the container with cold water. Mix this warm syrup with the fruit juice and another litre of plain cold water, or cold water mixed with ice-blocks. Stir and serve.

Vary the amount of citric acid to suit the age of the children. Use a little less for young children, and add a little more for teenagers. To 'dress up', serve with thin slices of lemon, and mint sprigs. Replace half the water with soda water, if desired.

Lemon and Barley Water

I was brought up to think that lemon and barley water is good for your kidneys; that you should always have a glass of it on the bedside table if you are sick; and that it is a thirst-quenching drink for hay makers.

I would not like to argue about the merits of this old-fashioned drink, but I do like it, and I make it at intervals during the summer when we are thirsty and want something a little different.

For 8 cups (2 litres/64 fl oz) of diluted drink:
½ cup (100 g/3½ oz) pearl barley
4 cups (1 litre/32 fl oz) water
2–3 lemons
¾ cup (165 g/6 oz) sugar

Simmer the barley in the water for 30–45 minutes, or until the liquid has slightly thickened.

While the barley cooks, grate the yellow part from the lemons, squeeze them, and mix them with the sugar.

Strain the hot barley liquid into the lemon mixture. Stir until the sugar dissolves, leave it to stand for about 10 minutes, then strain again, into the bottle in which you will store it. If there is less than 3 cups (750 ml/ 24 fl oz) pour extra boiling water over the barley, and make it up to volume.

To drink, dilute using three parts of water to one part of cordial, or add enough water to the total amount of cordial to make it up to 16 cups (4 litres/ 128 fl oz) altogether, if all the drink is to be used straight away.

Note:
Alter proportions slightly to suit your own taste.

Berry Cordials

I like to make my own fruit cordials when I have access to plenty of fresh ripe berries.

To serve, dilute it, one part cordial to about four parts of water or soda water.

The undiluted cordial makes a good ice-cream topping, too. In cooler weather I like to add a dash of fruit cordial to the syrup from canned or preserved fruit, then thicken the mixture with cornflour or custard powder. The resulting sauce makes a plain apple shortcake or steamed pudding much more exciting.

The following recipe is one that I use for wild blackberry cordial, but you can use other berries, fresh or frozen, to make similar cordials.

1 kg (2 lb/8 cups) blackberries
1 cup water (250 ml/8 fl oz)
sugar
citric acid

Crush the berries using a food processor or potato masher. Heat them, with the water, for 30 minutes, in a bowl over boiling water, stirring occasionally.

Strain through muslin or similar lining in a sieve or colander. Do not squeeze the bag. Leave overnight.

The next day measure the juice and add 1 cup sugar and 1 level measuring teaspoon citric acid to every 2 cups (500 ml/16 fl oz) juice. Stir until dissolved, without heating if possible.

Pour into small, clean soft drink bottles with screw tops, leaving 3 cm (1 inch) headspace. (Use bottles of the same height.) Put cleaned screw tops on loosely.

Stand bottles on a rack in a deep saucepan, with water up to the level of the cordial. Heat to 85°C (190°F). At this temperature little bubbles form on the sides of the saucepan, then burst on the surface of the water. The surface of the water should not be heaving with large bubbles, though. Keep at this temperature for 20 minutes. Lift out the bottles and screw tops on tightly. When cool, dip bottle tops and the necks of the bottles in melted wax, to make quite sure no air can get in. Store in a cool, dark place.

Once cordial has been opened, drink within 2–3 days, or store in the refrigerator for up to 6–8 weeks.

Note:
For blackcurrant cordial use 1 cup (250 ml/8 fl oz) water to 500 g (1 lb) fruit.

'Fifty-Fifty' Cordial

Anybody with school children knows how much fruit drink they can consume in hot weather. Here is an economical drink that you can make from fresh citrus fruit.

For 16 large glasses (4 litres/128 fl oz):
1½ cups (375 ml/12 fl oz) water
2 cups (440 g/16 oz) sugar
1 orange
1 lemon
1½ tsp citric acid
½ tsp Epsom salts

Boil the water and a cup of the sugar. Remove the coloured skin of the orange and lemon with a potato peeler, chop it very finely with the rest of the sugar, in a food processor, then add it to the hot syrup. Stir until the sugar is dissolved, then take it off the heat. Add the juice from both fruits, the acid and the Epsom salts, and leave to stand until lukewarm. Strain to remove the peel, then bottle and refrigerate for use as cordial, or dilute with 12 cups (3 litres/96 fl oz) of water to make a drink for immediate consumption.

Variation:
Boil all the sugar with the water, and grate all the coloured skin from the fruit using a grater.

Lemon Barley Water, Berry Cordials and 'Fifty-Fifty' Cordial

PRESERVES

Peach & Passn fr.
March '90

Basic Bottling

SEE PHOTOGRAPH ON PAGE 178

My bottling is quick and easy, often done one or two jars at a time. It would not win prizes at shows, but is none the worse for this. During the year I save empty jars which have metal lids that are lacquered inside, and which have a built-in ring of pliable material.

If you want to bottle fruit in such jars, clean them scrupulously when you get them. A dishwasher set on a hot cycle does a good job. When lid and jar are dry, screw on the lid and put it away. When you want to bottle fruit in it, put jar and lid, separately, in a saucepan full of water and let it boil while the fruit is prepared.

Peel, slice and cook the fruit as you like it for table use. (I often cook it in a little well-flavoured white wine instead of water, add a cup of sugar to each cup of liquid, and cut the fruit into thin slices. The mixture is usually rather solid, with much more fruit than liquid. It makes a good icecream topping, later.)

When the fruit is tender, lift the hot bottle from the boiling water with tongs, and stand it in a pie plate on a board. Ladle the boiling fruit and a little syrup into it until it is full to the brim, but not overflowing, make sure that the rim is clear of pieces of fruit, lift the top out of the boiling water, and screw it firmly on. When cool, wash and polish the jar, but do not loosen or tighten the lid.

When you want to use the fruit, run the lid under the hot tap before unscrewing it. Reuse the lid for other bottling only if it is unmarked inside.

Variations:

Bottle mixtures, e.g. Golden Queen peaches in passionfruit pulp.

Bottle lightly sweetened passionfruit pulp in tiny jars.

Note:

Lids should look slightly concave when fruit cools. If lids bulge up, or if the contents smell or look unusual, do not eat the fruit.

Do *not* use this method for bottling vegetables, meat or fish.

Crabapple and Japonica Jelly

Crabapples and small wild apples from trees that have grown from pips dropped by birds, make wonderful tart jelly, good for serving with meat or for spreading on bread. The fruit should have black seeds and a good colour. Fruit which is under- or over-ripe will not make good jelly. The fruit from spring-flowering japonica makes excellent jelly, too.

Wash and pick over the fruit, discarding any rotted or badly eaten pieces. Weigh it, and work with 1, or at the most 2 kg (2 lb 3 oz–4 lb 6 oz) of fruit at once, since small amounts make the best jelly. Chop large fruits roughly, then chop more finely, in small quantities, in a food processor. Include all skins and cores.

Tip chopped fruit quickly into water in a large saucepan, to prevent browning. Use 3–4 cups (750 ml–1 litre/24–32 fl oz) of water for 1 kg (2 lb 3 oz) of fruit. Boil vigorously, uncovered, until fruit is soft.

Pour through a sieve, banging it a few times to extract most of the liquid, then pour it through a fine cloth in a sieve, without any squeezing or shaking. Measure the juice into a large clean pan, and discard the pulp.

Add ¾ cup (185 g/6 oz) of sugar for each cup of juice. Boil rapidly, skimming off froth from the sides of the pot, until a little of the liquid, cooled on a saucer, forms a skin which wrinkles when a finger is run across it.

Pour into clean, heated (in a low oven) jelly jars, glasses, etc., and allow to set. Cover the surface of the set jelly with melted paraffin wax, then with cellophane covers.

Store in a cool dark place, and serve from the jar, or invert, like a sandcastle, on a small flat plate.

Kiwi Conserve

Kiwi fruit and pineapple may be combined to make a jam (or conserve) which may be used as a good breakfast spread and an interesting topping for cheesecakes. When you make this, add a little green colouring so that the finished jam is the same clear green as a fairly ripe, raw fruit.

2 cups (500 g/1 lb) chopped kiwi fruit flesh
1–3 tsp grated ginger root
juice of 1 lemon
1 cup (250 g/8 oz) canned pineapple (and juice)
2½ cups (550 g/1 lb 4 oz) sugar
green food colouring

If you like jam without too many seeds and are using kiwi fruit which are not too expensive, remove both the central core and the area with the most seeds before you chop the flesh.

First, halve the fruit lengthways. To cut out the central core and remove some of the seeds, use a sharp, serrated knife and cut a 'V' lengthways from each half. Hold the halved fruit in one hand and, with a teaspoon or dessertspoon, scoop the remaining flesh from the skin. Press this firmly into a two-cup measure, if you do not want to weigh it.

Peel the fresh root ginger and grate it finely. (If you use frozen root ginger, use at least twice as much, since it grates as a powdery dust.)

Boil kiwi fruit, ginger and lemon juice for 3–4 minutes. Add the pineapple juice and the pineapple, cut into small pieces. Boil for 5 minutes longer, then add the sugar. Boil briskly, stirring frequently, for about 10 minutes, or until a little jam sets when spooned on to a cold saucer.

Lemon Honey

Lemon honey is a smooth, easily spread, lemon-flavoured mixture with many uses. It is delicious when spread on pikelets, used as a filling for tartlets, between plain biscuits or the halves of a sponge sandwich, and is particularly tasty spread on pavlovas where its tartness counteracts the sweetness of the meringue.

Although lemon honey does not keep as well as jams or jellies, it can be kept, covered, in the refrigerator for several weeks.

50 g (2 oz) butter
1 cup (220 g/8 oz) sugar
2 tsp finely grated lemon rind
3 eggs, slightly beaten
½ cup (125 ml/4 fl oz) lemon juice

In the top section of a double boiler, or in a basin over a saucepan of boiling water, melt the butter and add the sugar and finely grated lemon rind. In another basin beat the eggs just enough to blend the yolks and whites, and strain with the lemon juice into the mixture over the boiling water. Heat, stirring occasionally, for 15–20 minutes or until the mixture has thickened. (Do not heat over direct heat once the eggs have been added.)

Pour into jars which have been cleaned and heated in a cool oven (100°C/225°F) for 30 minutes. Seal when cold with paraffin wax and cellophane covers.

Kiwi Conserve

Uncooked Mint Chutney

This is very quick to make, keeps well and is excellent served with cold meat, particularly lamb or mutton. It combines well with cheese, and is consequently useful in many savouries.

3 medium-sized firm red tomatoes
1 tablespoon salt
3–4 red-skinned apples
4–5 large onions
1 cup raisins
¼ cup mint, chopped
1 cup (250 ml/8 fl oz) vinegar, scalded and cooled

Remove the skins from the tomatoes, cut them in ½–1 cm (¼–½ inch) cubes, and sprinkle with the salt. Put aside for an hour if possible, to remove some of the liquid from the tomatoes and to make the pieces firmer.

Wash the polished apples, cut them into quarters and remove the cores and any blemishes. Remove the skin and roots from the onions and cut into large pieces. Put the apples, raisins and onions through the mincer, blender or food processor to chop roughly.

Pour the liquid from the tomatoes and discard it, and add the tomatoes, chopped mint and vinegar to the minced ingredients. Pack into jars which have been sterilised in boiling water or in an oven at 100°C (200°F) for 30 minutes. Remove any air bubbles, and seal with melted candle wax or paraffin wax and cellophane tops. (Since vinegar will evaporate through cellophane, the wax should not be omitted.) Keep for at least 1 week before using.

Late Summer Pickle

This pickle is pretty! I make it whenever I see cheap red peppers. It needs no salting or soaking. It is chopped, boiled and bottled in a matter of minutes. It disappears in a matter of minutes too, so make plenty!

2 cups cooked whole-kernel corn
6–8 cups chopped cabbage
3 onions, chopped
3 red peppers, chopped
3 green peppers, chopped
1 cup (220 g/8 oz) sugar
1 Tbsp salt
1 Tbsp celery seed
1 Tbsp mustard seed
1 Tbsp dry mustard
2½ tsp turmeric
2 cups (500 ml/16 fl oz) white vinegar
¼ cup (30 g/1 oz) cornflour
½ cup (125 ml/4 fl oz) water

Measure vegetables into a large saucepan. Use drained canned or fresh corn, and do not chop the cabbage too finely. Cut onions and peppers so that they are about the same size as the corn.

Add all remaining ingredients, mixing cornflour and water before adding them. Bring to boil, stirring con-

stantly. Simmer for 15 minutes, then pack into hot sterilised jars. Allow to cool. Seal with paraffin wax and cellophane covers.

Note:
Celery and mustard seeds are available in large grocery stores. Do not leave them out.

All Season Relish

This tasty relish can be made at any time of the year.

1 cup chopped celery
1 cup chopped onion
1 red pepper, chopped
1 tsp celery seed
1 tsp mustard seed
1 tsp turmeric
1½ cups (375 ml/12 fl oz) wine vinegar
1 (440 g/15½ oz) can whole-kernel corn
1 (425 g/15 oz) can sliced green beans
¾ cup (6 oz/165 g) sugar
1 Tbsp cornflour
2 tsp salt

Measure into a saucepan the celery, onion, red pepper, celery seed, mustard seed, turmeric and wine vinegar, and bring to the boil and boil for 5 minutes. Drain, add the corn, beans and sugar.

Bring back to the boil, stirring carefully, then add the cornflour and salt that has been mixed to a thin paste with a little extra vinegar.

Simmer for 2 minutes then bottle. Store in the refrigerator.

Variations:
Replace canned beans with 2 cups (200 g) of chunky cut frozen beans, or with fresh green beans if they are available.

Pineapple Chutney

This chutney can be made quickly and easily at any time of the year. With cheese, it makes good sandwiches and topping for crackers.

2 large onions
2 cups (500 g/1 lb) crushed pineapple
2 cups (440 g/1 lb) sugar
2 cups (500 ml/16 fl oz) white or cider vinegar
2 tsp curry powder
2 tsp turmeric
2 tsp salt
1 Tbsp cornflour

Chop onions into small pieces. Place in large saucepan with crushed pineapple, and simmer until onion is tender. Add sugar and nearly all the vinegar and bring to the boil. Mix remaining ingredients to a thin paste with the last of the vinegar, add to boiling mixture, stirring until it thickens. Taste, and add more curry powder if desired. Simmer for 10–15 minutes until thick, then pour into clean, hot jars and seal with paraffin wax.

Pesto

Pesto

Basil is a herb which has a wonderful flavour when fresh, but it loses most of its character when dried. For the last 15 years I have tried to grow enough to enjoy it fresh, or preserved as pesto, all year round.

Buying the plants in late spring, getting them established in a large pot on the kitchen windowsill, picking out the tips so the plants branch nicely, and generally cosseting them until early autumn has become a tradition in our house. Basil should be flourishing by the time that tomatoes ripen. Raw or cooked tomatoes and basil are a wonderful combination.

Pesto has a strong basil flavour and will turn plain pasta into something memorable. Spread on fresh, crusty bread and topped with tomatoes it transforms a simple sandwich.

3–4 cups lightly packed basil leaves
1 cup parsley leaves
4 cloves garlic
¼–½ cup Parmesan cheese
¼ cup pinenuts, almonds or walnuts
½–1 cup (125–250 ml/4–8 fl oz) oil (preferably olive)
about 1 tsp salt

Pick the basil leaves off the main stalks, using the stalks, flower and seed heads if they are young and tender. Break the parsley leaves into smaller pieces and remove the stalks.

Put all of this into the food processor, with the peeled garlic cloves, the Parmesan cheese and the nuts.

Traditionally olive oil is used to make pesto, but you can replace it with soya or corn oil, or use part olive oil and part other oil, if you choose. Start to process the leaves, adding up to half a cup of oil. Push the leafy mixture down if necessary, so that the leaves are finely chopped. Keep adding the oil until you have a dark green paste, just liquid enough to pour. The oil should form a layer on top of the chopped leaves. Add salt to taste.

Store the pesto you will use first in the refrigerator, in a lidded glass or plastic container. Freeze other jars, remembering to loosen lids before freezing. Pesto should keep up to a year, but may darken where it is exposed to the air.

Added to mayonnaise, hot, lightly buttered vegetables and pasta, or French dressings, the pesto will go a long way.

Tamarillo Chutney

1 kg (2 lb) tamarillos
250 g (9 oz) apples
500 g (1 lb 2 oz) onions
500 g (1 lb 2 oz) brown sugar
1 tsp mixed spice
1 tsp salt
¼ tsp cayenne pepper
1–1½ cups (250–375 ml/8–12 fl oz) malt vinegar

Blanch the tamarillos by dipping in boiling water for 15–20 seconds, then into cold water. Remove the skins and chop flesh fairly coarsely into a rather large, shallow saucepan. Add the apple, peeled and chopped in pieces of a similar size, the onions, chopped in fairly small pieces, the sugar, spices and seasonings. Mix with the vinegar and boil gently for 1–2 hours in the uncovered saucepan, until the mixture thickens to the correct consistency. Occasional stirring is desirable to prevent any sticking or scorching.

Pour into clean jars, remove air bubbles and leave to cool. Cover with melted paraffin wax and a cellophane seal. This pickle can be used immediately.

Tomato Relish

In this pickle the ingredients are boiled together for a longer peiod, and instead of staying as crisp pieces in a thin sauce the texture is softer, although pieces of tomato and onion can still be distinguished.

1.5 kg (3 lb 5 oz) tomatoes, ripe but firm
500 g (1 lb 2 oz) onions
2 Tbsp salt
2 cups (500 ml/16 fl oz) vinegar
2 cups (440 g/16 oz) sugar
2 tsp mustard
2 tsp curry powder
¼ tsp cayenne pepper
6 Tbsp flour

Blanch the tomatoes, remove their skins, and chop them coarsely. Chop the onions into pieces of similar size and spread the two vegetables together in a large shallow container (with a surface resistant to acid and salt). Sprinkle with the salt, and leave to stand for 8 hours or overnight.

Strain off the liquid (do not discard) and place the vegetables in a saucepan with the vinegar. Boil for 5 minutes, then add the sugar and the dry ingredients, mixed to a thin paste with the liquid formed when the vegetables and salt were left to stand. Stir until the mixture comes to the boil again, then leave to simmer gently in the uncovered pan for 45 minutes.

Pour into cleaned dry jars, seal carefully with paraffin wax when cold, and cover the tops of the jars with cellophane covers.

Flavoured Vinegars

Anyone who grows herbs knows how interesting it is to watch the way the herb garden changes in the course of the year. The tender little leaves of spring make way for a profusion of flowers in summer, the straggly long stems and seed heads of autumn, and the short spiky stumps of winter.

Generations of cooks and gardeners have preserved the herbs from summer and autumn, so that they can add an interesting herb flavour to some of their dishes in winter.

Herb vinegars have a strong flavour that you can appreciate without chewing through dried leaves and twigs. You can make them very easily, adding more herbs to the liquid as more leaves, seeds, etc. become available. Vinegars are particularly good for flavouring vegetables and salad foods.

Tarragon Vinegar

Chop up enough fresh tarragon stalks, leaves and seeds to fill half a cup. Put in a jar with 1–2 cups (250–500 ml/8–16 fl oz) wine or cider vinegar. Add a chilli, a clove of garlic, and/or some peppercorns if you like, put on the lid, and leave to stand in a warm place for about 2 weeks. Taste, add a little salt and sugar if desired, then strain off the flavoured vinegar into an attractive bottle containing several tarragon sprigs. The vinegar can be lightly tinted with a little food colouring.

Dill Vinegar

Make this in the same way as you would tarragon vinegar, using seed heads, flower and bud heads, and leaves. Chop using a food processor if desired. Put the chopped pieces in the jar alone, or with a few nasturtium leaves, seeds, and/or buds. Cover, shake at intervals for a week, then strain, and rebottle with a flower or seed head or two, and a few nasturtium flowers, if you like their colour. These will not keep their shape, but they will keep their colour. Use the vinegar sparingly, diluting if desired, in potato salads, cold carrot dishes, and with fish which needs flavour.

Mint Vinegar

Bruise sprigs of mint and pack them tightly into a coffee jar. Season with a little salt and sugar if desired, pour over enough cider vinegar to cover, then screw on the lid and leave to stand for three or four days, shaking the jar occasionally. Pour the strained vinegar over one or two flowering sprigs of mint in a pretty bottle. Colour pale green if colour is unattractive. Use for dressings with lamb, or on fruit salads.

Lavender Vinegar

Fill a jar with the heads of flowering English lavender. Cover with white wine vinegar, and leave in a warm place, away from direct sunlight for two or three days. Pour off the vinegar, which will be a startling purple, put more lavender flowers into the jar with the old ones and cover with more vinegar. Leave in a warm place for about a week, then pour off the liquid and mix with the earlier lavender vinegar. Add a few fresh sprigs of lavender for decoration. The colour fades after a few months, but the lavender flavour stays. A few drops on tomatoes gives them a lovely flavour.

Flavoured Vinegars

Strawberry and Raspberry Vinegar

Pour wine vinegar over clean, ripe, but not mushy berries in a jar, covering them generously. Screw on the cover and stand in a dark place at room temperature. Pour off the liquid after about a month, leaving any sediment behind. The colour will fade with time, but the flavour remains. A small amount in meat glazes gives the meat an interesting flavour.

Gas Barbecues

Gas barbecues will revolutionise your ideas about barbecues and barbecued food, and may well change your family's warm-weather eating habits completely.

Many people have happy memories of sitting round huge fires on the beach or river bank, as hot and perfect days faded into velvety evenings, while steaks, chops and sausages sizzled over the embers.

In fact, the memories of these barbecues are often better than the food actually was, and the meat may well have been charred or underdone. And the usual comment after the food was all cooked, was that the ashes looked perfect, now that there was nothing left to cook!

With gas barbecues, the long wait for the fire to burn down is eliminated. You can start to cook five minutes after you turn on the gas.

You don't have to buy special, often expensive, charcoal or compressed fuel, nor worry about liquid or gel starters.

It's as easy or easier than cooking on the stove in your kitchen. You turn your gas barbecue on in the same way, and cook on regulated heat that you can control easily and quickly.

You will probably find that your meal preparation time is reduced, because barbecuing tends to be a family occupation. In fact, you may be swamped by the offers of budding barbecue chefs!

Your gas barbecue may cause you to reorganise your yard, garden or patio so there is efficient movement between the kitchen where preparation is done, the sheltered area where your barbecue stands and where the barbecue chef holds court, and the place, indoors or outside, where you will eat.

Not only will you find your family wanting weekend breakfast and lunch barbecues as well as family barbecue dinners every night of the week, but you will find your entertaining is geared around this useful appliance. Barbecue entertaining suits our casual summer lifestyles, but you can most certainly show off your culinary skills with gourmet barbecued food, if this is what you want, while still retaining a relaxed, informal atmosphere.

That 'Real Barbecue' Flavour

When you cook food under the grill on your stove, its surface browns and cooks, and some juices drip off the food, to a cool area underneath the food, so your kitchen does not become smoky.

When you cook food on a rack above the hot coals of a charcoal-fuelled barbecue, the underside of the food cooks as the grilled food does, but the juices, instead of dripping on to a cool surface, fall onto the hot coals, where they sizzle and smoke. This smoke gives the food its unique barbecued smoky flavour.

When you cook on a gas barbecue you can choose to have the food plainly grilled, or give it a smoky flavour, to a greater or lesser degree.

On a rack just above the gas flames you can place a layer of lava rock (scoria), or a layer of pumice, or

of small ceramic bricks. The gas flames heat these until they glow and radiate heat. When juice from food drips on to them, it sizzles and smokes, and the smoke gives the food its 'barbecue' flavour.

You can increase this smoky flavour by putting soaked hardwood chips on top of the hot rocks. The wet chips smoke, rather than burn, and this extra smoke gives the food on the rack above a more marked flavour.

If you cover the cooking food with a tent of heavy foil, or with the domed lid that is sold with some barbecues, you surround it with a warm atmosphere, and it cooks more quickly. You also trap the smoke formed by the juices falling on the hot coals or from the smoking hardwood chips, so you intensify the smoky flavour.

The lava rock, pumice, and ceramic bricks may be reused many times. You will need a new supply of soaked hardwood chips each time you barbecue.

Ways to Cook

Cooking on a Grill Rack
The food is cooked on a rack or grid, or in a flat grilling basket over direct heat with the barbecue uncovered. The cooked food has browned outer surfaces and a slightly smoky flavour. Pieces of meat big enough for individual servings, small whole fish, quickly cooked vegetables brushed with oil mixtures, and breads which are to be warmed through and lightly toasted are cooked this way.

Cooking Large Pieces of Meat
Larger pieces of meat, which are to be cooked then carved, call for different techniques. Use one of the following methods:

- The meat is turned on a spit over the glowing rocks, so that it cooks evenly on all sides, and the centre heats through without the outside surfaces burning.

- The meat is covered with a domed lid which is bought with the barbecue (or less efficiently with a foil tent) so that the air around it is heated by the glowing rocks underneath, so the meat bakes as well as browning above the glowing rocks.

- The meat is covered by the barbecue's domed lid so that the air around it is hot, but it is protected from the direct heat of the glowing rocks by having a (foil) tray underneath it, between it and the rocks, or, on a two burner barbecue, it is positioned over the unlit burner, while the air under the dome is heated by the other burner. This method is suitable for fairly large covered barbecues. It is described as barbecuing by indirect heat.

Smoking Food
Smoked food is produced by putting soaked hardwood chips on the hot rocks. For maximum effect the food should be covered with the barbecue's domed lid, so the smoke surrounds the food while it cooks.

Wrapping Food in Foil
Foil-wrapping enables many low-fat foods to be heated

on the barbecue in a steamy atmosphere so that they do not burn before they have cooked. They do not have a browned surface or a barbecued flavour unless they are unwrapped and browned over the hot rocks after they are tender.

Cooking on a Hot Plate
A griddle or heavy, flat plate cooks food by pan-grilling. This food has little or no smoky flavour. Many foods which could not be cooked directly on a rack can be cooked on a hot plate. Your kitchen is kept free from spatters and heat, and the outside clean-up time will probably be considerably less.

Cooking in Pots and Pans
Heavy pots, pans and kettles can be used on a barbecue, too. In this situation, as when using the griddle, the barbecue is being used as an outdoor stove-top. The food will taste much the same as it would if cooked indoors. You may cook some foods in heavy pots earlier in the day and bring them outside to heat up on the gas barbecue and serve with your other barbecued foods.

Barbecue Utensils
A medium-sized stiff-bristled brush is important to remove residues from the grill rack.

A basting brush is a useful barbecue accessory. In fact, several are useful when you plan to use different glazes, marinades and sauces. Brushes the size of a small varnish brush work well.

Hinged, flat grilling baskets are very useful when you are cooking foods which need to be turned often, or which may stick, then break when turned over. These come in different shapes and sizes. Some hold only one or two hamburgers, others will hold a smallish flatfish. If you want to cook a butterflied shoulder or leg of lamb, you will need a basket which will take something longer and thicker. But, if you plan to barbecue whole large fish, you should get a proper fish-shaped basket. Although theoretically you can put small items in a large basket, you will find it easier to work with one that is only a little bigger than the food.

A griddle or thick flat metal plate can be put on top of a barbecue rack if you want to use one and do not have one as part of your barbecue.

A heavy frying pan of the cast iron variety, with a handle which will not burn, can be used in place of a griddle. A pan with a heavy, close-fitting lid can be used for cooking girdle scones, heating baked beans, etc, too.

Skewers are very useful for keeping cubes and small foods in place. Metal skewers are reusable. Those with flat sides stop food from slipping round.

Bamboo skewers are inexpensive and disposable. If they are to be used for cooking that will take longer than a few minutes over direct heat, they should be soaked in water for 15 minutes or longer before the food is threaded on to them.

A roll of aluminium foil is a very useful barbecue accessory. Aluminium foil containers have many uses.

They are unbreakable, heatable, may be used under the grill rack to catch drips, or filled with water to make steam. They come in many shapes and sizes and may be put on the grill rack in an unused corner.

Oven mitts and oven cloths will protect your hands. Barbecue aprons can be entertaining as well as protective! Chopping and carving boards and knives are as important by your barbecue as they are in the kitchen. Small, folding but stable tables are useful for situations where there is little working space. Covers protect barbecues from dust and grime if they are standing unused for some time.

Barbecue Recipes
Barbecued Bread Rolls   37
Barbecued Fish   42
   Fish Steaks   42
   Fish Fillets   42
   Whole Round Fish   42
   Shellfish   42
   Spiced Sole or Flounder   42
Lemon Butter Baste   42
Lemon and Garlic Dipping Sauce   45
Barbecued Foiled Fish   46
Garlic Herb Butter   55
Barbecued Chicken   56
Barbecued Chicken Breasts   56
Barbecued Chicken Legs   56
Barbecued Boneless Chicken Thighs   56
Barbecued Chicken Wings   56
Sesame Marinade and Glaze   57
Barbecued Lamb Forequarter   63
Barbecued 'Butterflied' Leg of Lamb   63
Barbecue Mini Leg Cuts   63
Barbecued Lamb Chops   65
Barbecued Stuffed Noisettes   66
Barbecued Lamb Kebabs   66
Spicy Barbecued Lamb   68
Barbecued Steak   72
Beef Satay   74
Barbecued Hamburgers   81
Sesame Onion Marinade   81
Minted Yoghurt Sauce   81
Soya and Sherry Dip   81
Apricot and Mustard Glaze   81
Barbecued Pork Ribs   87
Barbecued Pork Kebabs   87
Barbecued Ham Steaks   89
Super Snarlers   90
Barbecue Packs   111
Barbecued Potatoes   111
Barbecued New Potatoes   111
Barbecued Vegetables   124

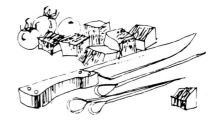

Eating for Health

We all want to look and feel our best, to be healthy and full of energy.

What's more, we want to stay this way for the rest of our lives, not just a few days or a few weeks. We also want to give our children the best possible start, guiding them towards all the good and healthy things in life.

This is, however, more easily said than done!

We are surrounded by top quality foods, but sometimes we make the wrong choices or eat more than we need. It is hard to eat less than we feel like eating. It is hard, too, to change our eating patterns.

What Should We Eat?

The message of the nineties is loud and clear.

- Eat a wide variety of food, from different food groups, each day.
- Eat only as much as you need. Keep a healthy weight with a good balance of regular exercise and healthy foods.
- Give more emphasis to wholegrain cereal foods, fruit and vegetables, and watch how much fat and salt you eat, or add to food.
- Check that foods and drinks that you buy ready to eat are not high in fat, sugar, or salt.
- Drink plenty of liquids, but drink alcohol in moderation.

A diet that contains generous amounts of wholegrain bread, potatoes, rice, pasta, and vegetables is good for everybody. A reducing diet based on the same foods with almost no added fat is likely to cause you to lose weight effortlessly, and keep you looking and feeling at your best.

A diet like this is high in complex carbohydrates. It is a diet which allows athletes to perform better, and is likely to help us function better, mentally and physically. It is a diet high in nutrients.

If you can modify your existing eating pattern, following these guidelines, you may well find yourself eating in a new way which you will find easy and satisfying to continue indefinitely.

When you prepare most of the food you eat you know exactly what foods you are eating. You do not have such control when you buy food which has been prepared commercially.

A diet high in complex carbohydrates is likely to give you the extra energy you need to start and continue with regular exercise.

When you decide to eat more grains and cereal foods, particularly those made with wholegrains, and to include more vegetables and fruit in your everyday meals, and at the same time, cut down on fats (and oils) you get some great bonuses.

Because unrefined cereals and vegetables are bulky, you will find that you are eating quite large amounts, so that you feel full before you have eaten too much. You do not feel 'half starved' or deprived!

You will find that you do not get hungry again an hour or two after you have eaten, because these are foods are are slowly digested. It is not hard to wait for the next meal.

You need not be involved in complicated cooking if you do not want to. You can buy very good wholegrain breads and ready-prepared baked beans, and it is easy to cook rice, pasta, and potatoes. Many vegetables and fruits are at their best when raw, and can be quickly turned into salads, or briefly cooked.

You can find a good range of complex carbohydrate foods which are inexpensive. This is not a pattern of eating which is likely to be expensive, especially if you choose fruits and vegetables which are at their best, and are in season. The foods that you are eating less of, or are cutting out of your regular diet, are those which are likely to be expensive. You will save money by not needing to buy snacks.

Complex carbohydrate foods are high in fibre. You will be unlikely to have any problems with constipation.

If you want to lose some weight, you will probably have to change some of your ideas about the foods that you serve and eat with breads, cereals, pasta, rice and vegetables, so that you cut down on the total amount of fats and oils that you eat. Many sauces, toppings, dressings and spreads are high in fat. It takes a while to change your ideas about these, and to switch to other accompaniments that will add flavour, texture and interest.

Don't try to change your family's and your own eating patterns overnight, but make changes gradually, without a big 'song and dance' about it. Because foods like bread, potatoes and pasta are likely to be favourites anyway, your family will probably be delighted to see more of them. Look for low-fat variations or alternatives of the foods that you serve, in smaller quantities, alongside these staples.

Have a long-term plan to encourage everyone in your house to see the advantage of a healthy eating pattern, so that they can all make good food choices when you are not around. You often need a very positive approach to counteract the not-so-good dietary advice to which your children are sure to be exposed!

There is no one perfect food. You need a wide variety of foods to get all the nutrients you need. You need more of some foods than others, however.

Food Groups

You need foods from all these groups, each day.

Bread and Cereals
Eat more of these!

It is now easy to buy a wide variety of different grains, and chopped or flaked or ground grain products.

When the outer coating of grains are left on, they are more nutritious, contain more fibre, and have a more definite, more interesting flavour.

Grains are used for bread and other baking, for breakfast cereals, and the whole or chopped grains (e.g.

rice), are cooked to serve with meat and vegetables.

Pasta of different shapes and sizes are made from grains.

Fruit and Vegetables

Eat more of these, too.

Eat a good range of different fruits and vegetables, to make sure that you get the nutrients from different varieties. Eat some of these raw, regularly, rather than cooking everything.

When you cook fruit and vegetables, take care to cook them for the shortest time they require, in a small amount of water, in a covered container. Think twice before adding too much salt, sugar or butter. Sometimes we add these by habit, when they are not really necessary.

Dairy Foods

We need dairy food in moderate amounts, and should look for low-fat varieties when we are concerned about reducing the amount of fat we eat.

Meat, Chicken and Fish

Buy lean cuts of meat and chicken.

Trim away visible fat before you cook meat and chicken.

Cook using methods that do not add more fat. Serve in moderate amounts, teaming them with generous amounts of cereals and vegetables. Pulses (dried peas, beans and lentils) may be used to replace meat.

Exercise

When you start to exercise gradually, you are likely to feel great! Your exercise should be an enjoyable activity. It is important, whatever your age.

Good exercise does not necessarily mean strenuous exercise, but it should be regular. Moderate exercise, for a relatively short time every day, is better than strenuous exercise once or twice a week.

Can you persuade a friend to walk with you, so your walk is actually a pleasant social activity?

Gardening may not seem strenuous, but keeping a garden in order involves quite a lot of different activities. A supply of home-grown fresh vegetables is a real bonus, too.

Riding a bicycle regularly is excellent exercise. You don't need the latest, most expensive model.

There are many exercise programmes to choose from if you like to exercise to music, or with a group of other people. If you like this idea, but can't get out of the house, look for regular exercise programmes on television, or find a video that you like. Friends who exercise like this are sure to encourage you by telling you how good it makes them feel.

It may take you some time to find the exercise pattern that is just right for you, but it is worth the effort. You'll feel fit and well, and look better for it.

Check that the younger people in your household are getting plenty of exercise, too. They may not be as active as you think they are.

Low-Fat Recipes

Old Fashioned Shank Soup 10
Pumpkin and Bacon Soup 12
Quick Hummus 25
Interesting Sandwiches 36
Bean Spread 37
Pita Bread Filling 37
Spiced Barbecued Sole or Flounder 42
Tomato-Baked Fish Fillets 45
Fish Fillets with Curry Cream Glaze 46
Barbecued Foiled Fish 46
Sautéed Groper 46
Orange Groper Steaks 49
Tomato Salsa 60
Beef Satay 74
Drip Stew 77
Pork and Apple Casserole 84
Peachy Pork Schnitzels 87
Porky Parcels 88
Quick Tangy Pork 89
Summer Spirals 96
Bacon Corn and Rice 101
Grainy Mix 101
Brown Lentil Pasta Sauce 102
Big Bean Burgers 102
Cooked Vegetables 124
Savoury Cabbage 126
Garlic Cucumber 126
Sweet Potato Cakes 126
Sautéed Mushrooms 127
Baked Fruity Sago 141
Brown Sultana Tea Break 151
Bran Bread 155
Fruit and Nut Balls 159
Yoghurt Smoothy 175

Tips for Losing Weight

Do you really know how much you eat? What about keeping a chart for yourself on the refrigerator door for a few days, and writing down everything that you eat? Then see if this ties up with the amount of food that you are buying each week. How much butter do you buy? How much oil? How many ready-prepared foods have you eaten? Perhaps looking at the lists of what you eat at home, what you eat out, and what you buy can help you see what changes you should make.

Remember, eat *more* fruit and vegetables, brown bread and wholegrain cereals, and dried bean dishes. Make sure that each of your three meals each day contains generous quantities of these. Apart from the fact that they are good for you, they will make you feel full, and stop you feeling hungry.

Eat as little added fat or oil, in any form, as you can. Watch for fat in hidden forms — in spreads, dressings, toppings, around meat, in nuts and snacks.

During the day, if you find yourself drawn towards the refrigerator from force of habit, be prepared! Keep a selection of raw vegetables ready and waiting. Cut celery, carrots, cauliflower, cucumber into snack-sized pieces, wash them and put them in closed plastic bags, so they are crisp and inviting, and ready for instant nibbling.

There are many low-fat varieties of dairy foods around these days. Choose low-fat yoghurt, low-fat cottage cheese and low-fat milk. Low-fat fruity yoghurt, in particular, can seem deliciously creamy.

Make sure that you eat plenty of vegetables raw, as salads. Instead of dressings use a sprinkling of lemon juice and chopped herbs with a grinding of pepper. If you feel the urge for a creamy dressing, mix low-fat yoghurt with a little tomato sauce. Season this further with lemon juice and herbs if you like.

Choose lean meat, and trim away all the fat you can see before you cook it. Keep serving sizes small. Make it look more by slicing it before you serve it.

Try to walk further, each day. Make your walk enjoyable, and buy walking shoes in which you feel as if you can walk for ever! If you have a brisk half-hour walk each day, you will notice the weight come off faster. See if you can change your pattern so that you *always* walk to buy your favourite magazine, to post the letters, or get a video. See if you can associate your walk with a non-edible treat!

See if you can turn water into a drink that you enjoy, and make a point of having several glasses of plain water each day. Serve yourself, for example, water poured over ice-blocks in a tall glass, with a wedge of lemon or lime, and maybe even a sprig of mint. Try carbonated water the same way — add a dash of bitters for a slightly aromatic flavour.

Don't skip meals. Plan to sit down and eat three meals a day, and don't rush any of them. It is much better to have three planned meals than unplanned snacks between meals or instead of regular meals. Make the most of each meal you have. Don't let any food slip down, unnoticed, while you stand at the kitchen bench, watch television, or read a book.

Invest in a good non-stick pan that has a lid, or that you can cover with a lid from your pot cupboard. With a pan like this you will find you can brown foods in almost no butter or oil, especially if you add a little water and put the lid on to keep the food in the pan surrounded by steam until it softens. You may well find that you can use half a teaspoonful of butter or oil, instead of one or two tablespoonfuls.

Nearly always use cooking methods that do not involve the food cooking in fat. Grilling, pan-grilling, barbecuing and roasting on a rack are much better choices than frying.

Look at your recipes critically and see whether you can modify them to remove steps which involve added fat. Try cooking a casserole or stew, for example, without browning the food in a couple of tablespoons of oil or butter before it is simmered. The flavour will not be quite the same, but it may not matter. Take extra care with flavourings to compensate.

Even though you are dieting to lose weight, keep eating a wide variety of foods. You have many vegetables, fruits, and cereal foods to choose from. It is important to eat a wide range of foods.

Make good use of a variety of herbs, spices and lemon juice, to flavour your food when you are removing fat-associated flavourings.

Eat as little salt as possible. You will become used to less and less if you cut down gradually. You will probably notice as you do this how strongly salted many bought snack foods are! Avoid these.

Acknowledgements

I would like to thank the following people and firms for their help.

SIMON HOLST, my son, is co-author with me of a very popular book, *Meals Without Meat*. A few of Simon's vegetarian recipes appear in this book.

CLARE FERGUSON, my sister, did the line drawings in this book, and came at short notice from London to help with the food styling of some of the photos.

J. WATTIE FOODS have allowed us to use some photos. These were produced for a campaign on low cost, good value foods, to accompany my recipes.

The NATURAL GAS CORPORATION own the photos which were used in three books I wrote, *Barbecue Cooking*, *Food for Healthy Appetites*, and *Food for Friends*. I cook with natural gas, and enjoy my association with the corporation.

SEASMOKE own some of the photos of fine seafood. They were originally used to accompany my recipes in their leaflets.

The NZ MEAT PRODUCERS' BOARD allowed the use of the photographs from my book *Lambtastic*.

SAL CRISCILLO photographed for all the work mentioned above. I would like to thank him for his unfailing good humour and endurance, as well as his competence. His permanent recordings of my cooking give me great pleasure.

Alison Holst

All Seasons Relish 182
Almonds, Spiced 171
Apple Cream Pie 134
Apricot and Almond Cake 164
Apricot Mustard Glaze 81
Asparagus Flan 32
Asparagus Squares 25
Aubergine, Barbecued 124

Bacon, Corn And Rice 101
Bagna Cauda 20
Baked Fish 49
Baked Fruity Sago 141
Baked Pizza Potato 108
Baked Rubarb Custard
  Pudding 137
Banana Muffins 148
Barbecue Packs 111
Barbecued 'Mini' Leg Cuts 63
Barbecued Bread Rolls 37
Barbecued 'Butterflied' Lamb 63
Barbecued Chicken 56
Barbecued Fish 42
Barbecued Fish Fillets 42
Barbecued Fish Steaks 42
Barbecued Foiled Fish 46
Barbecued Ham Steaks 89
Barbecued Hamburgers 81
Barbecued Lamb Chops 65
Barbecued Lamb Forequarter 63
Barbecued Lamb Kebabs 66
Barbecued New Potatoes 111
Barbecued Noisettes 65
Barbecued Pork Kebabs 87
Barbecued Pork Ribs 87
Barbecued Potatoes 111
Barbecued Shellfish 42
Barbecued Steak 72
Barbecued Vegetables 124
Barbecued Whole Fish 42
Barbecues, Gas 186
Barley Sugar 170
Basic Bottling 180
Bean Burgers 102
Bean Spread 37
Beans, Baked 30
Beany Pie 101
Beavertown Pâté 25
Beef Mini Roasts 77
Beef Port Casserole 78
Beef Satay 74
Beef, Corned 77
Beef, Drip Stew 77
Beef, Potted 30
Beetroot, Jellied 122
Berry Buckle 137
Berry Cordials 176
Berry Ice-Cream 142
Big Bean Burgers 102
Blender Mayonnaise 122
Blueberry Muffins 148
Boneless Chicken Thighs,
  Barbecued 56
Bottling, Basic 180
Bran Bread 155
Bread 153
Bread and Butter Pudding 138
Bread Sticks 153
Bread, Barbecued 37
Bread, Bran 155
Bread, Brown 154
Bread, Quick Yeast 154
Bread, Sultana 151
Brown Bread 154
Brown Lentil Pasta Sauce 102
Brown Rice 102
Brown Sultana Tea Bread 151
Buns, Hot Cross 152
Burgers, Bean 102
Burgers, Sausage 90
Butter, Garlic Herb 55
Butter, Lemon 42
Butterballs 170
Butterflied Leg of Lamb 63

Cabbage, Savoury 126
Cake, Apricot And Almond 164
Cake, Eating 162
Cake, Extra Fruity Christmas 167
Cake, Kiwi Layer 165
Cake, Orange 162
Cake, Simnel 165
Cake, Yoghurt 162
Candied Mandarin Peel 172
Canned Vegetable Salads 117
Caramel Peach Shortcake 136
Carrot And Parsnip Puree 126
Carrot And Tangelo Soup 12
Cashew Nuts, Salted 171
Casserole, Beef Port 78
Casserole, Layered
  Vegetable 130
Casserole, Orange Lamb 68
Casserole, Pork and Apple 84
Casserole, Whole Chicken 52
Cheese Rolls 37
Cheese, Potted 20
Cherry and Almond Slice 162
Chicken Breasts, Barbecued 56
Chicken Casserole 52
Chicken Legs, Barbecued 56
Chicken Wings, Barbecued 56
Chicken, Apricot 55
Chicken, Barbecued 56
Chicken, Festive Roast 52
Chicken, Lemon Roast 52
Chicken, Paprika-Baked 55
Chilli Beef and Beans 80
Chinese Lamb and Vegetables 68
Chocolate Crunchies 159
Chocolate Fondue 144
Chocolate Log 171
Chocolate Pear Custard 141
Chowder, Seafood 16
Chowder, Chunky 14
Chowder, Gardeners' 16
Chowder, Green Pea and
  Potato 15
Chowder, Oyster 16
Christmas Mince Pies 166
Chunky Chowder 14
Chutney, Mint 182
Chutney, Pineapple 182
Chutney, Tamarillo 184
Citrus Syllabub 144
Clare's Apricot Chicken 55
Conserve, Kiwi 180
Cooked Vegetable Salads 117
Cordial, Fifty-Fifty 176
Cordials, Berry 176
Corn Cobs, Barbecued 124
Corn Flan 32
Corn Rolls 37
Corned Beef 77
Cottage Cheese Potato Pie 107
Crab, Potted 23
Crabapple Jelly 180
Crayfish, Potted 23
Creamy Mashed Potatoes 113
Crème Caramel 142
Crêpes, Apple 38
Crêpes, Spinach 38
Cumin Bean Salad 118
Cumin Dressing 118
Curried Walnuts 171
Custard, Chocolate Pear 141

Dill Vinegar 184
Dip, Bagna Cauda 20
Dip, Hummus 25
Dip, Mexican Bean 22
Dip, Soya and Sherry 81
Dip, Taramasalata 20
Dipping Sauce 45
Dressing, Cumin 118
Dressing, French 122
Dressing, Mustard Cream 122
Dressing, Peanut 113
Drip Stew 77

Duchesse Potatoes 110

Easy Barbecue Scones 151
Easy Raclette 109
Eating Cake 162
Eating For Health 189
Economical Lasagne 98
Economical Meringues 161
Economical Orange Drink 175
Economical Roast Lamb 60
Extra Fruity Christmas
  Cake 167

Family Burgers 90
Feijoa Crumble Pie 134
Fennel Soup 12
Festive Roast Chicken 52
Fifty-Fifty Cordial 176
Filo Surprise Packages 109
Filo Triangles 127
Fish Fillet with Curry Cream
  Glaze 46
Fish Fillets, Baked 45
Fish Fillets, Barbecued 42
Fish Fillets, Oven-Fried 48
Fish Pie 45
Fish Steaks, Barbecued 42
Fish Steaks, Orange 49
Fish, Barbecued 42
Fish, Foiled 46
Fish, Smoked Roe 20
Fish, Whole Baked 49
Fish, Whole, Barbecued 42
Flan, Asparagus 32
Flan, Corn 32
Flan, Leek 33
Flap, Lamb 66
Florence Fennel, Marinated 122
Flounder, Spiced Barbecued 42
Fondue, Chocolate 144
Food Groups 188
Food Processor Nut Balls 159
French Dressing 122
Fresh Tomato Soup 10
Frittata, Onion 38
Fruit and Nut Balls 159
Fudge, Ginger 172

Gardeners' Chowder 16
Garlic Cucumber 126
Garlic Herb Butter 55
Garlic Roast Potatoes 110
Garlic, Roasted 60
Gas Barbecues 186
Ginger Fudge 172
Gingernuts 158
Glaze, Apricot and Mustard 81
Glaze, Sesame 56
Glaze, Soya and Sherry 81
Glazed Stuffed Noisettes 66
Gourmet Baked Potato 108
Grainy Mix 101
Grandmother's Chicken
  Casserole 52
Gravy, Mustard 77
Greek Summer Salad 118
Green Pea and Potato
  Chowder 15
Green Soup 15
Groper, Sautéed 46

Ham Cheese and Asparagus
  Quiche 34
Ham Steaks, Barbecued 89
Hamburgers, Barbecued 81
Herbed Baked Fish 49
Herbed Wine Sauce 128
Home-Style Baked Beans 30
Hot Cross Buns 152
Hummus, Quick 25

Japonica Jelly 180
Jellied Beetroot 122
Jelly, Crabapple 180

Jelly, Japonica 180
Juice, Spiced Tomato 25

Kebabs, Lamb 66
Kebabs, Pork 87
Kidney Pâté 25
Kiwi Conserve 180
Kiwi Layer Cake 165
Lacy Wafers 160
Lamb Chops 65
Lamb Chops, Barbecued 65
Lamb Cutlets, Lemon-Honey 65
Lamb Leg Cuts 63
Lamb Rack, Microwaved 60
Lamb Riblets 66
Lamb Steaks 66
Lamb, Chinese 68
Lamb, Roast 60
Lamb, Spicy Barbecued 68
Lasagne, Economical 98
Lasagne, Spinach and
  Mushroom 98
Late Summer Pickle 182
Lavender Vinegar 185
Layered Vegetable Casserole 130
Leek and Potato Soup 12
Leek Flan 33
Leg of Lamb, Butterflied 63
Lemon and Barley Water 176
Lemon and Garlic Dipping
  Sauce 45
Lemon and Herb Roast
  Chicken 52
Lemon Butter Baste 42
Lemon Honey 181
Lemon Meringue Pie 141
Lemon-Honey Lamb Cutlets 65
Lentil Sauce 102
Little Meatballs 81
Loin of Pork, Roast 84

Main Course Salads 116
Marinade and Glaze, Sesame 63
Marinade for Venison 74
Marinade, Mediterranean 63
Marinade, Sesame 56
Marinade, Sesame Onion 81
Marinade, Tex-Mex 63
Marinade, Wine 73
Marinated Florence Fennel 122
Mashed Potatoes 113
Mayonnaise, Blender 122
Meat Loaf 78
Meatballs 81
Mediterranean Marinade 63
Mediterranean Vegetable
  Stew 131
Meringues, Economical 161
Mexican Bean Dip 22
Microwaved Lamb Rack 60
Milk, Soya 175
Mince Pies, Christmas 166
Mincemeat Topping 143
Mini-Leg Lamb Steaks 66
Mint Vinegar 184
Minted Lamb Rack 60
Minted Yoghurt Sauce 81
Muffins, Banana 148
Muffins, Blueberry 148
Muffins, Orange Honey 148
Mushroom Quiche 33
Mushroom Salad 119
Mushroom-Filled Filo
  Triangles 127
Mushrooms Sautéed 127
Mushrooms, Barbecued 124
Mussels in Curried Tomato
  Sauce 43
Mustard Cream Dressing 122
Mustard Gravy 77
Mustard Sauce 128

New Potatoes, Barbecued 111
Noisettes, Barbecued 65

Noisettes, Glazed Stuffed	66
Oaty Fruit Pancakes	150
Old-Fashioned Fish Pie	45
Old-Fashioned Shank Soup	10
Onion Frittata	38
Orange and Lemon Drops	170
Orange Cake	163
Orange Drink	175
Orange Groper Steaks	49
Orange Honey Muffins	148
Orange Lamb Casserole	68
Oriental Steak Salad	74
Oriental Tofu and Noodles	96
Oven-Fried Fish Fillets	48
Oyster Chowder	16
Pan-Baked Scones	55
Pan-Grilled Venison Steak	73
Pancakes, Oaty Fruit	150
Paprika-Baked Chicken	55
Parsley Sauce	85
Pasta with Summer Sauce	96
Pâté, Kidney	25
Peach Crisp with Sauce	138
Peachy Ginger Steam Pudding	138
Peachy Mincemeat Topping	143
Peachy Pork Schnitzels	87
Peel, Candied	172
Peanut Dressing	113
Peanut Toffee	171
Peanuts, Roasted	171
Peppermint Chews	172
Pesto	183
Pickle, Late Summer	182
Pickled Pork	84
Picnic Pie	35
Pie, Apple Cream	134
Pie, Beany	101
Pie, Cottage Cheese Potato	107
Pie, Feijoa Crumble	134
Pie, Fish	45
Pie, Lemon Meringue	141
Pie, Onion	33
Pie, Picnic	35
Pie, Pork	92
Pie, Rhubarb	134
Pie, Steak and Kidney	78
Pies, Christmas Mince	166
Pineapple Chutney	182
Pita Bread Filling	37
Pizza, Potato	107
Pizza, Quick	30
Pork and Apple Casserole	84
Pork Pie	92
Pork Ribs, Barbecued	87
Pork, Pickled	84
Pork, Quick Tangy	89
Porky Parcels	88
Portuguese Potatoes	112
Potato Balls	110
Potato Cake, Swiss	106
Potato Cakes	124
Potato Pan Pizza	107
Potato Salad with Peanut Dressing	113
Potato Salads	120
Potato, Baked	108
Potatoes	106

Potatoes, Baked Pizza	108
Potatoes, Barbecued	111
Potatoes, Duchesse	110
Potatoes, Garlic Roast	110
Potatoes, Mashed	113
Potatoes, Portuguese	112
Potatoes, Special Scalloped	112
Potted Beef	30
Potted Cheese	20
Potted Crab	23
Potted Crayfish	23
Pudding, Bread and Butter	138
Pudding, Rhubarb	137
Pumpkin and Bacon Soup	12
Pumpkin and Coconut Soup	10
Purée, Carrot and Parsnip	126
Quiche, Ham Cheese and Asparagus	34
Quiche, Self-Crusting Mushroom	33
Quick Hummus	25
Quick Mini-Pizzas	30
Quick Tangy Pork	89
Quick Vegetable Salad with Cumin Dressing	121
Quick Yeast Rolls or Bread	154
Raclette, Easy	109
Raspberry Vinegar	185
Red Pepper Salad	118
Relish, All Seasons	182
Relish, Tomato	184
Riblets, Lamb	66
Rice Salad	120
Rice, Bacon and Corn	101
Rice, Brown	102
Rice, Potato and Pasta Salad	117
Roast Chicken, Lemon and Herb	52
Roast Lamb	60
Roast Lamb Forequarter	60
Roast Yams	127
Roasted Garlic Purée	60
Roasted Peanuts	171
Roasts, Beef Mini	77
Rock Cakes	159
Rollmops	26
Sago, Baked Fruity	141
Salad, Cumin Bean	118
Salad, Greek Summer	118
Salad, Mushroom	119
Salad, Potato	113
Salad, Quick Vegetable	121
Salad, Red Pepper	118
Salad, Rice	120
Salad, Shredded Carrot	118
Salad, Spinach	121
Salad, Steak	74
Salad, Tomato and Pasta	120
Salad, Venison	74
Salads, Canned	117
Salads, Cooked Vegetable	117
Salads, Main Course	116
Salads, Potato	120
Salads, Rice, Potato and Pasta	117
Salads, Undressed	119
Salmon Caviar	27

Salmon, Smoked	27
Salsa, Tomato	60
Salted Cashew Nuts	171
Sandwiches	36
Satay, Beef	74
Sauce, Brown Lentil	102
Sauce, Herbed Wine	128
Sauce, Lemon and Garlic	45
Sauce, Minted Yoghurt	81
Sauce, Mustard	128
Sauce, Parsley	85
Sauce, Summer	46
Sauce, Wine and Tomato	128
Sauces for Vegetables	128
Sausage Combo	93
Sausage Meat Roll	92
Sausages, Savoury	90
Sautéed Groper	46
Sautéed Mushrooms	127
Sautéed Potato Balls	110
Savoury Apple Crêpes	38
Savoury Cabbage	126
Savoury Sausages with Pineapple	90
Scalloped Potatoes	112
Schnitzels, Peachy Pork	87
Schnitzels, Veal	73
Scones, Easy Barbecue	151
Scones, Pan-Baked	55
Scones, Plain or Fancy	150
Seafood Chowder	16
Self-Crusting Mushroom Quiche	33
Sesame Bread Sticks	153
Sesame Glaze	56
Sesame Marinade	56
Sesame Onion Marinade	81
Shellfish, Barbecued	42
Shortcake, Peach	136
Shredded Carrot Salad	118
Simnel Cake	165
Smoked Roe Savouries	20
Smoked Salmon Slices	27
Snarlers, Super	90
Sole, Spiced Barbecued	42
Soup, Carrot and Tangelo	12
Soup, Fennel	12
Soup, Fresh Tomato	10
Soup, Green	15
Soup, Leek and Potato	12
Soup, Pumpkin	10
Soup, Pumpkin and Bacon	12
Sour Cream Onion Pie	33
South Pacific Meat Loaf	78
Soya and Sherry Dip	81
Soya Milk	175
Special Scalloped Potatoes	112
Speedy Spicy Spuds	113
Spiced Almonds	171
Spiced Barbecued Sole	42
Spiced Pumpkin and Coconut Soup	10
Spiced Tomato Juice	25
Spicy Barbecued Lamb	68
Spicy Potted Beef	30
Spinach and Cheese Crêpes	38
Spinach and Mushroom Lasagne	98
Spinach Salad	121
Spread, Bean	37

Spuds, Speedy	113
Steak and Kidney Pie	78
Steak Diane	73
Steak, Barbecued	72
Steamed Pudding	138
Stew, Vegetable	131
Strawberry Vinegar	185
Stuffed Roast Loin of Pork	84
Stuffing Balls	52
Summer Picnic Pie	35
Summer Sauce	46
Summer Spirals	96
Super Snarlers	90
Surprise Packages	109
Sweet and Sour Yams	127
Sweet Potato Cakes	126
Swiss Potato Cake	106
Swiss-Style Rhubarb Tart	134
Tamarillo Chutney	184
Tarakihi with Lemon Cream Sauce	49
Taramasalata	20
Tarragon Vinegar	184
Tart, Rhubarb	134
Tender-Crisp Zucchini	127
Tex-Mex Marinade	63
Tips for Losing Weight	190
Toasted Roll-Ups	37
Toffee, Peanut	171
Tofu-Shakes	175
Tofu, Oriental	96
Tomato and Pasta Salad	120
Tomato Relish	184
Tomato Salsa	60
Tomato Soup, Fresh	10
Tomato-Baked Fish Fillets	45
Tomatoes, Barbecued	124
Tortellini in Herbed Sauce	97
Uncooked Mince Chutney	182
Undressed Salad	119
Vegetables, Barbecued	124
Vegetables, Cooked	124
Venison Marinade	74
Venison Salad, Warm	74
Venison Steaks	73
Vinegar, Dill	184
Vinegar, Lavender	185
Vinegar, Mint	184
Vinegar, Raspberry	185
Vinegar, Strawberry	185
Vinegar, Tarragon	184
Wafers, Lacy	160
Walnuts, Curried	171
Warm Venison Salad	74
White Veal Schnitzels	73
Whitebait Patties	48
Wine and Tomato Sauce	128
Wine Marinade	73
Yams, Roast	127
Yams, Sweet and Sour	127
Yoghurt Cake	162
Yoghurt Smoothy	175
Zabaglione	144
Zucchini, Tender-Crisp	127